Supercharging C
with Assembly Language

Supercharging C
with Assembly Language

Harry R. Chesley and Mitchell Waite
The Waite Group

Addison-Wesley Publishing Company, Inc.

Reading, Massachusetts   Menlo Park, California
Don Mills, Ontario   Wokingham, England   Amsterdam   Bonn
Sydney   Singapore   Tokyo   Madrid   Bogotá
Santiago   San Juan

Many of the designations used by manufacturers and sellers to distinguish their products are claimed as trademarks. Where those designations appear in this book and Addison-Wesley was aware of a trademark claim, the designations have been printed in initial capital letters (i.e., Microsoft C Compiler, IBM, IBM PC, IBM PC/XT, IBM PC/AT, Microsoft, MS-DOS, PC-DOS, Digital Equipment Corporation, VAX, Cray Research Inc., Macintosh, Data Encryption Standard, and National Bureau of Standards).

Library of Congress Cataloging-in-Publication Data

Chesley, Harry R.
  Supercharging C with assembly language.

  Includes index.
  1. C (Computer program language)   2. Assembler language (Computer program language)   I. Waite, Mitchell.   II. Waite Group.   III. Title.
  QA76.73.C15C47   1987   005.13'3   87-943
  ISBN 0-201-18349-8

Typesetting by the H. S. Dakin Company, San Francisco. (Book design by Diana Davis and Kim Straitiff. Art production by Kim Straitiff.) Copy editing by Mary Goodell and Helen Berliner. Index by Helen Berliner. Proofing by K. D. Sullivan.

Cover design by Doliber Skeffington Design.

Text set in 10.5-point Century Schoolbook on the Allied Lintype 202/W. The listings are set in Bold Courier, the shadowed letters and numbers are set in PostScript® — both on the Allied Linotype L300.
Printed from camera-ready copy supplied by The Waite Group.

ABCDEFGHIJ-HA-8987
First printing, April 1987

Acknowledgements

I would like to thank Mitch Waite of The Waite Group for putting me up to the enjoyable, if challenging, task of writing this book, and to my wife, Suzana, for putting up with me while I wrote it. Also, Waite Group's Robert Lafore for being the best editor I could imagine having, and Jim Stockford for managing the project.

Harry Chesley

The Waite Group wishes to extend thanks to those people who helped us turn our manuscript into a final book we are proud of. At Addison-Wesley, thanks to Maeve Cullinane for dedicated production control, to Carole Alden for guidance throughout the project, and to Steve Stansel for his confidence in the original idea. The H. S. Dakin Company staff did a wonderful job of production: thanks especially to Diana Davis for patient management and design, to Kim Straitiff for assistance with the design and especially fine art, to Mary Goodell for her sensitive copy editing, Helen Berliner for assistance with copy editing and for indexing under fire, and to K. D. Sullivan for thorough proofing. Thanks to Lloyd Zusman for his technical review and to the staff at the Well for providing their on-line communications medium.

Mitchell Waite

Table of Contents

Preface

We had three goals in mind when we began to write this book. The first was to show how to speed up C code, to show how to outfox the C compiler, and to reveal the areas in which C routines are slow or limited. We wanted to demonstrate sophisticated techniques to analyze and increase hardware performance with concrete and non-trivial examples. Our second goal was to bring together all the relevant information about interfacing MS-DOS and C to 8086 Assembly Language. Over the course of years we found secrets in places such as the ROM BIOS listings, spec sheets for Intel's peripheral chips, and the schematics of the display adapters, but digging out the information and converting it into working programs was extremely difficult. Our third goal was to present this material so that it would be accessible to anyone interested in increasing the horsepower of the C programming language. We hope we have succeeded in showing IBM PC programmers how to make the leap from basic programming to advanced tweaking of the increasingly popular C programming language.

Mitchell Waite

Harry Chesley

Foreword

As an IBM PC software application developer, I spend at least 30 hours a week writing C code for clients. Frequently, I have to port my code to different machines, or find some way to make it go faster. But there are some things that the C language just can't do. Then I have to turn to assembly language and the internal environment of MS-DOS.

I have looked for a single source of information that addresses this black art of fine tuning, improving and tweaking final C code. After reading the manuscript for *Supercharging C with Assembly Language* by Harry Chesley and The Waite Group, I have now found that book.

Supercharging is what the author calls the entire subject of "optimization." Using example programs in Microsoft C and snippets from MASM, he teaches how to optimize a program from every possible angle. Chesley reveals not only the techniques of adding assembly language algorithms to your code, but especially how to identify when and where such routines should be used. He shows the tricky places to put assembly code and tells when you can actually do it wrong and slow a program down. After learning how to optimize with assembly language, Chesley goes on to present numerous examples of optimization by using the ROM BIOS directly.

There are plenty of example programs that reveal how to tap the power of the PC's screen, keyboard, and serial port. There are complete details on accessing the EGA, a program for doing fractals, and a program for a complete serial terminal.

The last section of the book discusses accessing the hardware directly and although this is condemned frequently as one of the main problems in portability of software, direct hardware access is indeed a necessary evil. For example, a windows program that talked to the bit mapped EGA via ROM BIOS would be a poor performer compared to one that directly accesses the chip. I am impressed that Chesley's book shows how to dive head first into the hardware and get the last drop of performance out of your code. He touches on all the major chips and concepts: direct screen access, high speed animation, interrupt driven serial I/O, direct sound access.

The final chapter of the book presents what he calls the IP Histogram program. This figures out which part of your code is consuming the largest execution time. With IP Histogram you can determine where the slow parts of the code are and then attempt to recode them using the numerous techniques presented in the earlier chapters.

Another invaluable part of the book is the set of C primitives Harry presents for doing graphics on the screen. I found these functions so well coded and easy to use that I am giving up on my commercial graphics library; and I am going to use these in my code from now on.

Lloyd Zusman
Master Byte Software

Chapter 1

Introduction

- Supercharging—A Definition and Our Examples

- What You Should Bring to this Book

- How this Book Is Organized

Supercharging is our synonym for optimizing, improving, and extending the capabilities of a program. This book will show you how to supercharge your C programs. This book will teach you how to optimize the execution time of your program with respect to both processor speed optimization and disk I/O optimization. It will show you how to call assembly language routines from C and how to write those assembly language routines. Finally, it will demonstrate how to call the ROM BIOS directly to access facilities your program couldn't use previously, and also how to speed up the execution of the program by cutting out the overhead of MS-DOS. Finally, it will demonstrate how to access and control the hardware itself directly. Direct hardware access, like direct ROM BIOS access, allows you to do more and to do it more efficiently. Along the way, you will learn a number of useful, real-world programs that illustrate the techniques being discussed. These programs are usable in their own right; they can also form a base from which you can develop more complex applications. And, just to make life a little more interesting, you will develop some game programs that are fun to play and that demonstrate the main principles at the same time.

The best way to learn new material about programming is to read the theory behind it, study the example code, compile and run that code, and finally extend it with new capabilities. Therefore, the example programs are complete, ready to be entered into the machine and run, and are stand-alone applications that perform useful functions. In addition, each chapter ends with a set of exercises that extend the functionality of the example programs in some way. The following set of complete, runnable programs is included in the book:

- ShowFile   Displays a text file and allows the user to display different parts of the file using the cursor keys.

- RAMSort   Sorts text files in RAM (similar to the MS-DOS SORT filter, but you have the source code to this one).

- ■ Encrypt   Encrypts and decrypts files.
- ■ TicTac   Plays a perfect game of tic-tac-toe.
- ■ Term   Emulates a simple terminal on the serial port.
- ■ Fract   Displays one class of fractals.
- ■ Pong   Plays video ping-pong.
- ■ Noise   Makes sound effects.
- ■ IP Histogram   Measures where the program is spending its time.

What You Should Bring to this Book

This book is written primarily for the programmer who is already comfortable with programming the IBM PC in the C language. It is designed to help you take the next step: mixing assembly language routines with your C code, directly using the ROM BIOS and the hardware of the machine, and tweaking the execution time of the program to the fastest possible speeds.

Supercharging C can be of use to a new C programmer as well. Although not intended for the completely naive beginner, the numerous examples can help a new programmer to understand the C language and how to program in it. This is particularly true if you are already familiar with programming the IBM PC in assembly language.

Everything found in this book can be applied to the IBM PC, the IBM PC/XT, and the IBM PC/AT. All of these programs have actually been run on those machines. Most of the material is also applicable to the IBM PCjr and the numerous existing IBM PC clones as well. The ROM BIOS section may not apply to PC clones that are not ROM BIOS compatible. However, all of the material will be applicable to any machine that is truly IBM PC compatible. The material presented here is independent of the version of the operating system since it largely bypasses that operating system. Throughout the book, the term "MS-DOS" is used to refer to the operating system, but all the programs work equally well with PC-DOS.

We used Microsoft C (version 3.0 or 4.0) and the Microsoft macro assembler, MASM, throughout this book. All of the theory and much of the specific code can also be used with other compiler/assembler combinations. Each time compiler- or assembler-specific information is introduced that fact is pointed out, and the important material in that section is presented more generally. Therefore, readers using other compilers or assemblers should find this book useful, but should be careful when applying specific information or when compiling the examples.

How this Book Is Organized

Chapters One and Two introduce and explain the concepts involved in super-charging. The main portion of the book is divided into three parts:

- Part I   Optimizing Execution Speed
- Part II   Accessing the ROM BIOS Directly
- Part III   Accessing the Hardware Directly

Each part begins with an introductory chapter that explains the techniques used in the type of supercharging described. Several chapters of examples follow, each of which develops its own stand-alone application. You can use the book in one of two ways: read the material in the order given, first studying the theory, then studying the examples that apply the theory; or, dive right into the examples and return to read the theory when questions arise.

Part I starts with "How to Call Assembly Routines from C" (Chapter Three), which describes the interface between C and assembly and shows how to write assembly language routines that can be called from a C program. Chapter Four uses this approach to optimize a RAM-based text file sorting program by recoding selected portions in assembly language. Similarly, Chapter Five does the same kind of optimization on a tic-tac-toe playing program. Part I concludes with Chapter Six, which illustrates how disk I/O can be far more significant than processor speed when optimizing a program.

Part II begins with "How to Call the ROM BIOS" (Chapter Seven), which describes the ROM BIOS and explains how to write ROM BIOS assembly language interface routines that can be called from your C program. Chapter Eight uses this approach to develop an efficient text file display program. Chapter Nine also uses this approach to demonstrate the ability of the Color/ Graphics Adapter to change the display background color. Chapter Ten then uses a ROM BIOS interface to a graphic display (either the Color/Graphics Adapter or the Enhanced Graphics Adapter) to display fractals. Chapter Eleven uses the serial port facilities of the BIOS to provide terminal emulation via the serial port.

In Part III, "How to Access the Hardware Directly" (Chapter Twelve) explains how to access the hardware directly from assembly language. This chapter covers direct access to memory, input/output ports, and interrupts. Chapter Thirteen uses this approach to place the text to be displayed directly into the display hardware memory. This is an improvement of the program that was developed in Part II. Chapter Fourteen uses the same technique with the graphics display. Chapter Fifteen extends the Term program developed in Part II by using hardware interrupts. Chapter Sixteen accesses the sound hardware by using input/output ports to produce sound effects. Finally, Chapter Seventeen presents a module that uses timer interrupts to record a histogram of where a program is spending most of its time. This information, together with the techniques developed in Part I, can be used to optimize the processor execution speed of the program.

Appendix A contains a quick introduction to assembly language programming for the programmer who already knows C. Programmers with no previous experience in assembly language should read, or at least skim, this appendix before reading the rest of the book. Appendix B explains the process of compiling or assembling a program and linking it with other routines to produce a runnable application. Appendix C contains a list of most of the available ROM BIOS calls and the parameters passed to or returned by them. Appendix D shows the ASCII and scan codes returned from the keyboard when different keys are pressed.

The supercharging techniques described in this book can help you get the most out of the IBM PC/XT/AT or compatible machines. Supercharging gives you more complete access to both hardware and software and increases the power and capabilities of your program as never before. Using supercharging techniques, you can improve the performance of your program by as much as several hundred percent.

Chapter 2

Supercharging: The Concepts

- IBM PC Overview
- Types of Supercharging
- Pros and Cons of Supercharging
- Measurement of Supercharging

W hat is "supercharging?" Supercharging enables a program to do something it couldn't do before, such as directly manipulating a part of the underlying hardware of the PC; couldn't do as much of, such as providing more detailed access to the keyboard; or couldn't do as fast, such as updating the screen. In this chapter, we'll discuss the various ways you can supercharge your own programs after you've read this book. We'll talk about the pros and cons of supercharging a program—why you should, why you shouldn't, and when. We'll explain how to design programs that are easy to supercharge. Finally, we'll talk about combining C and assembly language to supercharge your programs by directly improving the execution speed, and by allowing the program to access areas of the PC that are difficult to access using C alone.

IBM PC Overview

Most supercharging involves using resources already available but not easily accessible in the IBM PC. Other supercharging techniques involve bypassing parts of the PC's operating system to write less general but more efficient routines than those that come with the hardware, the operating system, or the compiler. In any event, an overall knowledge of the IBM PC, including its hardware and software components, is necessary to understand supercharging.

The IBM PC consists of a main system board and several add-on boards that are plugged into slots, as shown in Figure 2-1. The main system board contains the processor and its support chips, some of the memory available to the processor, interfaces to the keyboard and speaker, a timer, and the interface to the add-on boards. The add-on boards add more memory, interfaces to displays, connections to parallel and serial external devices, and a wide variety of other less standard hardware. There are two kinds of memory in the PC: RAM (random access memory) and ROM (read only memory). The contents of RAM can be changed by an executing program, but ROM is fixed and preset at the factory.

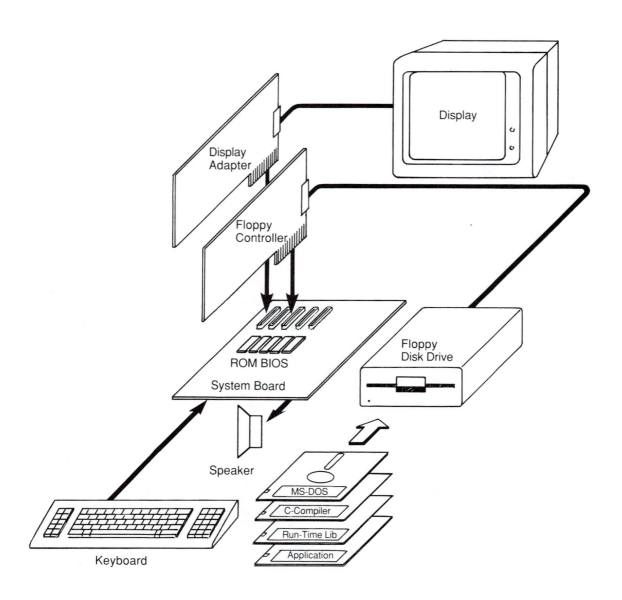

Figure 2-1. Components of the IBM PC

The software that runs in the PC comes from two sources: part of it is built into the ROM, and the other part is loaded from disk into RAM. The software in the ROM is called the "basic input/output system," or BIOS, or ROM BIOS. The software that is loaded from disk is either the operating system (MS-DOS) or an application program. Application programs written in C use MS-DOS, the ROM BIOS, and the hardware, as well as run-time libraries supplied with the compiler. In supercharging a C program, it is important to remember that all of these components together produce a running application on the IBM PC. Figure 2-2 shows the hierarchy of these components.

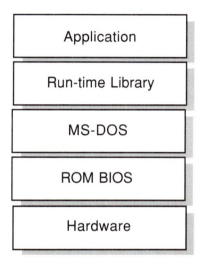

Figure 2-2. Components of a Running Application

The application is responsible for the specific task at hand: it knows what the task is and, at the highest level, how to accomplish it. The run-time library provides the interface between C and the rest of the system. In some cases, the interface is machine-independent, so programs can be ported easily to or from another machine. MS-DOS maintains the structure and consistency of the file system, and provides a common funnel through which applications access the underlying hardware of the machine. The ROM BIOS provides a low-level interface to the hardware, hiding the details of the hardware from the higher levels of the system. The ROM BIOS is literally the "*basic* input/output system" of the PC. Finally, the hardware carries out the physical actions that produce the desired results.

These components will be discussed in greater detail in later chapters of this book. For now, keep in mind that your program sits at the top of a hierarchy of software and hardware. When you call a function, such as reading data from a disk or writing characters on the display, you set in motion a chain of events that can be long and complicated. Sometimes it's hard to appreciate this, since the PC executes the chain in a fraction of a second, even if thousands of actions are involved. It's only when your program has to perform such a chain thousands of times in a row that the execution time becomes long enough for us slow humans to become aware of the process. And it's when the people who use the program are kept waiting for it to finish, that we start to think about supercharging the program.

Types of Supercharging

A number of different techniques can be used to supercharge a program. They fall into five general categories: optimizing processor execution speed, optimizing disk input/output, bypassing MS-DOS, bypassing the ROM BIOS, and accessing hidden facilities.

Optimizing Processor Execution Speed

This type of supercharging involves improving the efficiency of the code so that it runs faster. But in order to supercharge a program for processor speed, you must first find out where in the code the program is spending most of its time. Without knowing this, you'll optimize the wrong code—the part where the program only spends a small portion of its time. The classic rule of thumb is "a program spends 90% of its time in 10% of its code"—the trick is to find that 10%. One technique is to use IP Histograms, such as those produced by the module in Chapter Seventeen. Once you find the right area to optimize, you can take one or more of the following actions to make the code more efficient:

1. Declare some local variables to be register variables (assuming your C compiler supports register variables). This speeds up the program without changing its functionality at all, and is therefore the safest type of optimization.

2. Rewrite the C code to be more efficient. Often a routine can be rewritten in a more efficient manner with very little work.

3. Find a more efficient algorithm. A different algorithm may be more efficient in general, or else more efficient for the specific function, application, or type of input expected.

4. Rewrite the routine in assembly language. It is often possible to write tighter, more efficient code in assembly language than the C compiler

produces from your C source (though C compilers are getting very good at producing tight code).

Speeding up the code will be covered primarily in Part I of this book. In Chapter Three we will explain how to replace C routines with assembly language routines. In Chapters Four and Five, we provide examples of optimizing programs by rewriting them in assembly. In Chapter Seventeen, we discuss how to find the 10% of the code where the program spends 90% of its time, and we present a module that can be incorporated into programs to produce a histogram of where the program actually spends its time.

Optimizing Disk Input/Output

Another way to make a program run faster is to optimize disk input/output (I/O). With applications that read and write from the disk, disk I/O almost always consumes the bulk of the application's execution time. By carefully optimizing the way the program accesses the disk, the sizes of the buffers it uses, and the order in which it accesses data on different parts of the disk, you can make a much greater difference in total application running time than by optimizing processor speed. Simply changing the size of a buffer can sometimes have more impact than a week of recoding C routines into assembly language. This type of optimization is covered in Chapter Six, where a disk-bound program is developed and optimized.

Bypassing MS-DOS

The third way to improve the speed of an application is to bypass MS-DOS. While MS-DOS provides a very general interface to the hardware attached to the PC, it is not always the most efficient way to accomplish a given function. More general routines, like those provided by MS-DOS, are often less efficient for a specific use than a less general, special-purpose routine. Included in each IBM PC is a set of routines for directly manipulating the hardware. These routines are called the ROM BIOS (Read-Only-Memory Basic Input/Output System). By calling the ROM BIOS directly and bypassing MS-DOS, the overhead of MS-DOS's general purpose routines can be avoided.

Part II of the book discusses the ROM BIOS. Chapter Seven explains how to call it, and the rest of the chapters in Part II present examples that use the ROM BIOS. Chapter Eight, in particular, shows how an application can operate faster by bypassing MS-DOS and going directly to the BIOS.

Bypassing the ROM BIOS

The fourth way to increase the speed of the program is to bypass both MS-DOS and the ROM BIOS by directly programming the hardware of the PC. This approach removes all of the overhead that was introduced by the general purpose routines supplied with the machine or provided by MS-DOS or the run-time libraries. In fact, combining two optimization techniques—writing in assembly language and directly accessing the hardware—yields the most efficient program possible for an IBM PC, assuming the programmer is clever enough to write the most efficient possible assembly language program.

Part III covers direct access to the hardware. Chapter Twelve presents the theory, and the rest of the chapters in Part III give examples that use the hardware directly. Chapter Thirteen, in particular, shows how a program can run faster by using these techniques.

Accessing Hidden Facilities

This type of supercharging is concerned with functionality, not speed. It lets a program access facilities in the ROM BIOS and the hardware of the machine that are not accessible using the compiler run-time library or MS-DOS. No system allows access to every feature of the underlying hardware. Instead, it tries to choose those features that will be most needed by applications, and to provide a coherent and orderly interface to them, hiding the details of the hardware from the applications that use it. Usually this is desirable, but some applications need to use features in the hardware to which the operating system did not provide access. On the IBM PC, the application can either call the ROM BIOS, which provides more complete access to the hardware than MS-DOS does, or it can directly access the hardware itself if even the ROM BIOS does not provide the right functionality.

This aspect of supercharging is covered in both Parts II and III. Chapters Nine, Ten, and Eleven in Part II, and Chapters Fourteen, Fifteen, Sixteen, and Seventeen in Part III all provide examples of access to facilities not available through the run-time library and MS-DOS.

These five types of supercharging can also be combined to produce even more powerful and efficient programs. In particular, techniques that optimize speed work well when combined with techniques that provide access to facilities not previously available. The C programmer has, of course, started out with a very powerful language. Combined with the techniques presented in this book, the C language allows a programmer to build fast, efficient, and powerful applications for the PC.

Pros and Cons of Supercharging

The decision to spend the time and effort to supercharge a program is not a black and white one. Supercharging enables your program to run faster and to perform more tasks. But there are trade-offs, and you need to weigh the pros and cons carefully. Sometimes you have no choice but to supercharge, for instance, when your program needs direct access in order to perform its task. Still, there are potential side effects. Ultimately, the decision to supercharge depends on how and where the program will be used, how frequently it will be used, and the specific features it requires. In this section, we will discuss the advantages and disadvantages of supercharging an application.

The first disadvantage of supercharging is that it can limit the range of machines on which the program can run. Most of the techniques described earlier bypass some part of the IBM PC, its operating system software, the ROM BIOS, or the C compiler, to improve the program's efficiency. One of the functions of the software provided with the PC and the compiler is, however, to separate the application from the details of the specific hardware on which it's running. This is known as hiding the low level details from the high level portions of the program. In the case of the C compiler, this extends to the point of hiding the type of processor from the application—many C programs can run on anything from an IBM PC microcomputer to a Digital Equipment VAX minicomputer to a Cray supercomputer. If a function is rewritten in assembly language, it can run only on machines that use the 8086/8088/80286 series processors. Similarly, if an application uses the ROM BIOS, it can run only on machines whose ROM BIOS is exactly compatible with that of the IBM PC. The following table describes the effects of bypassing parts of the IBM PC software by supercharging:

Part	Isolates application from	Bypassed by	Bypassing causes program to run only on
C compiler	Kind of processor	Writing in assembly	8086/8088/80286 processors
C file I/O library	Local file system	Calling MS-DOS directly	MS-DOS machines
MS-DOS	ROM BIOS	Calling ROM BIOS directly	IBM PC ROM BIOS compatible machines
ROM BIOS	Hardware	Accessing the hardware	IBM PC hardware compatible machines

As this table indicates, there are different kinds of compatibility. Being IBM PC compatible does not guarantee that a machine can run your program. We can divide IBM PC "compatible" machines into three groups. The first group includes machines that are 100% hardware compatible. These will run any program that will run on the IBM PC. The second group includes machines with a ROM BIOS that is 100% compatible with the IBM PC, but whose lower level hardware may vary slightly. These machines will run programs that access the hardware only by going through MS-DOS or the ROM BIOS. The third group includes machines that run MS-DOS, but have a different ROM BIOS and underlying hardware. These will run only programs that access the hardware solely through MS-DOS. This explains why some programs will not run on all IBM PC "compatible" computers: there's more than one kind of "compatible."

From the point of view of compatibility, it would be nice to write programs that call only MS-DOS; then every program would run on every MS-DOS machine. Unfortunately, there are some good reasons to bypass MS-DOS and even the ROM BIOS. Bypassing can mean the difference between, say, a fast, responsive editor and one that can't display characters as fast as you can type them. It can mean a communications program that works 100% reliably, rather than one that loses characters occasionally. It can mean the difference between a game program with rich, full sound effects and one that only goes "beep." On the other hand, it can also mean a program that runs only on 100% IBM compatible machines—not very useful if your company has bought a large number of incompatible clones. Programmers who write applications for the IBM PC must make a series of decisions weighing features in the program versus the range of machines on which the program will run. And you, as an IBM PC programmer, must make the same decisions.

There is a second major disadvantage to supercharging: it often involves rewriting C code into assembly language. Since assembly language is harder to understand and change, this can increase the cost of both maintaining a program in the future and of adding new features to it. Whether rewriting in assembly language substantially increases the total cost of a program depends on the program, how much of it has been rewritten in assembly, and how well planned the split was between the C and assembly code.

We have discussed some disadvantages to supercharging and some situations in which only certain supercharging techniques should be used in a given application. On the other hand, there are two reasons to supercharge a program. The program isn't fast enough or it doesn't do enough. Both of these reasons are subjective—how fast is "fast enough?" If a thousand people instead of a dozen people are using a program, it is worth spending the extra time to polish the application thoroughly. If the program is used daily instead of once a month, supercharging is worthwhile. Only you, and the people who use your program, can decide whether supercharging is appropriate.

Some types of supercharging are harmless, or nearly so. Optimizing disk I/O and declaring variables to be registers do not change the functionality of the program, nor do they limit the machines on which the program can run. Rewriting selected sections in assembly language is also harmless if the program is to be run only on IBM PCs—i.e., it will never be ported to a VAX or a Macintosh—although assembly language code is harder to maintain and modify than C code. Directly accessing the ROM BIOS limits the program to ROM BIOS compatible machines, and directly accessing the hardware limits the program to hardware compatible machines. Here too, if the program in question is to be run only on IBM PCs, and not on clones with BIOSs that may be incompatible, then these supercharging techniques will not cause problems.

Sometimes you have no choice but to supercharge, regardless of the disadvantages. If your application needs access to a feature provided in the hardware but not accessible via MS-DOS, and perhaps not even via the ROM BIOS, then you must supercharge. It's no longer a matter of trading portability for efficiency; now it's a trade-off between portability and not doing it at all— and if you can't do it at all, you're not very likely to port it. This type of supercharging adds to new or existing programs functions that were previously impossible.

The point here is that you should not supercharge without first thinking through the consequences. Otherwise, you may end up with an unusable program—for example, one that runs on your development machine but not on the machines of the intended users of the program. If you think it through, you'll end up with a faster, better program that will impress everyone, not least of all yourself. Remember, once supercharged, a program makes a user's life a little easier every time it's run, and it takes no additional effort on your part.

Modular Programming

The first rule in writing a program that may later be supercharged is to write it in modules. When a program is written in modules, it's easy to rewrite any one of the modules to use a different, faster algorithm or to recode it in assembly language. If the program is not modular, supercharging it causes tremendous complications and confusion, and produces programs that are impossible to maintain.

The benefits of modular program design also apply to normal program development and maintenance, not just to supercharging a program. It is always a good idea to compose programs out of modules.

Designing a modular program is not simply a matter of breaking the design into chunks, with each chunk being limited to a specific size. The best way to learn how to write modular programs is to examine those written by others and to write your own. There are, unfortunately, no hard and fast rules for how to do it, but there are some general guidelines, which we discuss below.

Separate Function from Implementation

Every module has two faces. One face, shown to the other parts of the application, is its function. The other face, composed of the internal details seen only by the programmer and the compiler, is its implementation. The external face tells *what* a routine does, the internal face tells *how* it does it. Figure 2-3 illustrates this distinction using a television set. The external face includes the controls and display that interface to you, the user of the television set. The internal face includes the tubes and wires that react to the controls and generate the image to be displayed. When designing modules, it is important to separate the function of the module from its implementation. If the function remains constant, the implementation can be changed at any time without affecting the other modules in the program. Thus, we can rewrite one module to increase its efficiency without worrying about its impact on the rest of the program. It will speed up the routine and, therefore, the program as a whole, without changing its functionality.

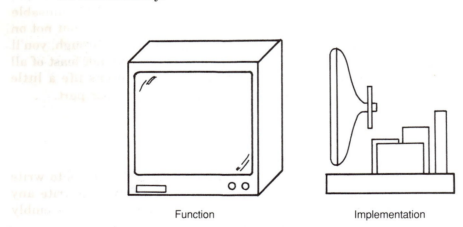

Function   Implementation

Figure 2-3. Function vs Implementation

Make Bite-sized Modules

Keep each module small enough so that you can understand its external function and internal algorithm all at once. One reason for making a program modular is to divide it into chunks that are understandable, even if the program is too large and complex to be understood as a whole. The modules themselves are composed of even smaller chunks of functionality, the functions.

Most of the programs we wish to create are too complicated to be fully understood all at once, but we can still deal with these large, complex systems by breaking them down into smaller problems. (See Figure 2-4.) This ability to deal with complexity by abstraction is one of man's most powerful intellectual tools. And it's equally useful whether we're writing an IBM PC application, building a bridge, or sending a person to the moon.

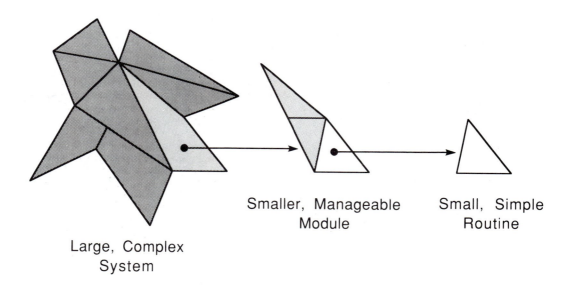

Smaller, Manageable
Module

Small, Simple
Routine

Large, Complex
System

Figure 2-4. Breaking Down Complexity

Minimize Inter-module Communication

Divide the program into modules so that the minimum amount of inter-module communication is required. This process is like cutting a diamond. Figure 2-5 illustrates how dividing a module properly into sub-modules minimizes the interconnections, while dividing it poorly complicates the design. Every problem or algorithm has lines along which it divides easily and naturally. Finding these lines is part of the art of programming. They most often run along the original conceptual boundaries of the machine or application. For instance, one natural division is between a display access module and a disk access module. For the same reasons that we design programs in modules, a piece of hardware is also designed in modules. The display and disk are two of the hardware modules in the IBM PC. The designers knew better than to design the whole PC system as one single, complex unit. Similarly, most applications inherit some of their design from the outside, real-world environment in which they'll be used. This external environment is also generally divided into modules in some way, which suggest lines along which our internal program modules can be split.

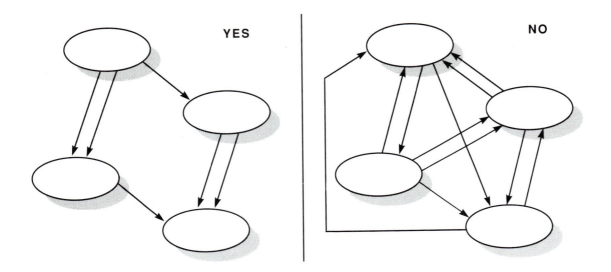

Figure 2-5. Minimize Interconnections

The divisions we've been talking about so far are horizontal: they separate parts of the program that are, in some sense, at the same level—for example, reading a block of data from a file and displaying it on the screen. Vertical divisions are also possible: they separate the different levels of sophistication— for example, controlling the disk drive on a physical level and dealing with it as a file system. Each of these can be an independent module. In the IBM PC, the ROM BIOS module controls the physical disk drive while the MS-DOS module treats the disk as a file system. (See Figure 2-6.) Subsequently higher modules add functionality for use by the higher levels of the application, simultaneously hiding the details of the operation by the lower levels. This keeps the higher levels from having to be concerned with the details of the lower levels; it also allows the lower level modules to be changed without affecting the higher levels.

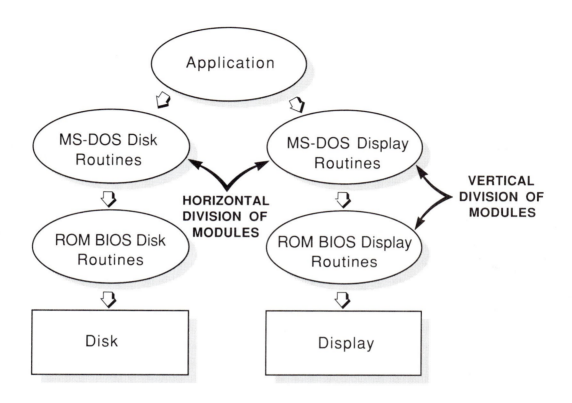

Figure 2-6. Vertical vs Horizontal Module Separation

Avoid Implicit Inter-module Communication

Always pass information between modules in parameters rather than in global variables. Someone looking at a module for the first time should not have to guess how information gets from one part of the program to another, or whether making a change in one part will affect another, seemingly unrelated part. If he can look at a well-defined interface, limited to the routines of the module and the parameters to those routines, this potential source of confusion and error can be reduced or eliminated. (See Figure 2-7.) There are times, however, when this is not possible or reasonable. Usually this happens because a large body of data simply must be exchanged between two modules; or, because a number of routines must all be passed the same piece of data, and setting a global variable is much more efficient than passing the same data to every routine called.

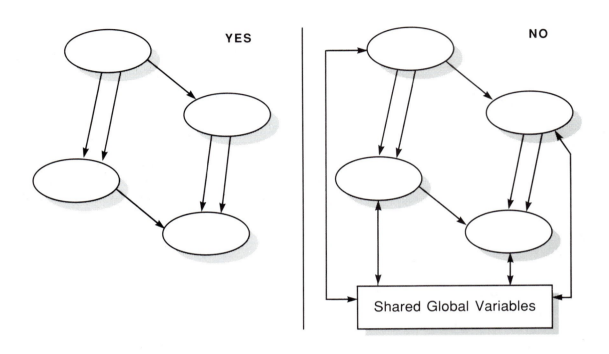

Figure 2-7. Pass Information Explicitly through Parameters

Measurement

The second rule of supercharging a program is to measure the program's performance, both before and after supercharging it. Sometimes it's obvious where the program is burning away processor time, for instance, when there is only one simple loop in the program. But it's easy to think you know where your program is spending its time and be completely wrong. Without actually measuring it, you can't really know. Similarly, without measuring the difference between the program's speed before and after supercharging it, you can't know whether or not you've done any good. Both of these types of measurement are easy to scoff at as unimportant, but both are essential to effective supercharging.

By their very nature, computers make it hard to see where they're spending their time. They execute much more rapidly than people can perceive, and there's no direct display of exactly what they're doing—not since the days of front panels with flashing lights, anyway. Luckily, computers are flexible enough to provide a solution to the problem: they can watch themselves, keep track of what they're doing, and report back to the programmer. Some compilers, in fact, will produce code that keeps track of how many times a function was called and how much time was spent in that function.

A more general solution to the problem is a module that collects and displays a histogram of what the value of the processor's instruction pointer (IP) was during the course of program execution. It can do this by interrupting the processor periodically (using the timer built into the PC), noting the value of the instruction pointer, then letting the program continue. When the program is finished, the module can display the histogram. This display is invaluable for pinpointing the 10% of the code in which the processor is spending 90% of its time. We will present a module that implements this IP sampling function in Chapter Seventeen. Figure 2-8 shows the basic idea.

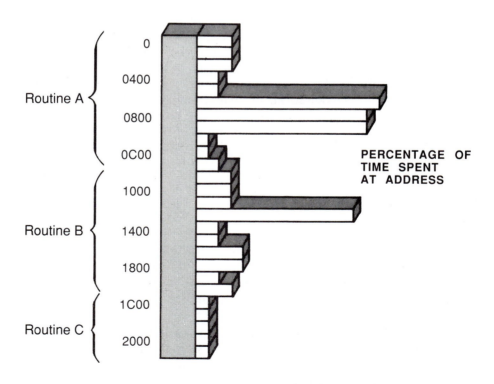

Figure 2-8. Instruction Pointer Histogram

While the IP histogram module helps the programmer to discover where the program is spending its time, it does not give an absolute measure of the total execution time. Therefore it isn't useful when comparing two versions of a program—the original versus the supercharged version. Total execution time can be determined using a somewhat cruder method: a stopwatch. To do this as simply as possible, it's a good idea to add to the program conditionally compiled code to do three things:

1. Display messages "starting execution" and "stopping execution." These messages tell when to start and stop the stopwatch, factoring out the initial loading time of the program, which is not under program control and therefore would bias the results of the measurement.

2. Generate test data. Most programs require external data for the program to read. It is easier to let the program generate fake data within the program than to locate or create a substantial amount of real data. The program can also generate "worst case" data to check the hardest input conditions.

3. Run the program code multiple times. To make program execution take long enough to be measured by a stopwatch and human reaction times, and long enough to factor out variations due to human error, it is often necessary to execute all or part of the program more than one time.

It is always easier to build measurement facilities into a program at the start than it is to add them in later. This is also true of generating test data. The best way is to use a constant, called CALIBRATE, which, if defined, enables compilation of the calibration and measurement code. This can easily be done using "#ifdef" directive.

Summary

Supercharging can improve an application in two ways: by increasing the speed of the application, and by adding features to it that previously were impossible. Increasing the speed of the program can be done a number of ways, from changing the algorithm or optimizing disk access, to rewriting the program in assembly language, to bypassing MS-DOS or the ROM BIOS and going directly to the hardware. Adding features involves bypassing the system software— MS-DOS or the ROM BIOS—in order to make use of facilities provided by a lower level of the system but not accessible to the application.

The decision to supercharge a program and the type of supercharging used depends on where and how the program will be used. Speed optimization must be traded off against limiting the types of machines on which the program can be run—IBM PCs only or clone PCs as well. Adding features, on the other hand, depends solely on the need for those features. If a feature is needed and cannot be implemented except by direct access to the ROM BIOS or hardware, the only trade-off is whether or not to write the program at all.

Once the decision to supercharge a program is made, and the type of supercharging is chosen, the programmer can do several things to make the job easier and less painful and, just as important, to make the application easier to maintain in the future. The first and most important thing is to write the program as a set of modules. This makes it easy to modify one part of the program without affecting the other parts. The second thing is to plan for performance measurement when the program is being written. This will allow you to compare the speed of two versions of the program without having to go to great lengths to create an environment in which such a comparison is possible.

The remainder of this book shows you how to go about supercharging programs using each of the techniques discussed above. It also provides numerous examples that should help you learn not only how to supercharge a program, but also how to write modular programs.

Exercises

1. Take a C program you've already written. Is it modular? Where could it be optimized?

2. Modify the C program from the first exercise to measure the speed. Measure it. After reading Part II of this book, try optimizing the program and remeasuring the speed.

Part I

Optimizing Execution Speed

Chapter 3

How to Call Assembly Routines from C

- Quick Introduction
- Assembly Segments and Groups
- Five Compiler Memory Models
- Interfacing C and Assembly
- Compiler Segment and Group Usage
- Calling Conventions
- Shortcuts

I n this chapter, we will explain how to call assembly language routines from C and how to call C functions from assembly language. These are, of course, really two sides of the same coin (or routine). We will also discuss segment and linker issues, such as where global variables are stored and how to access them. We will provide all of the information needed to write assembly language routines that can be called from a C program—the approach used most often in the rest of the book.

The reader should have a general understanding of assembly language programming and the underlying architecture of the IBM PC processor. A detailed knowledge of assembly language programming is not necessary to understand the material in this chapter, although it is needed to write any substantial routines in assembly, whether they're called by C code or stand by themselves. An introduction to assembly language for readers already familiar with C is available in Appendix A.

The specifics of how to call assembly routines vary from compiler to compiler. In this chapter, we present general information that applies to all compilers, and then give specific details using the Microsoft C compiler, version 3.0 or 4.0, and the Microsoft Macro Assembler (MASM).

A Very Quick Introduction to Calling Assembly Language

This chapter contains a great deal of information which is useful to programmers who want to mix C and assembly language programming. First, we will present a simple example and explanation of the most important aspects of interfacing C and assembly language. (See Listings 3-1 and 3-2 at the end of this chapter.) Impatient readers can then skip the rest of this chapter (for now!) and move directly on to Chapter Four. (We do recommend that, after reading the rest of Part I, you return and read all of this chapter.)

We will discuss a C callable assembly language routine on a line-by-line basis here, to give you a sense of how and why these routines are laid out the way they are. This will help to put the rest of the material in the chapter in its proper context.

Listings 3-1 and 3-2 explain how to call an assembly language routine from C. Listing 3-1 contains the C main program that performs the call, and Listing 3-2 is the assembly language subroutine. The program adds 1 plus 2 to produce 3 and then prints the result. This simple routine demonstrates the most important aspects of writing an assembly language routine called from a C program.

Most of the assembly language routines presented in this book have the same general format as the routine in Listing 3-2. They are all concerned with placing things in the proper segments, declaring the routine to be defined, saving registers, accessing parameters passed on the stack, restoring registers, and returning to the calling program. We will explain these concepts more fully later in this chapter.

The first statements in the example program are the SEGMENT and ASSUME pseudo-ops. They tell the assembler which segment to put the code and/or data into, and what to assume about the contents of the segment registers. The SEGMENT pseudo-op applies to everything between itself and the matching ENDS pseudo-op toward the end of the listing. This is a very simple example of only one segment. Additional data segments would require their own SEGMENT...ENDS pseudo-ops. The pseudo-ops in the example instruct the assembler to place the code between them in the _TEXT segment, which is where the C compiler places all code. The ASSUME pseudo-op then lets the assembler know that the code segment register (CS) will contain the base address of the _TEXT segment during the execution of the routine. We don't need to set this register: that's done by the code the compiler produces.

The next statement declares the function _add to be public, making it accessible to other modules. If this statement were not present, the routine would be private to this source code file. The linker would not be told the name, and therefore would not find the routine referenced by the main program. This would cause a linker error message to that effect. Note that the name of the function, as used in the C code, is preceded by an underscore (_). The C compiler automatically prepends this character to all names. Thus, even though you type "add" when entering the program, the compiler tells the linker that the name is "_add".

Next, we declare offsets to access the parameters to the routine. When the main program calls the function, it pushes the parameters onto the stack in reverse order. When the subroutine gets control, it saves the BP register and then sets BP to the current value of the stack pointer (SP). Once this is done, the parameters can be accessed at fixed offsets from BP. In this example, the a parameter is referenced as "[BP + a]" and the b parameter as "[BP + b]". We will discuss parameter passing in much greater detail later in this chapter.

The routine itself is now defined, starting at the PROC statement and continuing to the corresponding ENDP statement. These pseudo-ops surround a subroutine — PROC being short for procedure, another name for subroutine — and declare it to be either NEAR or FAR. This indicates whether a NEAR or FAR CALL should be used to invoke the routine, and consequently whether any RET instructions in the routine should do a NEAR or FAR return. We will use only one RET instruction, at the end of the function.

The routine itself first saves the BP register and then sets it to the contents of the SP register. Once this is done, the parameters are easy to access. The main function of the routine is then very simple: the a parameter is loaded into the AX register and the b parameter is added to it. C functions return their results in the AX register, as long as the results are 16 bits or less, so the answer is already in the proper place. All that is needed to finish the operation is to restore the BP register and execute a RET instruction.

The ENDP and ENDS pseudo-ops end the subroutine and segment. Finally, the END pseudo-op signifies the end of the assembly source code. This routine can then be assembled and linked with the C main program. (See Appendix B for details on how to assemble and link.) When run, it will print "1 + 2 = 3".

This example illustrates the rudimentary elements of writing an assembly language routine that is called from a C program. All of the assembly routines presented in this book will be similar to Listing 3-2. A complete discussion of interfacing C and assembly language is found in the rest of this chapter.

Segments and Groups

Before discussing the details of interfacing C and assembly routines, we need to discuss segments and groups. This material is not necessary for programming in C, but it is essential for assembly language programming, especially when the assembly language routines are used with C code.

There are two ways of viewing the memory of the IBM PC: as one large block, a megabyte in size, with absolute addresses ranging from 0 to FFFFF (hex); or as smaller blocks, each 64K bytes in size, which the program accesses by using a base address indicating the start of the block, plus an offset into the block that ranges from 0 to FFFF (hex). When we refer to the location of the memory-resident elements of the PC, such as display memory, the first view is more natural. The processor of the PC, however, unlike the processors of some other machines, forces us to use the smaller blocks when writing programs. These smaller, 64K-byte chunks are called "segments."

The processor contains internal registers that determine which segments can be accessed at any given time. These registers, called "segment registers," specify the base or starting address of the available segments. The base address can be virtually anywhere in the larger memory space, allowing the processor to access any part of memory by using the proper segment register value and offset. Segments, however, cannot begin at any arbitrary byte in the absolute memory space; they must start on a 16-byte boundary called a "paragraph." Since segments must begin on 16-byte boundaries, the bottom 4 bits of the absolute base address is always zero and does not need to be stored in the segment register. Figure 3-1 illustrates this arrangement. The value actually stored by the program in the segment register is the base address divided by 16. This means that both the contents of the segment registers and the offsets within the segments are 16-bit numbers. This is very convenient, since the 8086/8088/80286 is a 16-bit processor, making it the most natural size to deal with.

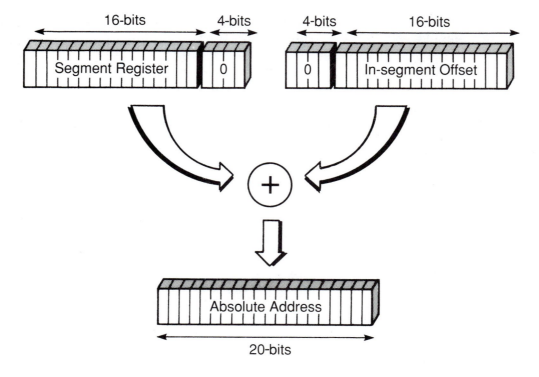

Figure 3-1. Segment Registers and Offsets

The processor contains several segment registers. One of these is used every time the processor accesses memory for any purpose, whether to fetch an instruction, read or write data, or push something onto the stack. The register used depends on the type of operation being performed. The following table lists all of the segment registers in the processor and the conditions under which each is used:

Segment	Register	Usage
Code	CS	Where instructions are taken from.
Stack	SS	Where the stack resides.
Data	DS	Where data is taken from and returned to.
Extra	ES	Used as a second DS in some instructions.

There is no reason why two segment registers cannot point to the same location (i.e., two segments are the same), or cannot point within 64K of the other (i.e., two segments overlap). For example, the data and stack segments could be the same, allowing pointers to point to data in either area without the pointer having to include a segment register value as well as the offset. In fact, the Microsoft C compiler does exactly this for exactly this reason. Similarly, if one of the segments is less than 64K bytes long, another segment can begin part way through it. Otherwise, we would be wasting the rest of the memory in that 64K block.

When code or data is taken from separately compiled modules—whether they're C modules, assembly modules, or a mix of the two—the code or data must often be combined into one or more segments. For example, two modules may each have global data which must be placed in the same data segment. It is possible to change the contents of the data segment register whenever a different module is entered or data from that module is referenced; but it is much more efficient to combine the data from the two modules into one segment and let the segment register contents remain the same. Similarly, if one function is to call another, it is better if both functions reside in the same code segment, even if they were compiled or assembled independently. Then the more efficient near type subroutine call can be used, rather than the more cumbersome far type call.

The program that combines segments from multiple modules is called the "linker." In assembly language, you can specify the segment in which you want a block of data or code to reside by using the SEGMENT...ENDS directives. The assembler then informs the linker by including this information in the object file it produces. The linker combines all of the code and data from the different modules into the appropriate segments, as directed by the information in the object files. The C compiler, unlike the assembler, automatically generates the appropriate segment information for the linker. The C programmer seldom needs to be concerned with it. That also means, however, that the programmer has less control over the segments and how they're used when writing in C.

Under some circumstances, a program may need to refer to any one of a number of segments using the same segment register value. This allows the data to be created using multiple segments, but to be referenced without having to change the contents of the segment register. As we will see later, the C compiler uses this facility to group different data classes together, while allowing references to data in any of the classes with the same data segment register value.

To accomplish this, you can request the linker to place several segments contiguously in memory; and to resolve references to those segments as offsets from the beginning of the whole group of segments, rather than from the beginning of the individual segment as it would normally do. This is done with the assembler GROUP directive. Of course, the combined size of all the segments in a group cannot be larger than 64K bytes—the size of a segment. Figure 3-2 shows multiple modules being combined into segments, and then multiple segments being combined into a group. You can think of the GROUP pseudo-op as a means of creating a new segment composed of multiple existing segments; a sort of "super segment."

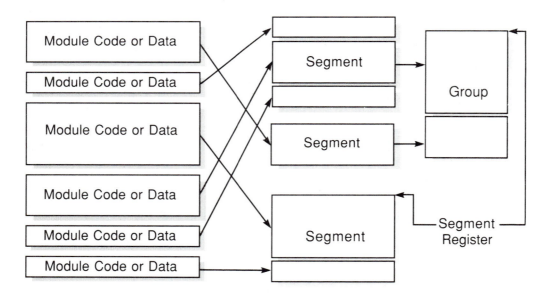

Figure 3-2. Segments and Groups

Compiler Memory Models

As we mentioned in the previous section, it is possible for different modules to use different segments, but it's more efficient for them to use a single segment and let the linker combine the code or data into that one segment. Sometimes, however, a program deals with more data than will fit in 64K bytes, and sometimes the program itself is larger than 64K bytes. Many compilers, including Microsoft's, allow programs to be larger than one segment and to use more data than 64K bytes, but at the cost of efficiency. Programs must use far rather than near calls, and pointers to data must be 32 rather than 16 bits. These different ways of dealing with segments are called the compiler "memory models."

We need compiler memory models because the segment addressing scheme of the IBM PC processor forces a decision on the programmer or compiler writer: He can either use 16-bit pointers and NEAR function calls, which are small and efficient but limit him to the four 64K segments available; or, he can use 32-bit pointers and FAR function calls that access the entire physical memory of the machine, at the expense of a slower and larger program. For assembly language programming, this decision can be made on a case-by-case basis, using whichever approach seems best for each variable or function. In the case of the code generated by the compiler, the choice of a default approach must be made first, although the programmer still has some flexibility. The default approach will be used unless the programmer explicitly overrides it. This decision is based on the programmer's choice of a memory model. Most compilers provide some combination of the following alternatives (See also Figure 3-3):

- Small model. All pointers are 16 bits in size. All function calls are NEAR. This model limits the program to 64K of code and 64K of data.

- Medium model. All pointers are 16 bits in size. Calls within a module are NEAR, calls between modules are FAR; each module is in a separate segment. This model permits the program to be as large as the available physical memory, but still limits the data to 64K.

- Compact model. All pointers are 32 bits in size; multiple segments are used as needed. All function calls are NEAR. This model limits the program to a single segment, but permits the data to be as large as the available physical memory. This model is not available in version 3.0 of Microsoft C, but is available in version 4.0.

- Large model. All pointers are 32 bits in size; multiple segments are used as needed. Function calls are the same as in the medium model. This model permits both the program and the data to be as large as the available physical memory.

■ Huge model. In the compact and large models, even though the total size of the data may be as large as physical memory, individual data items are limited to 64K. The huge model removes this restriction, but is otherwise identical to the large model. Huge model data items must, however, conform to certain size constraints. (See the C compiler manual for details.) This model is not available in version 3.0 of Microsoft C, but is available in version 4.0.

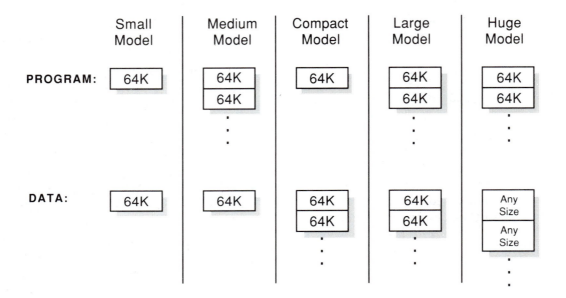

Figure 3-3. Memory Models

Some compilers leave you no choice of memory model: they only support one. Other compilers allow you to choose the model and to make selective exceptions to that choice. You can declare specific pointers to be 32 bits rather than 16, or 16 bits rather than 32. In the Microsoft C compiler, this is done using the key words "far" and "near". For example, "far int *pointer" would declare pointer to be a 32-bit pointer that can address anything in physical memory.

For most applications, the small model is sufficient. It is the simplest to deal with when writing assembly language routines that work with code produced by the C compiler. In this model, all the data is kept in the same segment, and the data and stack segment registers both point to that segment. The code resides in a single segment and all subroutine calls are near type calls. We'll use this model throughout the book.

Interfacing C and Assembly

To write assembly routines that are called by C functions or to call C functions from assembly, you need to know two things:

First, you need to know where in memory to place the segments in which the routines and variables belong. As we discussed earlier, objects from all the different modules, both C and assembly, must be combined into segments. References to these objects, both within a module and across modules, must be modified to reflect the final placement of the objects. The task of combining modules into the final application is the function of the linker. The linker performs this task based on instructions embedded in the modules it's linking. To write an assembly language module to be used with a C module, you must include information letting the linker know into which segment to place the code. You must also know where to find or place variables—local to this module and global to the program as a whole—that you want to use. When writing in C, the compiler automatically includes all this information for the linker. When writing in assembly, you must do it yourself.

The second thing you need to know is how to invoke a function: how to pass parameters to the function, what instruction to use to call the function, and where to find the result returned from the function. This is another area that is simple from the point of view of C, but more complex when viewed from assembly language. When writing in C, it's very easy to call a function. You just write something like "callIt(a,b,c)". The compiler then translates this simple call into a series of instructions which get or compute the parameters to be passed, push them onto the stack so the called function can find them, make a subroutine call to the function, and retrieve the result returned by the function. Similarly, the called function must be careful not to destroy information stored in the processor's registers that the caller still needs; it must access the input parameters as needed to perform its task, and it must place the result where the caller can find it. When writing in assembly language, all of this must be done by the programmer.

The conventions for calling a function are known as the "calling conventions" of the compiler. They include:

- Where to put the parameters to be passed to the called function.
- What assembly language instruction to use to call the function.
- What state the caller will find the system in when it regains control. This includes which registers in the processor the function is allowed to destroy.
- Where to put the value (if any) returned by the function.

In your compiler manual there should be a section on calling conventions —it may be called that or it may be called "Interfacing with Other Languages" or "Technical Information," or something similar. That section will include all the information described above. You should find that section in your compiler manual and read over it before continuing with this chapter.

We will be using the Microsoft C compiler, version 3.0 or 4.0, for all our examples. Other compilers have similar, but not necessarily identical, conventions. Also, we will be using the small memory model of the compiler, which is sufficient for most applications and simpler to deal with than the other models.

Compiler Segment and Group Usage

C allows the user to create several different types of program and data information:

Type	Includes
Code	All of the executable code produced by the compiler.
Global data	Variables accessible to all modules. They may be initialized or uninitialized.
Static data	Variables accessible only within a specific module or function. They may be initialized or uninitialized.
Parameters	Variables that are input (parameters) to a function.
Automatic data	Variables that exist only for the duration of the function. They are also called "local variables."

Examples of each of these types of program and data information are given in Listing 3-3, shown at the end of this chapter. Take a moment now to look through this listing. All these types of data are familiar to the C programmer, but not all of them are used every day. It is important to have a complete description of where the C compiler stores each of them in order to understand how to access global data for communication with other modules, and how to create variables that are local to the assembly language module. This information varies from compiler to compiler. The remainder of this section is specific to the Microsoft C compiler, version 3.0 or 4.0.

The Microsoft C compiler keeps these different types of data in several different segments:

Segment Name	Contents
_BSS	Uninitialized static data (except those declared far).
_DATA	Uninitialized global data and initialized global and static data (except those declared far).
Data segments	Global and static data declared far. Initialized items have a class name of FAR_DATA; uninitialized items have a class name of FAR_BSS.
STACK	Automatic variables.
CONST	Constants that are read-only (floating point constants, and segments values for far data items).
_TEXT	Code.

The _DATA, CONST, _BSS, and STACK segments are combined in a segment group called DGROUP. The data and stack segment registers both point to the start of this group during normal execution. In addition, a segment called NULL is included as the first segment in this group. This segment contains the compiler copyright notice and is used to detect invalid pointer usage. It is checked before and after the program executes; if the contents have changed, something has gone seriously wrong. Most likely the program has erroneously written indirectly to a zero pointer (which would point to the beginning of this segment). If this is the case, the error message "Null pointer assignment" is displayed. This group is, of course, limited to a total size of 64K bytes. All of these segments and the group DGROUP are shown in Figure 3-4.

To use C items from assembly or assembly items from C, they must be declared to belong to the proper segment and to be the same size as their corresponding declaration in the other module or language. Also, in the case of data segments, the segment must be declared to belong to the proper group. The one exception to this is external functions—that is, functions contained in another module but used in this one. They can be declared simply NEAR rather than as belonging to the _TEXT segment. This is all the assembler needs to know about the object, and the linker will correctly discover the segment in which the called function resides. By declaring the external function as NEAR, you are telling the assembler and linker that the called function is in the same code segment as the caller.

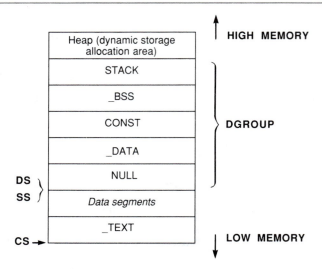

Figure 3-4. Compiler Segments and Groups

For C modules, this declaration of segments is handled automatically by the compiler. For assembly language modules, the programmer must declare them. Listing 3-4 shows the assembly language declaration of the variables shown in Listing 3-3.

One naming convention should be specifically noted: C variable names are preceded with an underscore (_) when referenced in assembly. This is because the C compiler automatically prepends an underscore to all function and data names defined. If you define a variable "xyz", the C compiler will actually name it "_xyz". Similarly, if you want to be able to reference an assembly variable from C, its name must begin with an underscore. Assembly language variables without an initial underscore, regardless of the segment in which they reside, are inaccessible from C.

Calling Conventions

All C compilers follow essentially the same sequence of actions when calling a function:

1. Save any registers that the called function may destroy and that are needed by the caller. Most compilers dictate that certain registers will always be preserved by the called function, so the caller does not need to save those registers.

2. Push the parameters to be passed to the function onto the stack. Most C compilers push the parameters in the reverse order from which they appear in the parameter list. This places the first parameter in the list (the last one pushed) at the top of the stack.

3. Call the function. This is always done with a CALL instruction, but it may be a NEAR CALL or a FAR CALL. The function then executes and eventually returns control to the caller.

4. Recover the return value. Most compilers return simple values in AX or AX/DX and larger values in static memory.

5. Pop the parameters off the stack.

6. Restore any saved registers.

In addition to these actions, certain conditions are assumed always to hold. In particular, the value of the segment registers CS, DS, and SS will always point to a particular set of segments.

The remainder of this section will discuss in detail the calling conventions of the Microsoft C compiler, version 3.0 or 4.0. Both versions of the compiler use the same calling convention, and probably all future versions will use it as well. However, earlier versions used a different set of conventions, not compatible with versions 3.0 and 4.0.

In Microsoft C, these conditions always hold: the DS and SS registers always point to the DGROUP group, and the CS register always points to the _TEXT segment, as discussed earlier in this chapter. A function can change these temporarily, but they must always be restored before the function returns. In addition, each function is required to preserve the contents of the BP, SI, and DI registers. The compiler does not, however, count on any of the other registers being preserved across function calls. Therefore, before calling a C function, all registers except BP, SI, and DI need to be saved if your assembly code is counting on the contents of these registers remaining unchanged. Also, an assembly routine called from C must save and restore the registers BP, SI, and DI if it changes them.

When calling a function, the parameters to the function are pushed in reverse order. For example, "callIt(a,b,c)" would push c, then b, then a, as shown in Figure 3-5. Variables of type char are converted to int before being pushed (char to int, unsigned char to unsigned int). Float type variables are converted to double. Structures are pushed entirely onto the stack, last word first. For arrays, a pointer to the array is pushed. Near pointers are 16 bits; far pointers are 32 bits, with the segment register value being pushed first, then the offset. The following table summarizes the sizes used when pushing parameters:

Type	Convert to	Size on stack
char	int	word
unsigned char	unsigned int	word
short		word
unsigned short		word
int		word
unsigned int		word
long		double word
unsigned long		double word
float	double	64 bits
double		64 bits
near pointer		word
far pointer		double word
array	pointer to array	word
structure		n words

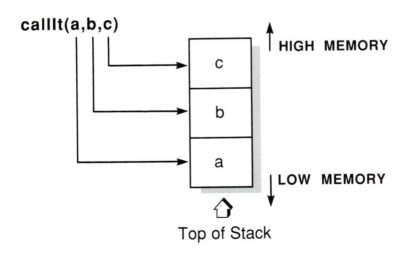

Figure 3-5. Order of Parameter Pushing

The main reason for pushing the parameters in reverse order is to allow for functions with a variable number of parameters, such as printf. By pushing the parameters in this order, the first parameter is left at the top of the stack. Even without knowing how many parameters there are, this first one can always be found by the called function. The first parameter can then specify the number of parameters that follow—as it does in the printf function.

When writing assembly language routines to be called by C functions, an easy way to remember the order of the parameters on the stack is to notice two things. First, the stack grows downward, toward lower memory. Second, the parameters are pushed in reverse order. These two facts cancel each other out, so the final arrangement of parameters in memory is in the same order as the original parameter list.

The CALL instruction is used to transfer control to the called function, whether an assembly function is being called from C—in which case the compiler generates the CALL instruction—or a C function is being called from assembly—in which case the programmer generates the CALL instruction. This will always be a NEAR CALL in the small memory model.

We recommend that you use the following set of instructions at the start of each function:

```
PUSH    BP          ; Save BP
MOV     BP,SP       ; Set BP from SP
SUB     SP,n        ; Reserve n bytes on the stack for local
                    ; variables (not needed if n is zero)
PUSH    DI          ; Save the DI and SI registers
PUSH    SI
```

This allows you to modify any registers you wish (except, of course, the segment registers). It also simplifies the task of accessing parameters, since they will always be at a constant offset from the BP register. If the program used the SP to access parameters, the offset would vary depending upon how much had subsequently been pushed onto the stack. This can be complicated to deal with and can lead to errors. Another advantage to using the BP register is that, if the function allocates local storage on the stack by subtracting the amount needed from the stack pointer as shown, the local variables can be accessed at a constant negative offset from the BP register. Figure 3-6 shows the stack when the program is in the middle of executing a function.

Before exiting, the following complimentary code should be used:

```
POP     SI          ; Restore the DI and SI registers
POP     DI
MOV     SP,BP       ; Restore the stack pointer
POP     BP          ; Restore the BP register
```

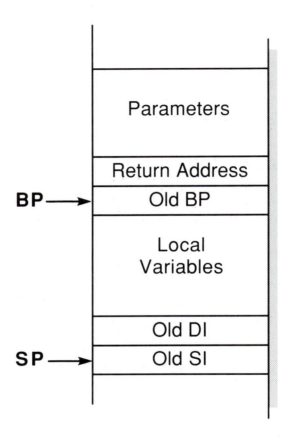

Figure 3-6. Stack Layout During Function Execution

If no local storage has been allocated on the stack, the "MOV SP,BP" instruction is not required. If storage has been allocated, however, this is a quick way to deallocate it.

The value returned from the called function is stored in the AX register for 16-bit or smaller values and the AX/DX registers for 32-bit values. Larger values—structures, floats, and doubles—are stored in a static memory area, and a pointer to them is returned in AX.

The following table summarizes where the resulting value is returned for each type. When AX/DX is used, DX holds the high order word in the case of numbers, or the segment register value in the case of pointers.

Type	Result Location
char	AX
unsigned char	AX
short	AX
unsigned short	AX
int	AX
unsigned int	AX
long	AX/DX
unsigned long	AX/DX
structure	static memory; pointer in AX
float	static memory; pointer in AX
double	static memory; pointer in AX
near pointer	AX
far pointer	AX/DX

For example, to call the retNext function (which was first shown in C in Listing 3-3) with a parameter of 10 ("retNext(10)"), the assembly code in Listing 3-5 could be used. On the other side, the function retNext, recoded in assembly, would look like Listing 3-6.

Shortcuts

Compared with a C program, there is a lot of text in an assembly language routine. There are also a number of concepts, such as segments and registers, which you don't have to deal with in C, but which are crucial to the proper operation of a piece of assembly code. All these complications provide additional areas where bugs can creep into the program, and bugs do creep in, given the least opportunity. Anything that can be done to simplify the job, therefore, will not only save you time, but also make it more likely that your code will work properly.

If you're going to be doing a lot of combined C and assembly programming, you can create a standard header file containing the segment definitions, ASSUME statement, and any other definitions you use regularly. This file can be included in the assembly code using the INCLUDE directive.

Another more powerful way to reduce the amount of work required to implement an assembly language routine is to write it first in C; then debug it, which is much easier in C than in assembly. Then use the compiler to translate it into assembly. Virtually all C compilers have an option that produces a file containing assembly language source code equivalent to the C source code. Often this file will need to be restructured, and comments will have to be added to make it more maintainable. The compiler does not produce the most well organized output, and certainly not the best commented. Nevertheless, using the compiler will take much less time than writing the file from scratch by hand.

Unlike a hand-coded assembly routine, this translated code is certain to work, since it's a translation of a C routine that worked. Starting from this point, changes can be made in the assembly code in small steps. If each step is tested thoroughly before the next step is taken, the probability of introducing bugs is dramatically reduced. We will present examples of this approach to assembly language recoding in the next two chapters.

[Warning! Version 3.0 of Microsoft C does not always produce an accurate assembly language translation of the C program. In particular, relative jumps that jump to the wrong location are sometimes generated. The assembly language should be checked carefully by hand and tested before being used. Version 4.0 corrects this problem.]

Summary

Different compilers use slightly different approaches to the interface between functions, but they all must standardize some things:

- Which segments to put the code and data in.
- What conventions to follow with regard to register saving and segment register contents.
- How to pass parameters to the called function.
- How to call the function.
- How to collect the result.

A programmer wanting to use both C and assembly must know and understand these conventions. Once he does, he understands both how to write assembly routines to be called by C programs, and also how to call C functions from assembly.

Assembly language programming is, however, much more prone to bugs than C programming is. It should not be used unless the desired function cannot be accomplished satisfactorily in C. If assembly language is used, you can take certain steps to reduce the chance of errors being introduced. One of the best allies of the programmer in this case is the compiler, which can be used to translate a C function into the equivalent assembly code. This gives the programmer a starting point, allowing incremental, rather than drastic, error-prone changes.

Exercises

1. Write a main program in C to drive the retNext function for testing purposes. This program should ask for a value to pass to retNext, call retNext, and then display the result returned by retNext. Try the C version of the function, then the assembly version.

2. Modify the assembly version of retNext to call printf, and display the value passed to it and the current value of count each time it's called.

3. Modify retNext to use the large memory model (assuming your compiler supports one).

Listing 3-1. "add1to2.c":

```
/*                    Example: Add 1 to 2 and Print It
 */

/*      main()

        Function: Add 1 and 2 and print the result.

        Algorithm: Call add to add the two numbers, and printf to print them.
*/

main()

{
        printf("1 + 2 = %d.\n",add(1,2));
}
```

Listing 3-2. "add.asm":

```
;                    Example Function to Add Two Numbers

_TEXT      segment byte public 'CODE'          ; Place the code in the code segment

           assume  CS:_TEXT                     ; Assume the CS register points to it

; _add(a,b)
;
; Function: Add together the two input parameters and return the result.
;
; Algorithm: Save BP and set it to SP to access the parameters. Add the two
; parameters together in the AX register. Restore the BP register. And
; return.

           public  _add                        ; Routine is available to other modules

           a = 4                               ; Offset from BP to the parameter a
           b = 6                               ; Offset to parameter b

_add       proc near                           ; NEAR type subroutine
           push    bp                          ; Save the BP register
           mov     bp,sp                       ; Set BP to SP; easier to access parameters
           mov     ax,[bp+a]                   ; AX = a (get the a parameter)
           add     ax,[bp+b]                   ; AX += b (add in the b parameter)
           pop     bp                          ; Restore the BP register
           ret                                 ; Return to caller
_add       endp                                ; End of subroutine

_TEXT      ends                                ; End of code segment

           end                                 ; End of assembly code
```

Listing 3-3. "typex.c":

```c
/*                  Examples of Types of Data & Code in C
*/

int a,b;                           /* Uninitialized global data. */

int x = {5};                       /* Initialized global data. */

static int i;                      /* Uninitialized static data local
                                       to this module. */

static int y = {9};                /* Initialized static data local to
                                       this module. */

/* retNext(inc): returns the current value of a count maintained by
    the routine, and then adds inc to the count. */

retNext(inc)

int inc;            /* Parameter data. */

{
        static int lastinc;        /* Uninitialized static data local
                                       to this function. */
        static int count = {0};  /* Initialized static data local to
                                       this function. */
        int retValue;              /* Automatic data. */

        lastinc = inc;             /* Code. */
        retValue = count;          /* Code. */
        count += inc;              /* Code. */
        return(retValue);          /* Code. */
}
```

Listing 3-4. "decl.asm":

```asm
;                    Assembly Equivalents for C Data

; First we declare the segments and groups:

_TEXT     SEGMENT    BYTE PUBLIC 'CODE'
_TEXT     ENDS

_BSS      SEGMENT    WORD PUBLIC 'BSS'
_BSS      ENDS

_DATA     SEGMENT    WORD PUBLIC 'DATA'
_DATA     ENDS

CONST     SEGMENT    WORD PUBLIC 'CONST'
CONST     ENDS
```

Listing 3-4. "decl.asm" *cont.*:

```
DGROUP   GROUP    CONST,_BSS,_DATA

; Next we declare the variables:

_DATA    SEGMENT

         EXTRN    _a:WORD        ; int a, b
         EXTRN    _b:WORD

         PUBLIC   _x             ; int x = {5}
_x       DW       5

_y       DW       9             ; static int y = {9}

_count   DW       0             ; static int count = {0}

_DATA    ENDS

_BSS     SEGMENT

_i       DW       ?             ; static int i

_lastinc DW       ?             ; static int lastinc

_BSS     ENDS

; Note that _y, _i, _lastinc, and _count are not accessible
; outside this module. Also note that the parameter inc and
; the automatic variable retValue are not declared here. They
; are allocated on the stack at run-time.
```

Listing 3-5. "caller.asm":

```
;        Assembly Equivalent of "retNext(10)"

         ASSUME   CS:_TEXT

         EXTRN    _retNext:NEAR

              .
              .
              .

; The following is the C function call "retNext(10)":

         MOV      AX,10          ; Push the parameter
         PUSH     AX
         CALL     _retNext       ; Call the function
```

Listing 3-5. "caller.asm" *cont.*:

```
        POP     BX                      ; Pop the parameter without destroying AX

; At this point, AX contains the return value from retNext(10).
                .
                .
                .
```

Listing 3-6. "called.asm":

```
;                       Assembly Equivalent of the retNext Function
;
; Note: The declarations in Listing 3-4 must precede this code;
; but the declarations of _a and _b should be removed.

; Let the assembler know what to assume about segment registers:
        ASSUME  CS:_TEXT,DS:DGROUP,SS:DGROUP

; Code goes in the _TEXT segment:
_TEXT   SEGMENT

; This function will be callable from other modules:
        PUBLIC  _retNext
_retNext PROC NEAR

        inc = 4                 ; Parameter inc offset from BP

        PUSH    BP              ; Save registers
        MOV     BP,SP
        PUSH    DI
        PUSH    SI

        MOV     BX,[BP+inc]     ; lastinc = inc
        MOV     _lastinc,BX

        MOV     AX,_count       ; retValue = count (AX is retValue)

        ADD     _count,BX       ; count += inc

        POP     SI              ; Restore the registers
        POP     DI
        POP     BP

        RET                     ; return(retValue)

_retNext ENDP

_TEXT   ENDS
```

Chapter 4

Processor Time Optimization: *RAMSort*

In this chapter we will develop and optimize RAMSort—a program that reads text into RAM from the standard input, sorts it in RAM, and writes it out to the standard output. The input data is sorted alphabetically by line. RAMSort duplicates the SORT function provided with MS-DOS, but also provides the source code, so you can make changes in what it does and how it does it. RAMSort can also be used as a base for other similar programs.

It is difficult to find the right place to optimize code, especially when recoding into assembly language. We will demonstrate how recoding ten lines in the right area is more effective than recoding a hundred lines in the wrong area.

RAM Sorts

Sorting is the process of ordering elements in a list according to certain criteria—numerically, alphabetically, chronologically, by degree of importance (which itself needs to be defined), and so forth. Independent of the criteria used for selecting the order, there are numerous algorithms for sorting lists. In this chapter, we use the "selection sort" algorithm because it is simple to understand and implement, it performs reasonably well, and requires a minimum amount of memory. The algorithm we describe is also a type of "RAM sort," which simply means that the data to be sorted will be read entirely into RAM, sorted, then written out. A RAM sort limits the amount of data that can be sorted to the amount of available RAM. Other kinds of sorts store the data on disk and can therefore sort much larger amounts of information.

In a selection sort, the array of data to be sorted is divided into two parts: the first contains the sorted elements (initially none), and the second contains the unsorted elements. The array is scanned *n-1* times, where *n* is the number of elements to be sorted. Each pass finds the lowest unsorted element and adds it to the end of the sorted portion of the array. This can be very easily implemented by maintaining an index to the beginning of the unsorted part of the array. When a new element is to be added to the sorted portion, it is simply exchanged with the first unsorted element. Then the index to the start of the unsorted part of the array is incremented, incorporating the new element into the sorted part of the array. This process is shown in Figure 4-1.

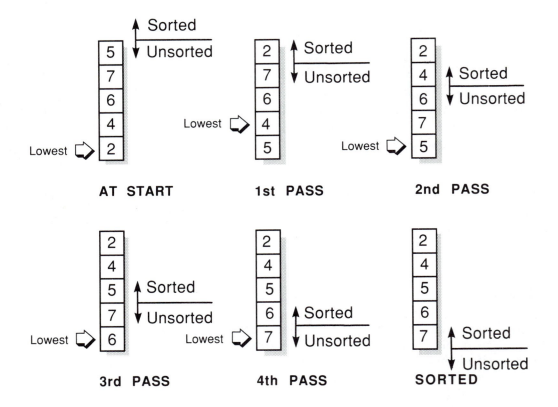

Figure 4-1. Selection Sort

Since each pass through the array removes one unsorted element, the program has one less element to search through on each successive pass. The algorithm, therefore, takes 0.5*n*(n-1) iterations of the inner loop (the loop that checks each element to find the lowest one). Because this number grows very rapidly as the number of elements to be sorted grows, it is important to implement the algorithm efficiently.

More information about this and many other sorting algorithms can be found in *The Art of Computer Programming, Volume 3: Sorting and Searching* by Donald E. Knuth.

The RAMSort C Program

Developing a fast and efficient program involves much more than just recoding parts of the program from C into assembly. It is far more important to choose the best algorithm and data structures, as demonstrated in our RAMSort program.

Sorting the text involves reordering the lines in RAM. If we were to simply reshuffle all of the characters each time, it would be very slow. Instead, we will keep an array of pointers to the initial byte of each line in RAM. When we need to shuffle the lines, we will exchange the pointers rather than moving the entire line. This arrangement of pointers and lines of text is shown in Figure 4-2. A line pointer array can also quickly locate the start of each line, which is the place to begin comparing two lines.

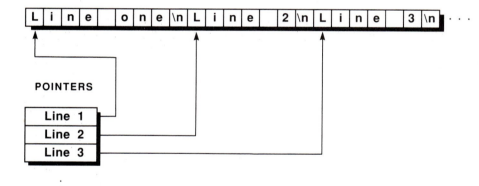

Figure 4-2. Pointers to Text Lines

The MS-DOS SORT program allows the lines to be sorted starting at a given column. RAMsort can provide this feature as well without sacrificing efficiency, by keeping a second pointer for each line. The second pointer points to the part of the line where sorting is to start. Having a second pointer also allows the program to be customized to start the sort at some place in the line other than a particular column; for example, you can divide the line into fields separated by tabs and start sorting after the *n*th tab.

Rather than ending the lines in the array with the newline character (\n), the individual lines will end with a null (zero) byte. This is the standard end of text string indicator for C and using it will simplify the job of comparing two lines. The lines will reside contiguously in a buffer, as shown in Figure 4-2.

The RAMSort program consists of three main phases:

1. Reading in the text.

2. Sorting the text.

3. Writing out the text.

"Reading in the text" means simply taking the text from the standard input and placing it into a buffer, building the pointer table as we go along. The standard gets function will read in one line at a time and store the line null-terminated (with a zero byte at the end). The column selection option adjusts the start-of-sort pointers to a place in each line a certain number of bytes after the start-of-line pointers.

Writing the sorted file is even easier — we just go through the pointer table and write each line to the standard output. Of course, the pointers no longer point to lines of text organized sequentially in memory. After being sorted, they jump all over memory, pointing at lines in the new order. But writing the lines out still means just writing each line referenced in the line pointer array, in the order in which it appears in the array.

Since we know we are going to be recoding into assembly, and that the most likely candidate for recoding is the sort routine, we will separate the sorting part of the code into a separate module. Later, we will replace the sort module with a functionally equivalent, assembly language version.

Listings 4-1, 4-2, and 4-3 contain the RAMSort program coded in C. Listing 4-2 is the main program; 4-3 is the functional heart, the sort routine; and 4-1 is an include file containing constants, structure definitions, and globals used by both C modules. We will describe the structure of the code in more detail below.

The lines of text are stored in the array called "buffer". A second array, lPtr, contains the pointers to the lines in the buffer. For each line, there is a structure in lPtr with two pointers. The first pointer, called start, points to the start of the line in the buffer. The second pointer, sortAt, points to the character at which to start sorting that line. The global variable nextLPtr points to the entry in lPtr where the next line pointer should go. If there are no lines, this variable points to the start of lPtr. The global nextLPtr is a pointer into the array of pointers to lines, and is not itself a pointer to a line.

The main function in RAMSort coordinates the sequence of operations to perform the sort. It starts by filling the buffer with lines, either by calling readLines or fillLines. The readLines function takes the data from the standard input, while the fillLines function generates the data internally for testing purposes. (This type of testing will be explained later in the chapter.) The main function then scans the command line arguments for a column number at which to start sorting. If it finds one, it calls offLines to set the sortAt field of each line pointer. Next, the lines are sorted by sortLines. And finally, writeLines writes the sorted lines of text to the standard output.

The function fillLines fills the buffer with hard-to-sort data. It starts with a line containing all Z's: "ZZZZZZZZZ"; the next line contains "ZZZZZZZZY"; then "ZZZZZZZZX"; etc. This is the worst kind of data to sort alphabetically. It's in reverse order and most of the initial characters of each line are the same, so a comparison of two lines must first compare all the identical initial characters.

The readLines function repeatedly calls the standard input function gets to read the lines to be sorted into memory from the standard input. The gets function null-terminates the lines it reads in, so the program needs only set the line pointers to the start of each line read. The readLines function also checks that the data to be sorted fits in memory. If not, it issues an error message and terminates execution of the program.

The writeLines function is one of the simplest in the RAMSort program. It simply goes through the line pointer array and call puts for each line.

The function offLines updates the sortAt portion of the line pointer structure. It is passed the number of characters into the line at which to start sorting. You might think that offLines merely involves setting sortAt to start plus the offset requested. But the line may be shorter than the desired offset. In that case, sortAt should be set to the end of the line. To detect such a case, RAMSort must scan the line, looking for the terminating zero byte.

The last routine in Listing 4-2 is fatal. This function reports fatal errors and then immediately returns to MS-DOS.

The algorithm used in RAMSort was discussed earlier in detail. It consists of two nested for loops. (See Listing 4-3.) The outer loop repeats n-1 times, where n is the number of elements to be sorted. The inner loop repeats once for each remaining unsorted element. It finds the lowest element available in the unsorted portion of the array, then moves it to the sorted part of the array.

Converting C to Assembly

At first glance, converting the sort routine in Listing 4-3 looks like a formidable task, especially since we are changing only part of it; but the C compiler can do the conversion for us. Most C compilers have an option that produces a file containing an assembly language equivalent of the C source code. Listing 4-4 is the assembly code produced by the Microsoft C compiler (version 3.0).

It includes:

- All the assembler directives needed.

- Definitions of the segments and groups used by the compiler.

- A set of working code from which to start optimizing.

The working code is especially important, because assembly language programming is more difficult and prone to error than C programming is. It is easier to make incremental changes to an existing program than to write a new program from scratch. Also, you are less likely to introduce mistakes.

Note: There is a line located two lines before label $F46 and near the beginning of the sortLines function that, as generated by the compiler, causes an error message when run through the assembler. To eliminate the error message, the line must be changed from "mov [bp-8],OFFSET DGROUP:_lPtr" to "mov WORD PTR [bp-8],OFFSET DGROUP:_lPtr".

Listing 4-5 shows the same code as above with a few changes that make it easier to use. Numeric references are replaced with symbolic names, and the original C code is inserted in comments. After converting C code to assembly, it's a good idea to keep the C code as well. It serves as additional documentation about the function, and the programmer can use it to port the program to a new machine. In the light of this more extensive example, the reader may wish to return at this point to Chapter Three and review the material presented there.

Measuring Performance

Before optimizing the RAMSort program, we need a means of measuring its performance. Without measuring, we won't know whether we've actually accomplished anything by optimizing the code. We have built into the RAMSort program a means of checking how much we've improved the performance of the program as we proceed. To use it, we recompile RAMSort with the CALIBRATE constant defined in the "rsort.h" include file.

The CALIBRATE option changes the way the program operates. Rather than reading its input from the standard input, it fills the buffer with a large amount of "fake" data. This data is chosen specifically because it is hard to sort. It consists of the string "ZZZZZ...ZZ", followed by "ZZZZZ...ZY", then "ZZZZZ...ZX", etc. Then it displays the message "Starting sort..." on the console. When the sort is finished, it displays "done". We can time the operation with a stopwatch, without having to find or generate a large input file of test data. The initial size of the buffer (9K) was chosen because it produces enough data that the CALIBRATE mode runs long enough to take meaningful timing measurements, but not so long that we have to wait all day for it. For normal use, this buffer size will be increased.

The CALIBRATE option also lets us time the program independent of the speed of the disk. This is important for three reasons. First, the type of disk can make a huge difference in the speed of the operation. Second, the disk I/O time can swamp the sort time, raising questions about the accuracy of the comparisons. Third, the placement of files on the disk can change the timing, also invalidating comparisons.

Running the original C program with CALIBRATE turned on, on an IBM PC, yields a run-time of 85 seconds. Remember that number, as we will be re-timing the program after each change.

Optimizing the Wrong Way

Optimizing is a difficult business. You have to hit exactly the right spot for it to do much good. Before we show the right place to optimize RAMSort, we'll show a couple of wrong places.

Optimization means writing better, tighter code than that written by the compiler. A lot of man hours went into making compiler-generated code as good as possible though, so it's hard, sometimes impossible to beat. Before reading further, take a look at the code produced by the Microsoft compiler. Can you do it better?

The most obvious candidate for improvement is the block of code below the label $L20001. This is where the pointer array entries pointed to by lowLPtr and srchLPtr are exchanged. We intended to use newLPtr only as a temporary storage location, but the compiler took our instructions literally and preserved the value after execution. Registers could have held the temporary value, but the compiler didn't realize that. This is an example of the compiler being dumber than we are. The compiler deals with each line of code individually. It doesn't look past the current line to see, for example, whether the variable being set to is ever referenced again. This sort of myopia is something we can improve on.

Listing 4-6 shows the original block of code and a more efficient replacement for it. We save five instruction execution times each pass through the loop. Now we assemble the sort module, link it with the main program, and run it again with CALIBRATE turned on. The result is 85 seconds—within a second of the original time. Something has clearly gone wrong!

What went wrong was our analysis of the program and how to optimize it. The sort routine has two loops. The outer loop is executed once for each line of input, or n times for n lines of input. The inner loop, however, is executed $0.5*n*(n-1)$ times—remember, this is the loop that finds the lowest line each time. So, if there are 900 lines of input (as is the case with the CALIBRATE option), the outer loop executes 900 times, while the inner loop executes 404,550 times, almost 450 times as much. No wonder optimizations in the outer loop don't do much good.

Now we've narrowed our aim to a handful of lines of code. So let's try once more to optimize the routine. This time we notice that the compiler-generated code did not use the SI and DI registers. If we keep the two variables used most often in the inner loop—lowLPtr and srchLPtr—in these registers, the program speed should increase considerably. As a side effect, the code we just optimized becomes even more efficient. Listing 4-7 shows this change. Note that if we use the DI register, it must be saved and restored so that the original contents are not disturbed. The DI register should be saved and restored at the same point in the program as the SI register.

Now using the CALIBRATE option produces a running time of 75 seconds, a definite, though not outstanding improvement over the original 85 seconds. So this seems to be a worthwhile, but slightly disappointing optimization. The version 3.0 compiler from Microsoft, however, has register variables. With this compiler, declaring a variable to be "register" type causes it to be kept in the SI or DI register. You can declare up to two variables to be register type. This is how the programmer can tell the compiler to perform the optimization we just did by hand.

If you add register declarations to the lowLPtr and srchLPtr definitions, then you will find the code produced by the compiler to be identical to that in Listing 4-7. Not only could we have saved time, we could have kept the program entirely in C, making it much easier to understand and change in the future. Also, we could have made the change without changing the functionality of the code at all, which would be much less prone to errors.

In short, we've run around in a circle, doing nothing of value, all because we didn't understand what the compiler could do for us.

Optimizing the Right Way

At this point, we have located the rather small area of code where optimization will be effective, and we know that the compiler has—with a little help from our register declarations—done virtually all the optimization there is to do. The one place we may yet improve things is in the strcmp call. If we replace this call with a tight loop in assembly, we may yet see some improvement in execution speed. Listing 4-8 shows the assembly language string comparison loop.

Now when we run the program with CALIBRATE turned on, we get a time of 56 seconds, a substantial improvement over the original 85 seconds, and a smaller, but still reasonable improvement over the register optimized version that took 75 seconds. And notice that we have only replaced six lines of the original assembly code.

Should we have tried replacing the strcmp call with C code before recoding it in assembly? Probably yes—it's always better to use C code if you can. Since we are limited to two register variables per function though, we could not declare lowLPtr, srchLPtr, and the char pointers required in string comparison all to be registers without putting the string comparison code in a separate routine, thus adding the overhead of a function call. The assembly version, therefore, is obviously faster than the C version could be—how much faster we don't know, because we went straight to the assembly version.

Final Tweaks

Some final adjustments are necessary before RAMSort is ready to be used. First, CALIBRATE must be turned off. But don't remove the code for it. You may want to return later and use it to measure future changes.

Second, the size of the buffer (set by BUFSIZE) and the size of the line pointer array (set by LPTRSIZE) determine the maximum size of the file, and the maximum number of lines in the file that RAMSort can handle. Both arrays must fit in a 64K data segment, along with the stack and other data used by the program. Experiment with them a bit to find out when they become too large.

Summary

Today's compilers are good at producing efficient code. As a programmer interested in optimizing a program, you should know what the compiler can do for you. If you are programming in C, you should be particularly aware of how to use register variables. Getting the most out of the compiler's capabilities can substantially improve the performance of a program without recoding it in assembly. If recoding parts of a program in assembly still seems like a good idea, the following guidelines should be followed:

- Choose your algorithm carefully. It will be much more difficult to change after it's recoded in assembly.

■ Separate the part to be recoded into a independent module.

■ Get the program working in C before attempting assembly recoding; it will be much easier to debug.

■ Identify the part of the program where optimization will help; indiscriminate recoding in assembly will simply waste time, not speed up the program.

■ Test carefully and thoroughly after recoding. It's easy to make mistakes when coding in assembly.

Only the programmer can decide whether the speed increase achieved is worth the added time of development and the increased cost of maintenance. Don't make that decision lightly—you'll be living with it for a long time.

Exercises

1. Code the in-line string comparison in C in the sort function and measure the timing against the assembly version given in the text.

2. Add an option to the RAMSort program to start sorting after the nth tab in each line; use a "/t·n·" switch to invoke it. Note that the design of the program keeps this addition from requiring changes in the assembly language module.

3. Add a "/r" option to RAMSort that reverses the order the lines are sorted in. Carefully consider the ways such an option can be added and the effects each way has on the efficiency of the program.

4a. The CALIBRATE option fills the buffer with a particular kind of data. Recode it with a different type of data—for instance, all bytes in a line the same. Compare the timing with the old CALIBRATE.

4b. Analyze the types of input data patterns which would invalidate the results given with the CALIBRATE mode.

5. [advanced] The string comparison code compares one byte at a time. Recode this to compare one word at a time in the inner loop, then compare the final byte(s) outside the loop. What speed improvement does this yield? Will it always improve the speed, or will some patterns of input make it less effective, even to the point of being worse than the original.

6. [very advanced] Change RAMSort to use all available memory, even that beyond 64K. You can either allocate a fixed size array of line pointers (of type FAR) and dynamically allocate the buffer outside the 64K data space; or, for maximum flexibility, dynamically allocate both the buffer and line pointer arrays. Particularly note the changes needed to the assembly code.

Listing 4-1. "rsort.h":

```
/*                      RAM Sort Definition File

        This file contains the global constants and structure
        definitions used in the RAM Sort program.
*/

#define CALIBRATE               /* Define this to run with fake input. */

#define BUFSIZE 9000            /* Size of buffer. */
#define LPTRSIZE 3000           /* Number of line pointers. */

char buffer[BUFSIZE];           /* The buffer of lines to sort. */

struct linePtr {                /* Line pointer type. */
        char *start;            /* Start of line. */
        char *sortAt;           /* Point to start sorting at. */
};

struct linePtr lPtr[LPTRSIZE];  /* Line pointers into the buffer. */

struct linePtr *nextLPtr;       /* Next entry in lPtr to use. */
```

Listing 4-2. "rsort.c":

```
/*                      RAM Sort Main Program

        This program reads the standard input into RAM, sorts
        it by line, and writes it back out again.
*/

#include <stdio.h>
#include <string.h>
#include "rsort.h"

/*      main(argc,argv)

        Function: Read the standard input into memory, sort it, and
        write it to the standard output. If there's a switch "/+<n>",
        then sort starting at column <n>.

        Algorithm: Call readLines to read it in, offLines to adjust
        the sort column if the appropriate switch is present, sortLines
        to sort it, and writeLines to write it out. If CALIBRATE is
        defined, skip the reading and writing and fill the buffer up
        with hard-to-sort stuff; this is used to check the timing.
*/

main(argc,argv)

int argc;
```

Listing 4-2. "rsort.c" *(cont.)*:

```c
char *argv[];

{
        int i;

        /* Read in the lines, or fill up the buffer with test data. */
#ifdef CALIBRATE
        fillLines();
        puts("Starting sort...");
#else CALIBRATE
        readLines();
#endif CALIBRATE

        /* Check for a starting column parameter. */
        for (i = 1; i < argc; i++)
                if ((argv[i][0] == '/') && (argv[i][1] == '+'))
                        /* Column sort switch found, so set the
                           columns to sort from. */
                        offLines(atoi(&argv[i][2])-1);

        /* Sort the lines. */
        sortLines();

        /* Write the lines back out again. */
#ifdef CALIBRATE
        puts("done.\n");
#else CALIBRATE
        writeLines();
#endif CALIBRATE
}

/*      fillLines()

        Function: Fill the buffer with fake (and hard-to-sort) data.

        Algorithm: Fill up ten-character lines until out of buffer space.

        Comments: Remember, this is intended to calibrate the speed
        of the sort, not to test it. This isn't necessarily the worst
        case for the program, just a case that takes time.
*/

fillLines()

{
        char *bPtr;             /* Pointer into buffer. */
        char fakeIn[10];        /* Current fill string. */
        char *fPtr;             /* Pointer into fakeIn. */

        /* Start with "ZZZZZZZZZZ". */
```

Listing 4-2. "rsort.c" (cont.):

```c
        for (fPtr = fakeIn; fPtr < &fakeIn[9]; *fPtr++ = 'Z');
        fakeIn[9] = 0;

        /* Fill in the buffer. */
        for (bPtr = buffer, nextLPtr = lPtr;
            (bPtr < &buffer[BUFSIZE-10]) &&
             (nextLPtr < &lPtr[LPTRSIZE]);
            nextLPtr++) {
                /* Set the line pointer entry for this line. */
                nextLPtr->start = nextLPtr->sortAt = bPtr;
                /* Get the next string ("Z...ZZ" -> "Z...ZY", etc.). */
                for (fPtr = &fakeIn[8]; fPtr >= fakeIn; fPtr--)
                        if ((*fPtr)-- == 'A') *fPtr = 'Z';
                        else break;
                /* Copy it into the buffer. */
                strcpy(bPtr,fakeIn);
                bPtr += 10;
        };
}

/*      readLines()

        Function: Read all the lines on the standard input into
        the buffer array, and set the lPtr array to point to each
        line in the buffer.

        Algorithm: Repeatedly call gets() until we've read the
        whole thing in. But make sure we don't overflow any of
        the arrays in the process.

        Comments: Note that there is no way with gets() to ensure
        that it doesn't overflow the buffer. For example, suppose
        we've almost filled up the buffer, and then get a very long
        line. Whatever is in memory after the buffer will get
        overwritten. This is a flaw in the standard I/O library,
        but not one we'll take the time to fix here. We will simply
        exit ASAP so it can't do very much damage.
*/

readLines()

{
        char *bPtr;    /* Pointer into buffer. */

        /* Fill in the buffer from standard input. */
        for (bPtr = buffer, nextLPtr = lPtr;
            (bPtr < &buffer[BUFSIZE]) &&
             (nextLPtr < &lPtr[LPTRSIZE]) &&
             (gets(bPtr) != NULL);
            nextLPtr->start = nextLPtr->sortAt = bPtr, nextLPtr++,
```

Listing 4-2. "rsort.c" *(cont.)*:

```
            bPtr += strlen(bPtr)+1);
        /* Check for errors. */
        if (bPtr >= &buffer[BUFSIZE])
                fatal("Input too large for RAM sort");
        if (nextLPtr >= &lPtr[LPTRSIZE])
                fatal("Input has too many lines");
}

/*      writeLines()

        Function: Write all the lines pointed to by the lPtr array
        (presumably they're in the buffer) to the standard output.

        Algorithm: Cycle thru the lines and call puts() for each one.

        Comments: This routine does not depend on the lines being in
        the buffer; they could be anywhere in the data segment. We
        don't use this feature - or rather lack of restriction - here,
        but it could be useful at some future date.
*/

writeLines()

{
        struct linePtr *lPPtr;  /* Line pointer pointer. */

        /* Write out each line. */
        for (lPPtr = lPtr; lPPtr < nextLPtr; puts((lPPtr++)->start));
}

/*      offLines(offset)

        Function: Start search from offset characters after the
        start of the line.

        Algorithm: Go thru the line pointer table and bump the
        sortAt field to point offset bytes past the start field;
        make sure, however, that it doesn't end up pointing past
        the end of the line.
*/

offLines(offset)

int offset;

{
        struct linePtr *lPPtr;  /* Line pointer pointer. */
        int i;                  /* Byte count. */
        char *cp;               /* Pointer into line. */
```

Listing 4-2. "rsort.c" *(cont.)*:

```
        /* If there's nothing to do, don't do it. */
        if (offset <= 0) return;

        /* Update each line in the array. */
        for (lPPtr = lPtr; lPPtr < nextLPtr; lPPtr++) {
                /* Find the byte, correcting for end-of-line. */
                for (i = offset, cp = lPPtr->start;
                        (i > 0) && (*cp != 0); i--, cp++);
                /* Set the sortAt pointer. */
                lPPtr->sortAt = cp;
        };
}

/*      fatal(s)

        Function: Report fatal errors and then exit to the system.
        s is a pointer to a string that describes the error.

        Algorithm: Calls fputs() to write the error message to the
        standard error output stream. Then call exit() to abort
        execution.

        Comments: The C library has perror() and abort() routines,
        but this is slightly more portable.
*/

fatal(s)

char *s;

{
        fputs("Fatal error: ",stderr);
        fputs(s,stderr);
        fputs(".\n",stderr);
        exit(1);
}
```

Listing 4-3. "sortl.c":

```
/*                      Sort Lines

        This file contains the function that sorts the lines that
        rsort.c read in.
*/

#include <stdio.h>
#include <string.h>
#include "rsort.h"
```

Listing 4-3. "sortl.c" *(cont.)*:

```
/*      sortLines()

        Function: Sort the lPtr array according to the lines pointed
        to by lPtr[].start; but sort from the column pointed to by
        lPtr[].sortAt.

        Algorithm: A selection sort. The smallest item is found and
        swapped with the first entry, then the smallest of the remaining
        items is found, then... Until the entire array is sorted.

        Comments: strcmp() is used to compare lines, which defines
        what we mean by "sorted." There are other definitions that
        could make sense here, from fairly simple ones like descending
        order to much more exotic ones.
*/

sortLines()

{
        struct linePtr *sortLPtr;       /* Start of unsorted lines. */
        struct linePtr *srchLPtr;       /* Line being checked now. */
        struct linePtr *lowLPtr;        /* Lowest line found so far. */
        struct linePtr newLPtr;         /* Temp for swapping sort/low. */

        /* For each line in the array... */
        for (sortLPtr = lPtr; sortLPtr < nextLPtr; sortLPtr++) {
                /* Find the lowest remaining line. */
                for (lowLPtr = srchLPtr = sortLPtr;
                     srchLPtr < nextLPtr; srchLPtr++)
                        if (strcmp(lowLPtr->sortAt, srchLPtr->sortAt) > 0)
                                lowLPtr = srchLPtr;
                /* Swap it with the first unsorted line. */
                newLPtr = *sortLPtr;
                *sortLPtr = *lowLPtr;
                *lowLPtr = newLPtr;
        };
}
```

Listing 4-4. "sortl.asm":

```
;       Static Name Aliases
;
        TITLE   sortl

_TEXT   SEGMENT  BYTE PUBLIC 'CODE'
_TEXT   ENDS
CONST   SEGMENT  WORD PUBLIC 'CONST'
CONST   ENDS
```

Listing 4-4. "sortl.asm" *(cont.)*:

```
_BSS     SEGMENT   WORD PUBLIC 'BSS'
_BSS     ENDS
_DATA    SEGMENT   WORD PUBLIC 'DATA'
_DATA    ENDS
DGROUP   GROUP     CONST,_BSS,_DATA
         ASSUME  CS:_TEXT, DS: DGROUP, SS: DGROUP, ES: DGROUP
PUBLIC   _sortLines
_DATA    SEGMENT
EXTRN    __chkstk:NEAR
EXTRN    _buffer:BYTE
EXTRN    _lPtr:BYTE
EXTRN    _nextLPtr:WORD
EXTRN    _strcmp:NEAR
_DATA    ENDS
_DATA        SEGMENT
;        .comm _buffer,02328H
;        .comm _lPtr,02ee0H
;        .comm _nextLPtr,02H
_DATA        ENDS
_TEXT        SEGMENT
; Line 29
         PUBLIC   _sortLines
_sortLines        PROC NEAR
         push   bp
         mov    bp,sp
         mov    ax,10
         call   __chkstk
         push   si
;        newLPtr=-4
;        srchLPtr=-6
;        sortLPtr=-8
;        lowLPtr=-10
; Line 36
         mov      WORD PTR [bp-8],OFFSET DGROUP:_lPtr
         jmp      SHORT $L20002
$F46:
; Line 39
         mov      ax,[bp-8]
         mov      [bp-6],ax
         mov      [bp-10],ax
         jmp      SHORT $L20001
$F50:
; Line 40
         mov      bx,[bp-6]
         push     WORD PTR [bx+2]
         mov      bx,[bp-10]
         push     WORD PTR [bx+2]
         call     _strcmp
         add      sp,4
         or       ax,ax
```

Listing 4-4. "sortl.asm" *(cont.)*:

```
        jle     $FC51
; Line 41
        mov     ax,[bp-6]
        mov     [bp-10],ax
; Line 43
$FC51:
        add     WORD PTR [bp-6],4
$L20001:
        mov     ax,_nextLPtr
        cmp     [bp-6],ax
        jb      $F50
        mov     bx,[bp-8]
        mov     ax,[bx]
        mov     dx,[bx+2]
        mov     [bp-4],ax
        mov     [bp-2],dx
; Line 44
        mov     si,[bp-10]
        mov     ax,[si]
        mov     dx,[si+2]
        mov     [bx],ax
        mov     [bx+2],dx
; Line 45
        mov     bx,[bp-10]
        mov     ax,[bp-4]
        mov     dx,[bp-2]
        mov     [bx],ax
        mov     [bx+2],dx
; Line 46
        add     WORD PTR [bp-8],4
$L20002:
        mov     ax,_nextLPtr
        cmp     [bp-8],ax
        jb      $F46
; Line 47
        pop     si
        mov     sp,bp
        pop     bp
        ret
_sortLines      ENDP

_TEXT   ENDS
END
```

Listing 4-5. "sortl.asm":

```
;       RAM Sort Function

_TEXT   SEGMENT   BYTE PUBLIC 'CODE'
```

Listing 4-5. "sortl.asm" *(cont.)*:

```
_TEXT      ENDS
CONST      SEGMENT   WORD PUBLIC 'CONST'
CONST      ENDS
_BSS       SEGMENT   WORD PUBLIC 'BSS'
_BSS       ENDS
_DATA      SEGMENT   WORD PUBLIC 'DATA'
_DATA      ENDS

DGROUP     GROUP     CONST,_BSS,_DATA

           ASSUME    CS: _TEXT, DS: DGROUP, SS: DGROUP, ES: DGROUP

PUBLIC     _sortLines

_DATA      SEGMENT
           EXTRN     __chkstk:NEAR
           EXTRN     _buffer:BYTE
           EXTRN     _lPtr:BYTE
           EXTRN     _nextLPtr:WORD
           EXTRN     _strcmp:NEAR
_DATA      ENDS

_TEXT      SEGMENT

; sortLines()

           PUBLIC    _sortLines

_sortLines PROC NEAR
           push   bp
           mov    bp,sp
           mov    ax,10
           call   __chkstk
           push   si

;          struct linePtr *sortLPtr;
;          struct linePtr *srchLPtr;
;          struct linePtr *lowLPtr;
;          struct linePtr newLPtr;

           newLPtr = 4
           srchLPtr = 6
           sortLPtr = 8
           lowLPtr = 10

;          for (sortLPtr = lPtr; sortLPtr < nextLPtr; sortLPtr++) {
           mov    WORD PTR [bp-sortLPtr],OFFSET DGROUP:_lPtr
           jmp    SHORT $L20002
$F46:
```

Listing 4-5. "sortl.asm" *(cont.)*:

```
;                   for (lowLPtr = srchLPtr = sortLPtr;
;                        srchLPtr < nextLPtr; srchLPtr++)
        mov     ax,[bp-sortLPtr]
        mov     [bp-srchLPtr],ax
        mov     [bp-lowLPtr],ax
        jmp     SHORT $L20001
$F50:

;                           if (strcmp(lowLPtr->sortAt,srchLPtr->sortAt) > 0)
        mov     bx,[bp-srchLPtr]
        push    WORD PTR [bx+2]
        mov     bx,[bp-lowLPtr]
        push    WORD PTR [bx+2]
        call    _strcmp
        add     sp,4
        or      ax,ax
        jle     $FC51

;                               lowLPtr = srchLPtr;
        mov     ax,[bp-srchLPtr]
        mov     [bp-lowLPtr],ax

$FC51:
        add     WORD PTR [bp-srchLPtr],4
$L20001:
        mov     ax,_nextLPtr
        cmp     [bp-srchLPtr],ax
        jb      $F50

;                   newLPtr = *sortLPtr;
        mov     bx,[bp-sortLPtr]
        mov     ax,[bx]
        mov     dx,[bx+2]
        mov     [bp-newLPtr],ax
        mov     [bp-newLPtr+2],dx

;                   *sortLPtr = *lowLPtr;
        mov     si,[bp-lowLPtr]
        mov     ax,[si]
        mov     dx,[si+2]
        mov     [bx],ax
        mov     [bx+2],dx

;                   *lowLPtr = newLPtr;
        mov     bx,[bp-lowLPtr]
        mov     ax,[bp-newLPtr]
        mov     dx,[bp-newLPtr+2]
        mov     [bx],ax
        mov     [bx+2],dx
```

Listing 4-5. "sortl.asm" *(cont.)*:

```
;           };
            add     WORD PTR [bp-sortLPtr],4
$L20002:
            mov     ax,_nextLPtr
            cmp     [bp-sortLPtr],ax
            jb      $F46

; }
            pop     si
            mov     sp,bp
            pop     bp
            ret

_sortLines ENDP

_TEXT   ENDS

            END
```

Listing 4-6.

```
;               newLPtr = *sortLPtr;
            mov     bx,[bp-sortLPtr]
            mov     ax,[bx]
            mov     dx,[bx+2]
            mov     [bp-newLPtr],ax
            mov     [bp-newLPtr+2],dx

;               *sortLPtr = *lowLPtr;
            mov     si,[bp-lowLPtr]
            mov     ax,[si]
            mov     dx,[si+2]
            mov     [bx],ax
            mov     [bx+2],dx

;               *lowLPtr = newLPtr;
            mov     bx,[bp-lowLPtr]
            mov     ax,[bp-newLPtr]
            mov     dx,[bp-newLPtr+2]
            mov     [bx],ax
            mov     [bx+2],dx
```

is replaced with:

```
;               newLPtr = *sortLPtr;
;               *sortLPtr = *lowLPtr;
;               *lowLPtr = newLPtr;
            mov     bx,[bp-sortLPtr]
            mov     si,[bp-lowLPtr]
```

Listing 4-6. *(cont.)*

```
        mov     ax,[bx]
        mov     dx,[si]
        mov     [bx],dx
        mov     [si],ax
        mov     ax,[bx+2]
        mov     dx,[si+2]
        mov     [bx+2],dx
        mov     [si+2],ax
```

Listing 4-7.

```
;               for (lowLPtr = srchLPtr = sortLPtr;
;                    srchLPtr < nextLPtr; srchLPtr++)
        mov     ax,[bp-sortLPtr]
        mov     [bp-srchLPtr],ax
        mov     [bp-lowLPtr],ax
        jmp     SHORT $L20001
$F50:

;                       if (strcmp(lowLPtr->sortAt,srchLPtr->sortAt) > 0)
        mov     bx,[bp-srchLPtr]
        push    WORD PTR [bx+2]
        mov     bx,[bp-lowLPtr]
        push    WORD PTR [bx+2]
        call    _strcmp
        add     sp,4
        or      ax,ax
        jle     $FC51

;                           lowLPtr = srchLPtr;
        mov     ax,[bp-srchLPtr]
        mov     [bp-lowLPtr],ax

$FC51:
        add     WORD PTR [bp-srchLPtr],4
$L20001:
        mov     ax,_nextLPtr
        cmp     [bp-srchLPtr],ax
        jb      $F50
;               newLPtr = *sortLPtr;
;               *sortLPtr = *lowLPtr;
;               *lowLPtr = newLPtr;
        mov     bx,[bp-sortLPtr]
        mov     si,[bp-lowLPtr]
        mov     ax,[bx]
        mov     dx,[si]
        mov     [bx],dx
        mov     [si],ax
        mov     ax,[bx+2]
```

Listing 4-7. *(cont.)*

```
        mov     dx,[si+2]
        mov     [bx+2],dx
        mov     [si+2],ax
```

is replaced with:

```
;               for (lowLPtr = srchLPtr = sortLPtr;
;                    srchLPtr < nextLPtr; srchLPtr++)
        mov     si,[bp-sortLPtr]
        mov     di,si
        jmp     SHORT $L20001
$F50:

;                       if (strcmp(lowLPtr->sortAt,srchLPtr->sortAt) > 0)
        push    WORD PTR [si+2]
        push    WORD PTR [di+2]
        call    _strcmp
        add     sp,4
        or      ax,ax
        jle     $FC51

;                           lowLPtr = srchLPtr;
        mov     di,si

;               newLPtr = *sortLPtr;
;               *sortLPtr = *lowLPtr;
;               *lowLPtr = newLPtr;
$FC51:
        add     si,4
$L20001:
        cmp     _nextLPtr,si
        ja      $F50
        mov     bx,[bp-sortLPtr]
        mov     ax,[bx]
        mov     dx,[di]
        mov     [bx],dx
        mov     [di],ax
        mov     ax,[bx+2]
        mov     dx,[di+2]
        mov     [bx+2],dx
        mov     [di+2],ax
```

Listing 4-8.

```
;                       if (strcmp(lowLPtr->sortAt,srchLPtr->sortAt) > 0)
        push    WORD PTR [si+2]
        push    WORD PTR [di+2]
        call    _strcmp
```

Listing 4-8. *(cont.)*

```
        add     sp,4
        or      ax,ax
        jle     $FC51
```

<u>is replaced with:</u>

```
;                       if (strcmp(lowLPtr->sortAt,srchLPtr->sortAt) > 0)
        push    di                      ; Save si/di
        push    si
        mov     di,WORD PTR [di+2]      ; di = lowLPtr->sortAt
        mov     si,WORD PTR [si+2]      ; si = srchLPtr->sortAt

loop:   lods    BYTE PTR [si]           ; Get the next byte to compare
        scas    BYTE PTR [di]           ; Compare it
        jne     noteq                   ; If they don't match
        or      al,al                   ; End-of-string?
        jnz     loop                    ; If not
        pop     si                      ; Pop si/di
        pop     di
        jmp     $FC51                   ; The strings are equal
noteq:  pop     si                      ; Pop si/di
        pop     di
        ja      $FC51                   ; Jump if string 1 is more than 2
```

Chapter 5

More Processor Optimization: *TicTac*

In this chapter, we will develop and optimize a tic-tac-toe playing program. The program will play a perfect game of tic-tac-toe—that is, it will make the best possible move at each turn, or more commonly, it will pick one of several best moves. In a sense, the program simulates a large number of possible futures, and based on an analysis of that simulation, it makes the move that leads to the future that is best for it—the one that will win the game. The program's approach to selecting the right move is applicable to many kinds of problems, both games and non-games. It tries all the possible next moves, and for each such move, it tries all possible replies; then all possible replies to the replies, and so on, until it has found a move either guaranteed to win or one that will tie. Failing either, it will pick one of the losing moves since it has no other choice.

To pick the best possible move, the program must examine a large number of possible moves and counter moves. This takes time. In this chapter we will also show you how to optimize the program to reduce the time required to choose the best move.

Tic-Tac-Toe

First, just in case anyone doesn't know how tic-tac-toe is played, we'll explain the game. Tic-tac-toe is played on a board like that shown in Figure 5-1A, with nine spaces arranged in a three-by-three grid. Players take turns placing marks in one of the spaces. The player who goes first marks with Xs, and the other player marks with Os. The object of the game is to get three of your marks in a row, either vertically, horizontally, or diagonally before the other player can do it.

The rest of Figure 5-1 shows an example game. Figure 5-1B shows the board after the first move has been made; the X player marks the center space.

Figure 5-1C shows the reply to this—the O player marks the lower left corner. In Figure 5-1D, X has marked two spaces in a row—he could hardly have avoided it, since his first move was in the center. This forces O to mark the space that would otherwise allow X to get three in a row and win. Now O is within one move of winning, so X is forced to mark the space between O's two marks. X marks the left center space in Figure 5-1F. This, in turn, gives him two in a row again, so O is forced to make the move shown in Figure 5-1G. By now the game is pretty well determined. X's move is shown in Figure 5-1H, and O blocks

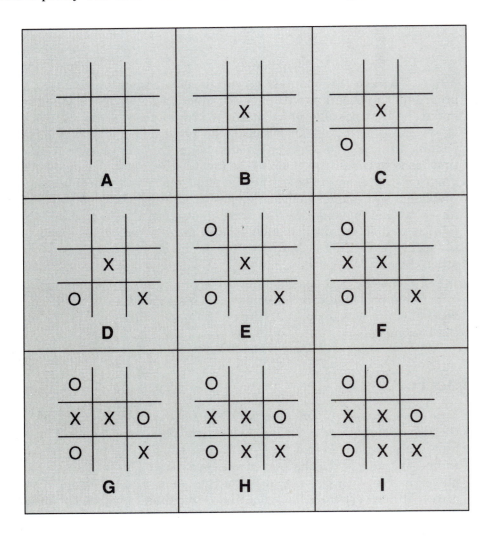

Figure 5-1. Tic-Tac-Toe

the attempted three-in-a-row as shown in Figure 5-1I. Only one move remains for X, and the game ends in a tie. Most tic-tac-toe games end in a tie, especially if your opponent plays a perfect game, as our computer program will.

To play tic-tac-toe with a computer, we must find a way to tell the computer which space we want to mark. We do this by numbering the spaces as shown in Figure 5-2. The player can then specify a move simply by typing a digit, and the computer marks the space the player selected. On the other hand, we'll have the computer print out the board after its move, rather than forcing the player to decode digits.

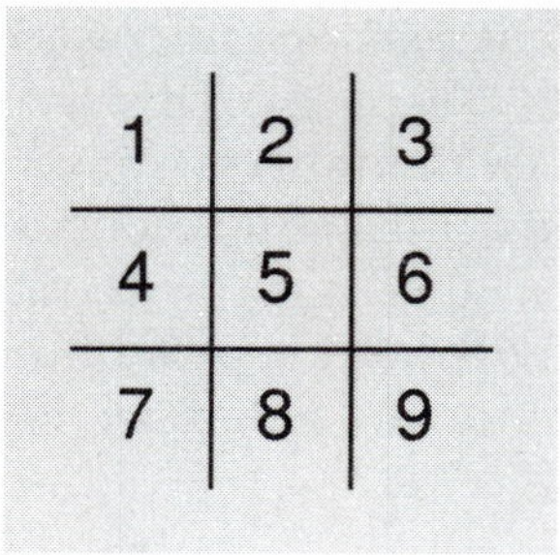

1	2	3
4	5	6
7	8	9

Figure 5-2. Board Numbering

Search Strategies

One way to look at the problem of finding the best move in a game is to think of the potential moves as forming an inverted tree, with board positions at the nodes of the tree and moves forming the branches. The first moves form the topmost branches. For each first move, there are a number of possible replies which form the second-level branches of the tree. For each of those replies, we will make a counter-reply, forming the third-level branches. The branching process ends under two circumstances: one player wins, or there are no more legal moves, and the game ends in a tie. Finding the best possible move can be thought of as searching this tree for the branch that leads to the best set of terminal, or final, branches.

Figure 5-3 shows a small part of the tree for tic-tac-toe. It shows all the first-level branches, and one set of the second level of branches. There are eight other second-level branches that are not shown. In fact, the entire tree has nine factorial (9*8*7*6*5*4*3*2 = 362,880) separate nodes, because there are nine possible first moves. There are then eight possible replies for each of those moves, since one space was taken by the first move. To each of those replies, there are seven possible third moves, and so on until only one possible move remains.

Actually, this is not a complete analysis of the game. There are fewer than 362,880 nodes in the tree, because nodes that have three in a row for one side or the other terminate the tree—i.e., there is no reason to search further down that branch. It isn't easy to analyze how much smaller this makes the tree, so we will use nine factorial to give us an order-of-magnitude idea of the complexity of the problem. If it took one millisecond to check each node, we could check the whole tree in 363 seconds. This is probably more time than we will actually need. If, on the other hand, it took one microsecond to check each node, we could check the tree in only 0.363 seconds. This is certainly less time than we will actually need. With these two numbers, we have a rough idea of the complexity of the problem: between one-third of a second and six minutes. We will find out later that it actually takes 90 seconds (without optimization). This is a reasonable time frame, since it will not keep the human player waiting so long that he loses patience, but long enough that we have an incentive to improve the performance of the program.

The program must search the move tree to find the best top-level branch, where "best" is defined as any branch guaranteed to win, or failing that, guaranteed to tie, or failing that, one that may lose. There are two ways to conduct the search: breadth first and depth first. Breadth first searching computes all the branches at the top level; then those at the next level; then at the next; etc. In other words, the program searches the whole tree in parallel, as illustrated in Figure 5-4A. Depth first searching goes all the way down the first series of branches until it finds a tie, win, or lose; then it tries the next path to the bottom of the tree; then the next. With depth first, therefore, the program searches the tree by considering each path from the top to the bottom in turn. This is illustrated in Figure 5-4B.

For the purpose of writing a program, depth first searching is much easier, especially because recursion can be used to traverse the tree. That is, we can write one routine that goes through each branch on a given level in turn, and for each branch the routine calls itself to analyze each of the sub-branches:

"Search tree":

1. If this is a terminal node (i.e., win or tie), return "win" or "tie".

2. For each branch from this node:
   a. Call "search tree" to check the node at this branch.
   b. If this is the best branch seen so far, remember it.

3. Return best branch found.

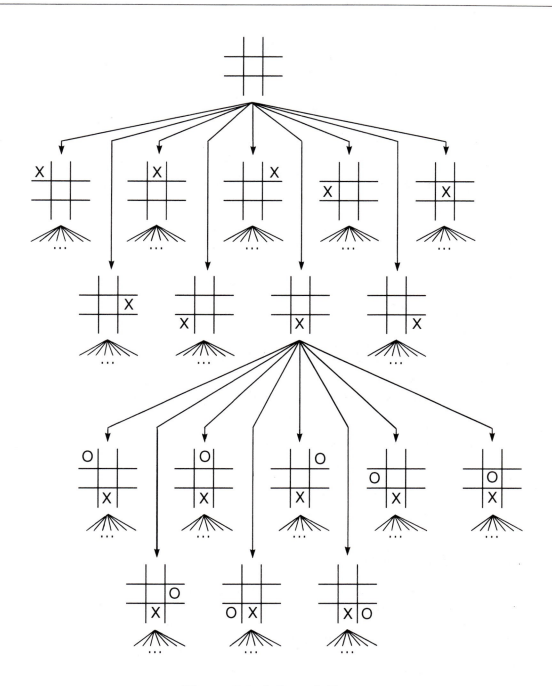

Figure 5-3. A Search Tree

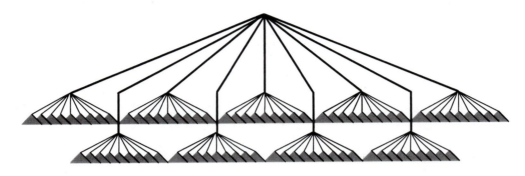

A: Breadth First

In A, notice that the first level lines are all of heavy thickness, searching breadth first.

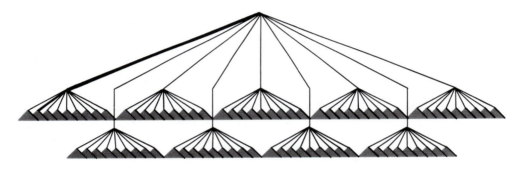

B: Depth First

In B, notice that the single heavy line continuing to the bottom of the second level of the first branch, searching depth first.

Figure 5-4. Search Strategies

The TicTac Program

The TicTac program consists of two parts: The first part is the user interface, which asks the player whether the computer should play Xs or Os, and at each turn asks him which move he wants to make. The user interface also displays the board after each move and decides when the game has been won or tied. The second part of the program is the move generation function, which finds the best available next move to make. These two parts share functions to determine if the current board position is a tie or a win.

Listing 5-1 contains the TicTac program in C. The array named board holds the current board state: it includes one entry for each space on the board. Each entry can be one of three possible values: zero if the space is not yet taken; 1 if the space is taken by X; or -1 if the space is taken by O. The program is quite straightforward, the only complex areas being the main and bestMove functions. These are also the functional heart of the program.

The main function first establishes which side (or sides) the computer will play. The program allows all possibilities: human versus human, computer versus human, and computer versus computer. This information is kept in humanX, which is TRUE if the human will play Xs; and humanO, which is TRUE if the human will play Os. Both can be either TRUE or FALSE. The main loop of the program alternates making moves on each side. The variable named side indicates which side's turn it is: 1 for X or -1 for O. This variable is switched between 1 and -1 each cycle through the loop. Within the loop, the humanX and humanO variables are checked to see if the user should be asked for the move or if the bestMove function should be called instead. After each move, the printBd function prints out the current state of the board.

The intelligence of the program resides in the bestMove function, along with the isTie and hasWon functions. bestMove knows how to find the best possible next move in the game. It makes that move and also returns the "value" of the move. The value is 1 if the move can win regardless of the other player's response; 0 if the move can tie regardless of the response; or -1 if the move can lose. Even if bestMove returns 1, it is still possible to lose the game if poor moves are made in the future. A return value of 1 means only that a win is guaranteed if the best possible moves are made in the future as well. Similarly, a return value of -1 means a lose only if the other player plays a perfect game.

First, bestMove checks the current board position. If the game is tied, bestMove returns a value of 0 (tie). In a tie, the move is irrelevant since the game is already over. If the game is not tied, bestMove must find the best remaining possible move. The for loop cycles through each of the possible moves and tries it out. The trial moves will be taken back before the function exits, and the board will not be displayed to the user while this hypothetical move is present. The for loop is analogous to trying each move on paper and then erasing it before trying the next one. With the potential move in place, hasWon is called to determine if it is a winning move. If not, bestMove is called recursively to determine how well the other side can do given this move — passing "-p" to this new bestMove call causes the function to find the best move for the other side, whatever the original value of p was. If bestMove returns -1, the other side can do no better than lose, so this is a winning move. If bestMove returns 0, this move guarantees a tie. The bestMove function remembers this move, in case it can't find one that will win. Next, the hypothetical move is taken back, restoring the board to the same state it was in when we entered the function. If, at this point, bestMove has found a winning move, the function returns immediately, without searching the rest of the branches—it knows it won't find anything better. On the other hand, if after searching all the branches, bestMove hasn't found a winning move, it returns the best move it can find, which will result in a tie, or failing that, losing the game.

bestMove is a recursive function, written assuming that it's already been written—i.e., that defines itself in terms of itself—and it seems circular and impossible at first. But it does work, and it is a powerful tool in solving these types of problems. When writing this kind of function, there are two important things to watch out for. First, make sure the program doesn't recurse forever, that there is something to stop it eventually. In bestMove, this is the check for isTie at the beginning. And second make sure that when the program does stop, it hasn't eaten up all the available stack space: in our tic-tac-toe program, we know it will never recurse more than nine levels deep, since that's the maximum number of possible moves (also known as the depth of the tree). If the board were 100x100, this approach wouldn't work as well, since then the depth of the tree would be 10,000.

To know how large the stack can get, you must know how much is pushed onto it at each step of the recursion. In the tic-tac-toe program, there are the two parameters, p and v, the return address for the function call, the registers we expect the compiler to save on the stack—bp and possibly si and di (if we use any register variables)—and the local variables i, lastTie, lastMove, and subV. Altogether, that's a maximum of 20 bytes per recursion or 180 bytes for nine levels of recursion. With our compiler, the default stack size is 2K bytes, so the 180 bytes is well within safe limits. But remember that previous routines have already used up part of the stack, so always leave a healthy safety margin.

Optimizing TicTac

As always, the first step in optimizing a program is to measure it. With TicTac, we can measure the time it takes to find the first move when the computer plays the Xs. To find this first move, the program must search the entire tree—or at least down to those points where ties and wins occur. For this program, we don't need a CALIBRATE mode, as we did for RAMSort, because TicTac naturally produces prompts before and after the processor-intensive period and because disk I/O is not involved.

If we time the program, we find that it takes 90 seconds to discover the best first move. That move is one of several that lead to a tie if the other side also plays a perfect game. TicTac returns the last such move found, a play in space number 9 (the lower right hand corner).

The next step in optimizing TicTac is to declare some of the variables to be registers. If this is done to the i variables in every routine, the side variable in main, the w variable in hasWon, and the lastMove variable in bestMove, the running time is reduced to 70 seconds. The next step is not quite as obvious: we can declare board to be type char rather than type int. This saves time because we frequently refer to board by indexing into it. If board is int, an expression such as "board[i]" requires that i be multiplied by two before being used as an index. If board is char, i can be used without modification as the index into the array. Redeclaring board as char reduces the execution time to 64 seconds. This is as far as we can optimize the program in C. Next, we'll have to use assembly language.

The most frequently called routines in TicTac are hasWon and bestMove. Since bestMove is composed primarily of calls to other functions, an area that the C compiler usually handles very efficiently, we'll concentrate on hasWon. Listing 5-2 shows the C version of hasWon translated into assembly language. This was produced by having the compiler generate the assembly equivalent of the C code.

The important thing to notice in this listing is that the compiler never realized that the expressions being evaluated could be computed using byte registers. Instead, it converts the bytes to words, generating a lot of unnecessary code. You might suspect that this is because the variable w is declared to be int. But if you look at the code produced with w declared to be type char, the same conversion to words is done, and the compiler further refuses to accept a char variable in a register. Instead, it places the variable on the stack, creating even more code. (Note: the compiler does this because it uses the SI and DI registers to store register variables, and these registers cannot be accessed as bytes.)

We can easily improve on the code generated by the compiler. First, we can use a byte register to store w—we will use the BL register. Second, we can add up the board entries without first converting them to words. And third, we can eliminate some of the function entry/exit code by not calling _chkstk. This version of hasWon is shown in Listing 5-3—its execution time is down to 55 seconds. This is only a 14% improvement over the previous version, but if we consider the entire set of optimizations, our total increase in performance is 38.8% over the original 90 seconds.

Summary

We have presented a program that plays a perfect game of tic-tac-toe. It searches a tree of possible future moves to find the best next move in a game. This kind of exhaustive search can be useful in many problem areas that involve responding to potential future events, but it can consume a great deal of processor time.

The program was then optimized by using register variables, by redeclaring the board array to be char rather than int, and by recoding one of the most frequently called routines in assembly rather than C. The total execution speed improvement was 38.8%.

Exercises

1. One more optimization can be made easily in hasWon. Find it, make it, and measure it.

2. Add a feature to TicTac to display the progress of the search. As each hypothetical move is made, display it using 'printf(" %1d",i)'. When it's retracted after being tried, erase it from the screen using 'printf("\010 \010")' (that's equivalent to backspace, space, backspace).

3. Change TicTac to tell the value of its computer selected moves. That is, tictac should tell whether it expects to win, lose, or tie.

4. Add a feature so that if the user enters a move of -1, the program tells him what it thinks the best move is, but does not make the move.

5. [advanced] Change the program to play 3D tic-tac-toe on a 4x4x4 board. This involves major changes in the program. The size of the tree will now be so large that finding the perfect move will take far too long. Some other definition of "best" must be used, for example, three in a row might be "better" than two in a row.

Listing 5-1. "tictac.c":

```
/*                       TicTac

        This program plays a perfect game of tic-tac-toe.
*/

#define FALSE 0
#define TRUE 1

int board[9];    /* The playing board; for each space, 0 is not used,
                    1 is X, -1 is O. */

/*      main()

        Function: Ask the user which side(s) he wants to play. Then
        make or ask for moves one each side until one side wins.

        Algorithm: First, set humanX and humanO to indicate which
        side(s) the human is playing. Then init the board and print
        it out. Then iterate making or asking for a move, printing
        it out, and testing for a win. Each pass thru the main loop,
        the program switches sides.
*/

main()

{
        int side;                /* Which side is playing (1 or -1). */
        int move;                /* Next move. */
        int val;                 /* Value of move. */
        int humanX, humanO;      /* TRUE if human is playing X/O. */
        char str[20];            /* Input are for yes/no. */

        /* Ask the user if the computer should play the Xs. */
        printf("Should the computer play Xs? ");
        gets(str);
        if ((str[0] == 'y') || (str[0] == 'Y')) humanX = FALSE;
        else humanX = TRUE;
        /* Ask about playing the Os. */
        printf("Should the computer play Os? ");
        gets(str);
        if ((str[0] == 'y') || (str[0] == 'Y')) humanO = FALSE;
        else humanO = TRUE;

        /* Initialize the board. */
        initBd();

        /* Show the empty board. */
        printBd();

        /* X goes first. */
```

Listing 5-1. "tictac.c" *(cont.)*:

```
        side = 1;

        /* Loop until a win or the player quits. */
        while (TRUE) {
                /* If this side is played by the human... */
                if ((humanX && (side == 1)) || (humanO && (side == -1))) {
                        /* Query for move; repeat until legal. */
                        do {
                            if (side == 1)
                                    printf("X's move; enter 1-9, or 0 to quit: ");
                            else
                                    printf("O's move; enter 1-9, or 0 to quit: ");
                            scanf("%d",&move);
                        } while ((move != 0) && (board[move-1] != 0));
                        /* Check for quit. */
                        if (move == 0) break;
                /* Otherwise, decide on the best move to make. */
                } else move = bestMove(side,&val)+1;
                /* Make the move. */
                board[move-1] = side;
                /* Show the new board to the user. */
                printBd();
                /* If that one won it, say so and exit. */
                if (hasWon(side)) {
                        printf("That move won!\n");
                        break;
                };
                /* If it was a tie, say so and exit. */
                if (isTie()) {
                        printf("Tie game!\n");
                        break;
                };
                /* Switch sides for the next move. */
                side = -side;
        };
}

/*      initBd()

        Function: Initialize the board to all empty.

        Algorithm: Set each board entry to zero.
*/

initBd()

{
        int i;

        /* Zero (empty) each square in the board. */
```

Listing 5-1. "tictac.c" *(cont.)*:

```
        for (i = 0; i < 9; i++) board[i] = 0;
}

/*      isTie()

        Function: Return TRUE if the current board position is a tie.

        Algorithm: See if we can find an untaken board position  If not,
        it's a tie. Otherwise, there's still hope.
*/

isTie()

{
        int i;

        /* Check each space on the board. */
        for (i = 0; i < 9; i++) if (board[i] == 0) return(FALSE);
        /* If none found, return tie. */
        return(TRUE);
}

/*      hasWon(p)

        Function: Return true if player p has won, where p is 1 for X
        and -1 for O.

        Algorithm: Check for every possible three in a row. If any are
        found, it's a win, so we return TRUE; otherwise, we return FALSE.
*/

hasWon(p)

int p;

{
        int i;
        int w;

        /* Calculate the sum of three in a row. */
        w = 3*p;

        /* Check for three in a row horizontally. */
        for (i = 0; i < 9; i += 3)
                if ((board[i]+board[i+1]+board[i+2]) == w) return(TRUE);

        /* Check for three in a row vertically. */
        for (i = 0; i < 3; i++)
                if ((board[i]+board[i+3]+board[i+6]) == w) return(TRUE);
```

Listing 5-1. "tictac.c" *(cont.)*:

```
        /* Check the diagonals. */
        if ((board[0]+board[4]+board[8]) == w) return(TRUE);
        if ((board[2]+board[4]+board[6]) == w) return(TRUE);

        /* If nothing, then return a non-win. */
        return(FALSE);
}

/*      bestMove(p,v)

        Function: Return the best possible move for player p. p is 1
        for X or -1 for O. Also return the value of that move (1 for
        a win, 0 for a tie, and -1 for a loss) in v.
*/

bestMove(p,v)

int p;
int *v;

{
        int i;
        int lastTie;
        int lastMove;
        int subV;

        /* First, check for a tie. */
        if (isTie()) {
                *v = 0;
                return(0);
        };

        /* If not a tie, try each potential move. */
        for (*v = -1, lastTie = lastMove = -1, i = 0; i < 9; i++) {
                /* If this isn't a possible move, skip it. */
                if (board[i] != 0) continue;
                /* Make the move. */
                lastMove = i;
                board[i] = p;
                /* Did it win? */
                if (hasWon(p)) *v = 1;
                else {
                        /* If not, find out how good the other side can do. */
                        bestMove(-p,&subV);
                        /* If they can only lose, this is still a win. */
                        if (subV == -1) *v = 1;
                        /* Or, if it's a tie, remember it. */
                        else if (subV == 0) {
                                *v = 0;
                                lastTie = i;
```

Listing 5-1. "tictac.c" (cont.):

```
                        };
                };
                /* Take back the move. */
                board[i] = 0;
                /* If we found a win, return immediately (can't do any
                    better than that). */
                if (*v == 1) return(i);
        };
        /* If we didn't find any wins, return a tie move. */
        if (*v == 0) return(lastTie);
        /* If there weren't even any ties, return a loosing move. */
        else return(lastMove);
}

/*      printBd()

        Function: Display the board for the user.

        Algorithm: Iterate thru each square and print it out.
*/

printBd()

{
        int i;

        /* For each square... */
        for (i = 0; i < 9; i++) {
                /* Print X, O, or space. */
                if (board[i] == 0) printf(" ");
                else if (board[i] == 1) printf("X");
                else printf("O");
                /* If this is the last square in the line... */
                if ((i % 3) == 2) {
                        /* Print the adjacent numbered board. */
                        printf("      %1d|%1d|%1d\n",i-1,i,i+1);
                        if (i != 8) printf("-+-+-      -+-+-\n");
                } else printf("|");
        };
        printf("\n");
}
```

Listing 5-2. "haswon.asm":

```
;                       hasWon(p)
;
; Returns TRUE if side p has won the game.

_TEXT   SEGMENT  BYTE PUBLIC 'CODE'
```

Listing 5-2. "haswon.asm" *(cont.)*:

```
_TEXT    ENDS
CONST    SEGMENT   WORD PUBLIC 'CONST'
CONST    ENDS
_BSS     SEGMENT   WORD PUBLIC 'BSS'
_BSS     ENDS
_DATA    SEGMENT   WORD PUBLIC 'DATA'
_DATA    ENDS

DGROUP   GROUP     CONST,_BSS,_DATA

         ASSUME  CS: _TEXT, DS: DGROUP, SS: DGROUP, ES: DGROUP

         PUBLIC  _hasWon

_DATA    SEGMENT

         EXTRN   _board:BYTE
         EXTRN   __chkstk:NEAR

_DATA    ENDS

_TEXT       SEGMENT

; hasWon(p)
;
; int p;

         p = 4

         PUBLIC  _hasWon

_hasWon PROC NEAR
         push    bp
         mov     bp,sp
         mov     ax,4
         call    __chkstk
         push    di
         push    si

;        w = 3*p
         mov     ax,3
         imul    WORD PTR [bp+p]
         mov     di,ax

;        for (i = 0; i < 9; i += 3)
         xor     si,si
$F13:
;                if ((board[i]+board[i+1]+board[i+2]) == w)
;                        return(TRUE);
         mov     al,BYTE PTR _board[si+2]
```

Listing 5-2. "haswon.asm" *(cont.)*:

```
        cbw
        mov     cx,ax
        mov     al,BYTE PTR _board[si+1]
        cbw
        add     ax,cx
        mov     cx,ax
        mov     al,BYTE PTR _board[si]
        cbw
        add     cx,ax
        cmp     cx,di
        je      $L20001
        add     si,3
        cmp     si,9
        jl      $F13

;       for (i = 0; i < 3; i++)
        xor     si,si
$F18:

;               if ((board[i]+board[i+3]+board[i+6]) == w)
;                       return(TRUE);
        mov     al,BYTE PTR _board[si+6]
        cbw
        mov     cx,ax
        mov     al,BYTE PTR _board[si+3]
        cbw
        add     ax,cx
        mov     cx,ax
        mov     al,BYTE PTR _board[si]
        cbw
        add     cx,ax
        cmp     cx,di
        je      $L20001
        inc     si
        cmp     si,3
        jl      $F18

;       if ((board[0]+board[4]+board[8]) == w) return(TRUE);
        mov     al,BYTE PTR _board+4
        cbw
        mov     cx,ax
        mov     al,BYTE PTR _board
        cbw
        add     ax,cx
        mov     cx,ax
        mov     al,BYTE PTR _board+8
        cbw
        add     cx,ax
        cmp     cx,di
        jne     $I23
```

Listing 5-2. "haswon.asm" *(cont.)*:

```
$L20001:
        mov     ax,1
        jmp     SHORT $EX10
$I23:

;       if ((board[2]+board[4]+board[6]) == w) return(TRUE);
        mov     al,BYTE PTR _board+4
        cbw
        mov     cx,ax
        mov     al,BYTE PTR _board+2
        cbw
        add     ax,cx
        mov     cx,ax
        mov     al,BYTE PTR _board+6
        cbw
        add     cx,ax
        cmp     cx,di
        je      $L20001

;       return(FALSE);
        xor     ax,ax
$EX10:
        pop     si
        pop     di
        mov     sp,bp
        pop     bp
        ret
_hasWon ENDP

_TEXT   ENDS

        END
```

Listing 5-3. "haswon2.asm":

```
;                       hasWon(p)
;
; Returns TRUE if side p has won the game.

_TEXT   SEGMENT  BYTE PUBLIC 'CODE'
_TEXT   ENDS
CONST   SEGMENT  WORD PUBLIC 'CONST'
CONST   ENDS
_BSS    SEGMENT  WORD PUBLIC 'BSS'
_BSS    ENDS
_DATA   SEGMENT  WORD PUBLIC 'DATA'
_DATA   ENDS

DGROUP  GROUP    CONST,_BSS,_DATA
```

Listing 5-3. "haswon2.asm" *(cont.)*:

```
        ASSUME  CS: _TEXT, DS: DGROUP, SS: DGROUP, ES: DGROUP

        PUBLIC  _hasWon

_DATA   SEGMENT

        EXTRN   _board:BYTE

_DATA   ENDS

_TEXT       SEGMENT

; hasWon(p)
;
; int p;

        p = 4

        PUBLIC  _hasWon

_hasWon PROC NEAR
        push    bp
        mov     bp,sp
        push    di
        push    si

;       w = 3*p
        mov     ax,3
        imul    WORD PTR [bp+p]
        mov     bl,al

;       for (i = 0; i < 9; i += 3)
        xor     si,si
$F13:
;               if ((board[i]+board[i+1]+board[i+2]) == w)
;                       return(TRUE);
        mov     al,BYTE PTR _board[si+2]
        add     al,BYTE PTR _board[si+1]
        add     al,BYTE PTR _board[si]
        cmp     al,bl
        je      $L20001
        add     si,3
        cmp     si,9
        jl      $F13

;       for (i = 0; i < 3; i++)
        xor     si,si
$F18:

;               if ((board[i]+board[i+3]+board[i+6]) == w)
```

Listing 5-3. "haswon2.asm" (cont.):

```
;                       return(TRUE);
        mov     al,BYTE PTR _board[si+6]
        add     al,BYTE PTR _board[si+3]
        add     al,BYTE PTR _board[si]
        cmp     al,bl
        je      $L20001
        inc     si
        cmp     si,3
        jl      $F18

;       if ((board[0]+board[4]+board[8]) == w) return(TRUE);
        mov     al,BYTE PTR _board+4
        add     al,BYTE PTR _board
        add     al,BYTE PTR _board+8
        cmp     al,bl
        jne     $I23
$L20001:
        mov     ax,1
        jmp     SHORT $EX10
$I23:

;       if ((board[2]+board[4]+board[6]) == w) return(TRUE);
        mov     al,BYTE PTR _board+4
        add     al,BYTE PTR _board+2
        add     al,BYTE PTR _board+6
        cmp     al,bl
        je      $L20001

;       return(FALSE);
        xor     ax,ax
$EX10:
        pop     si
        pop     di
        pop     bp
        ret
_hasWon ENDP

_TEXT   ENDS

        END
```

Chapter 6

Input/Output Speed Optimization: *Encrypt*

I n this chapter, we will develop and optimize an encryption/decryption program. The Encrypt program takes the data from the standard input, encrypts it using a key from the command line, and writes it to the standard output. Encrypting a file twice restores it to its original state, so the same program can be used for both encryption and decryption. You can use encryption to ensure the confidentiality of files on your computer even if other people have physical access to it. Encryption also maintains confidentiality if you use telecommunications services. You can transfer files without worrying about other people reading them.

Thus far, we have discussed optimizing processor performance. Now we will concentrate on optimizing disk input/output (I/O). This type of optimization usually makes a greater difference in applications involving disk access than recoding C functions in assembly language, even though it is often simpler to implement. Both recoding in assembly and optimizing disk I/O are useful techniques, but, as always, the programmer must understand when and where to apply them to achieve the most benefit.

Encryption

Cryptography is much older than computer science, and although the use of computers has introduced some new wrinkles in the subject, the basic principles have remained the same for centuries. Cryptography is the science of modifying a piece of information according to a set of rules such that the information is no longer intelligible, but no information has been lost, so that applying another set of modifications will restore it to its original state. Formerly, the rules had to be simple enough that the person receiving the encrypted information could easily recover it. Computers have relaxed this constraint because they can perform a large number of transformations in a relatively short period of time; cryptographers are no longer limited to what they can manage with only pencil and paper. Nevertheless, simplicity is still a good guideline.

The amount of information to be transferred between the sender and receiver of the message to tell the receiver how to decode the message should be small. Generally, one uses a "key," which is a word composed of a small number of characters. The confidentiality of this key is crucial to the security of the message system.

In the terminology of cryptography, encryption is the process of transforming "plain text" into "cipher text" and back again. With the program we're developing, the plain text is the data read from the standard input and the cipher text is the encrypted data written to the standard output. Most systems of cryptography use one algorithm to encrypt a message and another to decrypt it. Some systems use a single algorithm for both, as does the one we will use. In this case, encrypting a message twice returns it to its original unencrypted state.

There are two basic forms of cryptography: substitution and transposition. We will use a pure substitution cipher, but we will describe both types here. Most ciphers are a combination of the two.

In a substitution cipher, the message is divided into pieces—bytes are often used in computers, and characters in normal text. Each part is replaced with a unique substitute. The key determines which of the many possible sets of substitutions to use. Figure 6-1 shows an example of a substitution cipher.

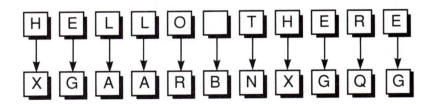

Figure 6-1. Substitution Encryption

In a transposition cipher, the order of the parts is rearranged as shown in Figure 6-2. In this type of cipher, the key determines how the elements are moved around.

We can derive more complex ciphers by combining substitution and transposition of ciphers, by variations within them, and by variations in how the particular substitutions and transpositions are chosen. Probably the best known contemporary computer cipher is the Data Encryption Standard (DES) of the National Bureau of Standards. This cipher encrypts 64-bit blocks at a time, using a 56-bit key. The DES is basically a complex, multi-stage substitution cipher.

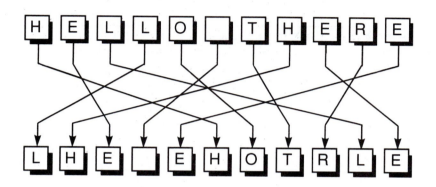

Figure 6-2. Transposition Encryption

Controversy has arisen regarding the security of the DES cipher. The original version of the cipher, designed by IBM, used a 128-bit key which made it much more difficult to break. The key size was reduced to 56 bits at the request of the National Security Agency. The Agency did not disclose its reasons to the general public, and this has inevitably led to speculation that the NSA would like a cipher weak enough that they can break it, but strong enough to keep everyone else out. We may never know the real reason, but perhaps the lesson to be learned is this: if organizations like the NSA want to read your mail, there's no way you're going to stop them.

More information on the DES algorithm and computer cryptography in general can be found in the book *Computer Networks* by Andrew S. Tanenbaum.

A very simple form of computer encryption is the exclusive-or substitution cipher. This algorithm takes bytes from the key and exclusive-ors them with bytes from the plain text to produce the cipher text. When the key is exhausted, the algorithm starts over at the first byte of the key. This is a very fast algorithm on most modern computers and provides a high level of security. Figure 6-3 illustrates exclusive-or substitution encryption. In our encryption program, the key is modified before being used, to increase the security of the cipher even further.

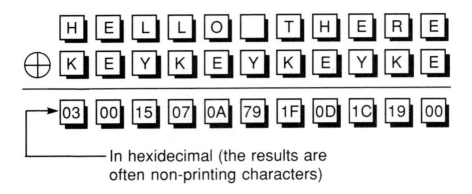

In hexidecimal (the results are
often non-printing characters)

Figure 6-3. Exclusive-Or Encryption

The Encrypt Program

Encrypt uses a simple, cyclical key, exclusive-or substitution cipher. It takes advantage of the efficient exclusive-or operation on the PC to implement the substitution cipher. Encrypt performs an exclusive-or on each byte of the text together with one byte from the key. Each byte in order is exclusive-ored with the next byte of the key. When the program runs out of key bytes, it starts over at the beginning of the key. This is a very simple form of encryption, but it is proof against 99% of the people who are liable to try to read your confidential files.

Before the program starts the encryption, it reworks the key a little. First, it takes the last character of the key and spreads the bits into the top bits of each of the other bytes. This is necessary since we want to be able to encrypt binary (8-bit data) files, but the key is composed of ASCII characters (7 bits). Second, we invert selected bits in each byte of the key. This reduces the likelihood of getting a key with a lot of zero bits, in which case the encrypted bits would be identical to the original ones. The encryption itself is a simple matter of reading a block of data from the standard input, exclusive-oring each byte with a byte from the key, and then writing the block to the standard output. The process continues until there are no more bytes to be read.

The Encrypt program is presented in Listing 6-1. It starts by defining the size of the buffer it will use, and the maximum size of the key. It also defines CALIBRATE here for debugging purposes, just as it was used in Chapter Four.

The main function gets the key from the command line and modifies it to make the encryption more secure. Then it puts both the standard input and the standard output into "binary" mode, for two reasons: first, to allow the encryption program to work on either binary or text files, and second, to allow the encryption program to produce binary files when reading text files.

The encrypt function is, of course, the heart of the program. It reads, encrypts, and writes blocks until there is nothing more to be read. It must also deal with the last block in the file, which may be smaller than the buffer size. The encryption process is performed in the for loop in the middle of the function. It exclusive-ors each byte in the buffer with a byte from the key.

Operating System and C File I/O

Before we can talk about optimizing the Encrypt program, we need some background information about how the operating system and the C run-time library perform disk I/O.

An operating system provides several features for programs wishing to read from or write to the disk:

- It hides the details of the hardware and low level software from the program, simplifying the program and at the same time making it portable across different types of hardware.

- It imposes a structure on the data stored on the disk, providing directories and files, and it prevents the application from violating this structure.

- It provides features such as translation between fixed and variable sized blocks to help the application.

The C compiler comes with a run-time library which adds another layer of insulation for the programmer. These routines allow the programmer to access the disk in even simpler, more convenient ways than those allowed by the operating system. Also, they provide a degree of independence from the operating system, which can be a great help when porting a C program to another machine. Taken all together, however, this hierarchy of function calls and facilities available either directly or indirectly to the programmer can be confusing. The entire hierarchy is shown in Figure 6-4. We will discuss it from the bottom up.

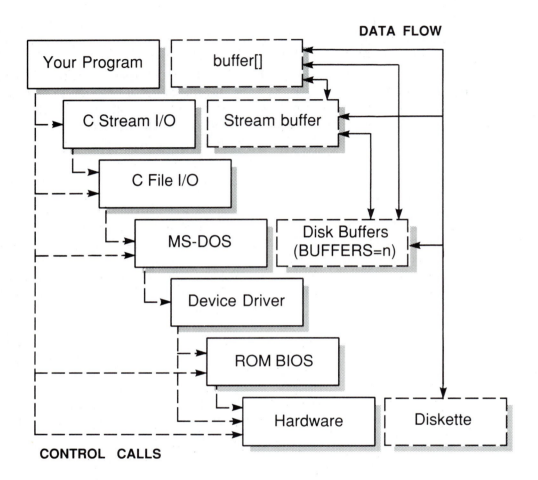

Figure 6-4: Disk Access Hierarchy

The physical hardware that moves data from the diskette into memory is at the lowest level of the hierarchy. The hardware is controlled by commands issued to it via input/output instructions. It generally transfers data directly between the processor's RAM memory and the external device using direct memory access (DMA). DMA is a hardware facility that transfers data into memory without the active participation of the processor. The commands available at this level are extremely simple: There are no files or directories yet, and the data is transferred in fixed size blocks.

The next level of the hierarchy, the ROM BIOS, contains routines for accessing some of the available types of hardware. In the PC/XT, for example, there are routines for accessing the floppy disk and the hard disk, and a certain level of disk access is required in the ROM to boot the computer in the first place. The ROM BIOS determines the details of the specific hardware level commands to be sent to the external device to access the data within it. The calling routine—generally a device driver, but sometimes an application program—doesn't need to know these details. At this level still, there are no files or directories. The data to be accessed is specified by the physical drive, head, track, and sector numbers where it resides on the disk and it is transferred in fixed size blocks.

Device drivers provide a uniform interface between MS-DOS and both disk (block) devices and non-disk devices such as serial ports, mice, etc. They allow the operating system to deal with a wide range of different types of devices, as long as the devices can be made to conform to a common structure at this level. Device drivers are not usually called directly from the user program; rather, they are called indirectly by MS-DOS. When MS-DOS calls a device driver, it specifies data by its logical offset on the disk rather than its physical location. MS-DOS does not concern itself with heads and tracks, only with blocks of data which are still of fixed size.

The next level in the hierarchy is MS-DOS—the heart of the disk I/O system. Below the MS-DOS level, several different device drivers and corresponding devices may be used. Above this level, each language has a somewhat different interface. But all data transfer goes through MS-DOS, except when it is accessed directly from an application to the ROM BIOS or hardware, generally only in the rare instances of disk patch utilities.

MS-DOS imposes the directory and file structure on the disk, keeping track of all the blocks and allocating them as necessary. It maintains directories of which blocks compose which files and in what sequential order. MS-DOS records the names of files and the directory or subdirectory in which they reside. At this level in the hierarchy, calls can open a file by name, and then can read or write a block of any size of data at a given offset from the start of the file. The file may or may not be physically contiguous on the disk; MS-DOS takes care of finding or allocating the blocks wherever they may be.

MS-DOS reads disk blocks into its own internal buffers, then copies the portion of the block requested into the calling routine's area. This allows the program to access the disk without having to use the fixed size blocks. The number of buffers available for this is set in the CONFIG.SYS file by the BUFFERS parameter. MS-DOS remembers the last several blocks that were read or written. If they are needed again, it can find them in one of these buffers and therefore won't need to read them again from disk.

MS-DOS functions are invoked by interrupts, which are available only at the assembly language level, with parameters passed in registers.

The C compiler comes with a run-time library that includes routines to interface with MS-DOS. These routines provide basically the same functionality as MS-DOS, but with two important features. First, they are called as C functions, not interrupts, allowing a C program to use them directly and efficiently. Second, they follow a convention and format consistent with C libraries on other machines, allowing programs written for one machine to be run on other machines with the same type of library. Examples of these functions include open, close, read, and write.

Since programs often want to deal with data in chunks of one character or one line at a time, the C run-time library also provides a set of routines for dealing with files in this fashion. This style of file access is known as stream I/O. The functions available include getchar, putchar, gets, puts, fgets, and fputs. The stream I/O routines read data into an intermediate buffer in large chunks, and return the data to the program in smaller sizes as requested. Because of the intermediate buffering, the disk I/O is still efficient, but the program gets to access the data in the manner most convenient to it.

Following the chain of data movement, you'll notice that a byte of data could potentially go from the disk to the MS-DOS buffer, then to the stream I/O buffer, and finally to the application buffer. This would involve copying the same data three times, which could be quite a waste of time. Luckily, shortcuts are available. First, you can call the C file I/O routines rather than the stream routines, bypassing one copy operation. Needless to say, this is a bad trade if the facilities provided by the stream routines are needed by the application. Second, if transfer requests to MS-DOS are in 512-byte multiples (the size of the fixed blocks on disk), MS-DOS will not use its internal buffer, but instead will transfer the data directly between the application buffer and the disk. So, by calling the C file routines and using a buffer size that is a multiple of 512 bytes, we will achieve the most efficient possible transfer of data, copying it only once —and that transfer is done by hardware DMA, not the CPU.

Optimizing the Program

As with the RAMSort program, we've built a CALIBRATE option into Encrypt to make it easier to measure the performance of the program. In Encrypt, CALIBRATE simply displays starting and ending messages, so we can separate the program loading time from the actual execution time.

Timing the program in Listing 6-1 with a stopwatch, on an IBM PC with floppy disks and an input file size of approximately 33K, yields an execution time of 34 seconds. Let's see if we can improve on this time.

The BUFSIZE constant determines how much data will be read from disk each iteration, and, in turn, how much will be written back again. To pick the optimal number for this buffer size, we need to know two important facts about personal computer disks.

First, data is ultimately transferred to and from the disk in fixed size blocks. The size of the blocks varies from computer to computer, and sometimes from disk drive to disk drive. In virtually all cases, though, the size of each block is a multiple of 128 bytes, and most often 512 bytes. MS-DOS uses the latter size as illustrated in Figure 6-5.

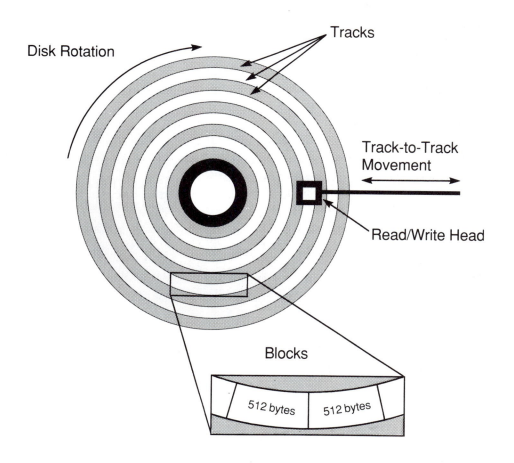

Figure 6-5: Disk Tracks and Blocks

If less than a full 512-byte block is written to the disk, the operating system must preserve the existing data in that block. It transfers the existing data into memory, changes the part of the block being written, and then transfers the block back out again. If the rest of the block is then written, the entire block must again be transferred to the disk. If, on the other hand, 512-byte multiples are written, the operating system can perform a single operation to transfer the data to disk, and it doesn't need to bother to get the existing block from disk, since all of it will be changed.

In addition, when the operating system gets a read or write request of a multiple of 512 bytes, it takes the shortcut we noted earlier: it reads or writes the data directly between the program's buffer area and the disk. If fractional blocks are involved, the operating system can't do this, because it must move them into its own buffer area and then transfer only the appropriate sub-part to or from the program. This is true during both reads and writes.

Using this information about the system, we can increase BUFSIZE from 1,000 bytes to 1,024 bytes, a multiple of 512 bytes. Now we run the program again and measure it. This time we get an execution time of only 21 seconds — an amazing improvement over 34 seconds, considering that we increased the buffer by only 24 bytes.

The second important fact about disks is that data on a diskette is physically organized into tracks, which is also shown in Figure 6-5. The rotation of the disk very quickly brings data on the "current" track to the read head. But to read data on another track, the head must be moved sideways. This movement is the slowest operation the disk performs, and therefore should be minimized as much as possible.

Encrypt deals with two files, the input file and output file. These files almost always reside on different tracks on the disk. By making the buffer size 1,024 bytes, therefore, we're asking the head to switch from the input file track to the output file track and back again for every 1,024 bytes of input. On our 33K test file, this means 66 track-to-track movements.

If we increase the buffer size to 20,480 (still a multiple of 512), we will have 20 times fewer head movements to slow us down. Timing the program with this change yields an 8 second run time — less than one-quarter of our original 34 seconds! And all we've done is change the value of BUFSIZE!

CPU Optimization

Now that we've optimized the disk I/O, we can concentrate on optimizing the CPU. Declaring the variables keyPtr and bufPtr to be register further reduces the execution time to 6 seconds. Had we done this at the start, we would have achieved an unimpressive 2 seconds improvement out of 34. Now, however, it's a 25% improvement from 8 seconds to 6.

Disk I/O time often swamps the CPU execution time. So, you should look for ways to optimize the disk accesses before looking for ways to speed up the code.

Why didn't we take this approach in Chapter Four? First, because the RAMSort application used the stream I/O functions, which read the data into an internal buffer, freeing the application from concerns about buffer sizes, and returning the data to the application in blocks of the size the application wants. Second, RAMSort reads everything into memory, sorts it, then writes it back out, preventing unnecessary head movement due to concurrent input and output.

Other Disk Drives

We used a floppy disk for the trial runs presented above because it gives the clearest, most substantial results. A hard disk will have faster track-to-track head movement and also faster data transfer times. But although the hard disk will reduce the effect of our optimization, we will still see substantial improvement.

Summary

Changing the way a program accesses the disk can dramatically affect the overall speed of the program. Depending upon the degree to which the program uses the disk, and the manner in which it operates, disk I/O time can affect the total speed of the program more than any other single factor. For this reason, you should attempt to optimize disk I/O before optimizing the CPU performance. Often, disk optimization will be so dramatic as to eliminate the need for additional improvements in performance.

Once again, we have illustrated that very small changes in the right part of the program can improve it much more than substantial changes in the wrong part. This is perhaps the most important lesson to be learned about optimization.

Finally, the Encrypt program also illustrates a general principle: it is often possible to trade RAM space for execution time. In this case, the larger the buffer, the less time Encrypt will take to execute. If we're willing to wait, we can make do with much less space.

Exercises

1. If you have access to a hard disk, try running the program on it, for each of the values of BUFSIZE used above. Compare the timings to those of the floppy disk.

2. Recode the inner loop, where the buffer is encrypted, in assembly language — but first make it a separate module. How much improvement do you find relative to the 20,480-byte version? How much relative to the 1,000-byte version?

3. Change Encrypt to use fread/fwrite. Use a 1,000-byte buffer. Compare the timings to the read/write version. What conclusions can you draw about stream I/O?

4. Change Encrypt to use getchar/putchar. This change eliminates the application buffer entirely. Time it and compare it with the original and the variation from Exercise 3. Note that this version uses very little run-time memory.

Listing 6-1. "encrpt.c":

```
/*                    Encrypt

        This program encrypts the standard input and writes it to
        the standard output. It requires one parameter: the key for
        the encryption, which can be up to eight characters long.
        Decryption is done by simply running the program again on the
        encrypted file with the same key -- i.e., encryption and
        decryption are the same operation.
*/

#include <fcntl.h>
#include <io.h>
#include <stdio.h>

#define BUFSIZE 1000    /* I/O buffer size. */
#define KEYSIZE 9       /* Maximum size of key (plus one for null). */

#define CALIBRATE       /* Define for start/end prompts. */

char buffer[BUFSIZE];   /* The I/O buffer. */

#define STDINFILE 0     /* Standard input non-stream file number. */
#define STDOUTFILE 1    /* Standard output file number. */

#define TRUE 1
#define FALSE 0

/*      main(argc,argv)

        Function: Encrypt the standard input and write it to the
        standard output, using the single command line parameter
        as the key.

        Algorithm: Get the key and rearrange it to improve security,
        then encrypt using exclusive-or with the key.
*/

main(argc,argv)

int argc;
char *argv[];

{
        char key[KEYSIZE];      /* The key. */
        char *cp, *cp2;
        char c;

        /* Check if we've got the right number of command line
           parameters. */
        if (argc != 2) {
```

Listing 6-1. "encrpt.c" *(cont.)*:

```
                  /* If not, remind him how to use this program. */
                  fputs("Usage: encrypt key <plainText >cipherText",stderr);
                  exit(1);
          };

          /* Check if we've got a decent sized key. */
          if ((argv[1][0] == 0) || (argv[1][1] == 0)) {
                  /* If not, tell him he needs a bigger key. */
                  fputs("Key must be at least 2 characters in size.",stderr);
                  exit(1);
          };

          /* Get the key. */
          for (cp = key, cp2 = argv[1];
               (cp < &key[KEYSIZE-1]) && (*cp2 != 0); *cp++ = *cp2++);
          /* Distribute the last byte among the top bits of the earlier
             ones, and toggle some of the bits in each key byte. All of
             this helps ensure a more secure key. */
          for (c = *(--cp), *cp = 0; cp >= key; cp--) {
                  *cp |= (c & 1) << 7;
                  *cp ^= 0x55;
                  c >>= 1;
          };

          /* Use binary I/O mode. For two reasons: (1) We want to be
             able to encrypt binary files; (2) characters may be
             turned into LFs in the encryption process, which would
             erroneously be translated into CRLF. */
          setmode(STDINFILE,O_BINARY);
          setmode(STDOUTFILE,O_BINARY);

          /* Encrypt it. */
#ifdef CALIBRATE
          fputs("Starting...",stderr);
#endif CALIBRATE
          encrypt(STDINFILE,STDOUTFILE,key);
#ifdef CALIBRATE
          fputs("done.\n",stderr);
#endif CALIBRATE
}

/*      encrypt(inFile,outFile,theKey)

        Function: Encrypt the file specified by inFile, using
        theKey, and write it to outFile.

        Algorithm: Exclusive-or the bytes with theKey, recycling
        theKey as needed.
*/
```

Listing 6-1. "encrpt.c" *(cont.)*:

```c
encrypt(inFile,outFile,theKey)

int inFile;
int outFile;
char *theKey;

{
        char *keyPtr;
        char *bufPtr;
        int bufCnt;
        int sizeRead;

        keyPtr = theKey;
        /* Cycle until nothing left to read. */
        while (TRUE) {
                /* Read in a bufferfull. */
                sizeRead = bufCnt = read(inFile,buffer,BUFSIZE);
                if (sizeRead <= 0) break;
                /* Encrypt it. */
                for (bufPtr = buffer; sizeRead-- > 0; *bufPtr++ ^= *keyPtr++)
                        if (*keyPtr == 0) keyPtr = theKey;
                /* Write it out. */
                write(outFile,buffer,bufCnt);
        };
}
```

Part II

Accessing ROM BIOS Directly

Chapter 7

How to Call the ROM BIOS

- Interrupts — Hardware, Processor, INT, Pointer Storage

- Operation of Interrupts and Jumbled Organization

- The ROM BIOS — Facilities Available

- Calling the ROM BIOS — C to BIOS Interface

- Interface Library to ROM BIOS Text Functions

- Avoiding Microsoft's C int86 Function

Every IBM PC comes with a set of built-in routines. These routines are present in the machine even before MS-DOS is booted (initially read in from diskette). In fact, they include the code that does the booting. These routines are stored in ROM (read-only memory) and are called the ROM BIOS, or "Basic I/O System." The ROM BIOS includes routines that interface with the keyboard, display, floppy disk, hard disk, printer port, and serial port. In most cases, when you issue a call to MS-DOS involving one of those devices, it in turn calls the ROM BIOS to carry out the request.

In this chapter, we will discuss how to call the ROM BIOS directly. Calling these routines directly serves two purposes. First, it is potentially much more efficient, since it bypasses the execution of the MS-DOS routines, for instance, when writing data to the display. This can dramatically improve the performance of the progam. Second, it allows access to some of the features of the computer that MS-DOS does not. This can add features to an existing program or make a previously impossible program feasible. The drawback to calling the ROM BIOS is that not all MS-DOS machines have a ROM BIOS with the same calls as the IBM PC. To run a program that calls the ROM BIOS directly, a machine must be not only MS-DOS compatible, but ROM BIOS compatible.

Interrupts

The ROM BIOS is not called using the same CALL instruction used for C functions. A slightly different facility, interrupts, is used instead. Before we can discuss the ROM BIOS itself, therefore, we need to explain the interrupt facility of the processor.

Interrupts are similar to subroutine calls: the instruction execution, or control flow of the machine, is temporarily transferred to a different part of memory. But rather than specifying a memory location to transfer control to, interrupts are invoked by specifying which one of several possible preset interrupt routines to call. Control is then transferred to a location found in an interrupt table in low memory. The entries in this table are known as interrupt vectors. By separating the interrupt type from its memory location, neither the code nor the hardware that invoke the interrupt need to know anything about the current layout of memory, which may change if the application or operating system changes. Unlike subroutine calls, interrupts can be invoked either by the program, the processor, or the external hardware.

Interrupts on the 8086/8088/80286 serve four purposes:

- Notifying the processor that some event has occurred in the hardware.
- Handling of error conditions (e.g., divide by zero).
- Calling MS-DOS and the ROM BIOS.
- Storing pointers to tables.

A different mechanism invokes the interrupt for each of these different types except the last one. Once invoked, however, the processor handles the interrupts in the same manner.

The first type of interrupt is used by the hardware. Hardware devices attached to the IBM PC bus operate independently from the processor. While the processor is executing your application, the disk drive controller may be simultaneously writing data to the disk, or the serial port hardware may be sending a character out the serial port. When one of these independent activities ends, or when an external condition arises requiring the attention of the processor, the hardware must notify the processor in some manner. This can be done by having the processor occasionally check the device to see if it needs attention. This approach is called "polling." It is the simplest way to control devices, but it isn't very efficient. Most of the times the processor checks the device, nothing needs to be done, so the processor has wasted its time asking. On the other hand, the device often finishes a task while the processor is busy doing something else, and so sits idle until the processor gets around to asking if it's finished.

Interrupts are more efficient because they "interrupt" the processor to let it know that a task is finished or that something significant has changed. Hardware interrupts of this type can occur at almost any time, possibly in the middle of the execution of an application program. They can occur between any two instructions (but not in the middle of an instruction). Don't worry, however, interrupt routines are always very careful to return to the application without disturbing anything. The application is never even aware that an interrupt has occurred.

Hardware interrupts are also used because the hardware does not know where an interrupt routine may reside in memory. The program could tell the hardware the location of the interrupt routine, but this would add much more complexity to the design of the device. It is much simpler to use an interrupt number, which can often be hard-wired into the device.

Hardware interrupts are most often used by the operating system and its device drivers. Interrupts of this type must be explicitly enabled in the hardware before they'll occur. Writing interrupt code is a challenging task, since it must be designed to generate the minimum possible interference with the executing application. We will present some examples of hardware interrupts in Part III of this book.

The second type of interrupt is known as a processor interrupt. These interrupts are used to handle special cases that arise during program execution, or to provide additional processor capabilities. They are called processor interrupts because either they originate within the processor and not in the external hardware, or they are explicitly invoked by the executing program. Occasionally during the execution of a program, an error condition occurs. Processor interrupts are used to catch these error situations. On the 8086/8088 there are only two such cases: divide by zero and arithmetic overflow. Processor interrupts are also used to allow a debugging program (such as DEBUG) to single-step the program execution.

The third type of interrupt can be invoked by executing the INT instruction. These are called software interrupts, and are used, among other things, to call the operating system and ROM BIOS from an application program. By using interrupts rather than CALL instructions to invoke the operating system, it becomes possible to change the operating system and the addresses it uses without having to recompile or reassemble all of the applications that use it. Only the interrupt table, which is part of the operating system, needs to change.

Finally, some interrupt vectors are not used to transfer control to subroutines at all. Instead, they are used to store pointers to tables used by other routines. By storing these pointers at known locations, it is possible to replace them with pointers to other tables, changing the operation of the system. For example, one interrupt vector points to the table that contains the image of characters on the screen for use in graphic character display; the character set can be changed simply by changing this vector to point to a different table.

Interrupt Operation

Once the processor recognizes that an interrupt should be performed, it takes the following actions:

1. The FLAG, CS, and IP registers are pushed onto the stack.

2. The interrupt flag (IF) is cleared, which disables further interrupts.

3. The interrupt number is used to index into the interrupt table in low memory — interrupt 0 chooses location 0, interrupt 1 chooses location 4, interrupt 2 chooses location 8, etc. — from which a new CS and IP are loaded.

4. Execution continues at the new CS/IP.

When the interrupt service routine begins executing, the processor has already saved the Flag, CS, and IP registers; but the interrupt service routine must be careful to save and restore any other registers that it modifies. When the routine is finished, it executes an IRET instruction, which restores the Flag, CS, and IP registers from the stack and then continues execution of the interrupted application. This entire sequence is diagrammed in Figure 7-1. By restoring the Flag register, the interrupt flag is restored to the value it had before the interrupt occurred. This usually re-enables interrupts. An application might, however, disable interrupts and then invoke a software interrupt, in which case interrupts would not be re-enabled after the completion of the software interrupt service routine.

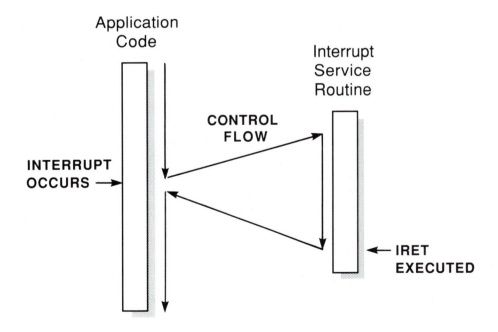

Figure 7-1. Interrupts

One of the hardware interrupts, the non-maskable interrupt (NMI), is immune to the effect of the interrupt flag (IF). It can occur at any time, even if interrupts have been disabled by clearing the IF. This interrupt is very seldom used on the IBM PC.

There are 256 separate interrupt vectors in the 8086/8088. Each consists of four bytes, two for the CS value and two for the IP value. The interrupt table, therefore, occupies the first 1,024 bytes of physical memory. Most of these interrupts are already reserved. The following table lists the assigned usage of these interrupts on the IBM PC by interrupt number (0-FF hex):

Class	Numbers (hex)	Usage
Processor	0	Divide by zero
	1	Used by debugger to single-step
	4	Arithmetic overflow (from INTO)
Hardware	2	Non-maskable interrupt
	8, 9, B-F, 40, 70-77	Device interrupt
Software	3	Used by debugger for breakpoints
	5, 10-1C	ROM BIOS
	20-3F	MS-DOS
	80-F0	BASIC
	60-67	General usage (by application)
Pointer	1D-1F, 41, 46	ROM BIOS
Reserved for Future use	6-7, A, 42-45 47-5F	

If you are thinking that this assignment of interrupts seems a bit jumbled, you're right. But once you assign an interrupt number, you can never take it back. As the design of a computer system evolves, new needs for interrupts arise that cannot be foreseen, leading inevitably to a jumbled assignment of numbers. By now, thousands of programs have been written that assume that some subset of these interrupts use the numbers given above. The moral: Be thankful that it isn't much more jumbled than it is.

The ROM BIOS

The ROM BIOS provides two main services: starting or "booting" the computer initially, and interfacing it to the attached hardware devices. On the IBM PC there is also a Basic interpreter built into ROM, which is not found on most compatible computers. In this chapter, we will cover the booting process, but not the Basic interpreter. We will mainly be concerned with those device-interface routines that can be called from an application program. A listing of the ROM BIOS can be found in the IBM *Technical Reference* manual. This listing is an invaluable resource when working extensively with the ROM BIOS.

Most ROM BIOS functions are provided within the ROM built into the IBM PC's main printed circuit board. This ROM resides in memory at physical addresses F0000-FFFFF; and different versions of the PC use differing amounts of this block, from 40K to the full 64K. Facilities are also included in the ROM BIOS design for extending it by using additional ROMs on other boards. The most notable of these are the ROM BIOS extensions for the hard disk (at address C8000), and the Extended Graphics Adapter (EGA) (at C0000). Figure 7-2 shows the general layout of the ROM BIOS in memory.

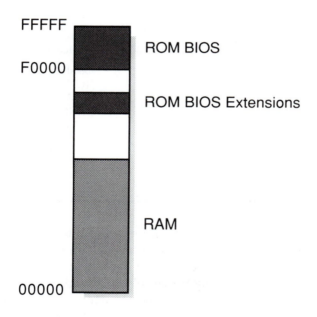

Figure 7-2. ROM BIOS Memory Locations

When you first turn the power on, it is a part of the ROM BIOS that begins executing. It starts by performing a series of diagnostic tests called the "Power-On Self Test," or POST. These tests are kept in ROM rather than on disk for two reasons: first, because a hardware failure might occur in an area that prevents data from being read from the disk, and second, because this is part of the function of interfacing to the attached devices, which is the principle job of the ROM BIOS. Once the tests have been run, the ROM BIOS boots the machine by loading a block of data from a preset position on disk and executing it. This fixed-position block of data is called the "boot block." The boot block begins execution, and then reads in the operating system, or perhaps an individual, stand-alone application. The machine is then up and running.

Once the machine is booted, the main job of the ROM BIOS is to provide an interface to the hardware available in the IBM PC. Thus, the ROM BIOS hides the low-level details of the hardware from the software loaded from disk. The ROM BIOS contains routines for accessing and controlling the following devices:

Device	Routines
Keyboard	Read a character
	Check whether a character is available
	Read current shift key states
Display	Set display mode
	Set cursor type
	Set cursor position
	Read cursor position
	Read light pen position
	Select active display page
	Scroll active area up or down
	Read character/attribute from display
	Write character/attribute to display
	Write character only to display
	Set color palette
	Write dot
	Read dot
	Write character to display, TTY style
	Get current video state
	Write string (AT only)
Floppy or Hard Disk	Reset disk
	Read status
	Read sectors into memory
	Write sectors from memory
	Verify sectors
	Format track
Hard Disk only	Return drive parameters
	Initialize drive pair characteristics
	Read long
	Write long

Device *(cont.)*	**Routines**
Hard Disk only *(cont.)*	Seek Alternate disk reset Read sector buffer Write sector buffer Test drive ready Recalibrate Run controller RAM diagnostic Run drive diagnostic Run controller internal diagnostic
Printer Port	Print character Initialize printer port Read printer status
Serial Port	Initialize serial port Send character Read character Read status
Clock	Read clock count Set clock count Read real time (AT only) Set real time (AT only) Read date (AT only) Set date (AT only) Set the alarm (AT only) Reset the alarm (AT only)
General	Get memory size Get attached equipment list
AT Extensions (all AT only)	Device open Device close Program termination Event wait Read joystick System request key pressed Wait Move block Extended memory size determination Switch to virtual mode Device busy loop Interrupt complete flag set

Later in this chapter, we will show how to call these facilities from C by using assembly language interface routines. In this and later chapters, we will present libraries of routines that interface to most of the functions listed above. We will concentrate on the display, but will also show how to work with the keyboard, printer, and serial ports.

We will not show the ROM BIOS disk interface because we don't recommend that the programmer access the disk directly using the ROM BIOS. There are several reasons for this: MS-DOS provides a much better interface; it's very easy to damage the data on the disk using these routines; and these routines are only required when doing low-level disk repairs, for which there are much better, much safer programs available commercially. In short, accessing the disk directly via the ROM BIOS invites serious and disk-destroying mistakes. Avoid doing so unless you have no other choice. Finally, we will not discuss the AT-specific functions, since these functions produce programs that only run on the IBM PC/AT. We want to write programs that will run on any member of the IBM PC family of computers.

Calling the ROM BIOS

The ROM BIOS was designed to be called from assembly language, not from C. It uses interrupts to transfer control to the BIOS routines, and it passes parameters to and from the routines in processor registers. This is quite straightforward to program in assembly, but impossible to program directly from C. The main function of the C-to-ROM BIOS interface routines, therefore, is to convert from the C calling and parameter passing conventions to the ROM BIOS calling and parameter passing conventions. It is also possible to call the ROM BIOS using the int86 function provided with the Microsoft compiler. This alternative approach will be discussed later in this chapter.

Interfaces to two of the simplest ROM BIOS functions are presented in Listing 7-1. These routines return the size of the memory in the system and a list of the equipment which is attached to it:

Function

memSz() — Returns the number of 1K byte blocks of memory in the system.

getEq() — Returns a word indicating the type and quantity of equipment attached, as shown in Figure 7-3. Listing 7-2 contains an include file that makes it much simpler to use the information returned by this function. (Note that the maximum system board memory reportable by this function is 64K bytes, which was the maximum possible in the original PC.)

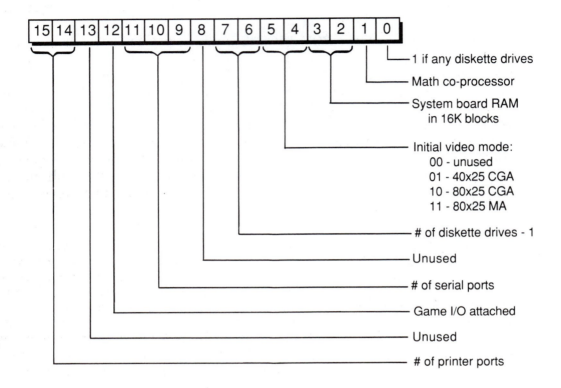

Figure 7-3. Equipment Listing Bit Meanings

Listing 7-3 contains a program that uses these routines to display the configuration of the machine on which it's run.

Most of the ROM BIOS functions are more complex, requiring additional input parameters and potentially returning more results. Each device type handled by the ROM BIOS has its own individual interrupt. Different functions within that device type are selected by passing different values to the routine in the AH register. For example, to set the cursor position to row 5, column 17, the following assembly language code can be used:

```
mov     dh,5      ; Set dh to the row number
mov     dl,17     ; Set dl to the column number
mov     bh,0      ; Set bh to the page number
mov     ah,2      ; Function 2: set cursor position
int     10H       ; Call the ROM BIOS display routine
```

The row and column number are passed to this routine in the DH and DL registers, and the display page number is passed in BH. AH is used to select the display function—in this case, function number 2, set cursor position. A different function sets the mode and is selected by setting AH to 0:

```
mov     al,2    ; Set mode 2 (80x25 B&W)
mov     ah,0    ; Function 0: set display mode
int     10H     ; Call the ROM BIOS
```

The same interrupt is used, but a different value in AH selects a different function to be executed. The different function also requires a different set of parameters. The register usage for most of the ROM BIOS routines is given in Appendix C. The remainder of Part II of this book will present additional interface routines for other parts of the ROM BIOS, as well as examples of how to use them.

Listing 7-4 contains an interface library to the text display functions of the ROM BIOS. This library contains routines for each of the 13 text display functions of the normal PC. The PC/AT has several extended string write functions that are not included here. If you want your program to run on the entire line of the IBM PCs, it's best to stay away from these functions. The following summarizes the routines provided:

Function

---

setMod(mode)—Set the display mode:

Mode	Meaning
0	40x25 B&W
1	40x25 color
2	80x25 B&W
3	80x25 color
4	320x200 color
5	320x200 B&W
6	640x200 B&W
7	Monochrome adapter (fixed mode)

setCTyp(start,end)—Set cursor type. Cursor extends from line number start to line number end within the character.

setPos(page,row,col)—Set cursor position to the row and column given, in the page specified. The upper left hand corner is row zero, column zero.

Function *(cont.)*

---

getPos(page,&row,&col,&start,&end) — Get the cursor position and type from the page specified. After the call, row and col will contain the row and column; and start and end will contain the cursor type — row, col, start, and end are all of type int.

getLite(&row,&col,&raster,&pixCol) — Return FALSE if the light pen switch is up. Otherwise, return TRUE and the row and column of the character pointed to in row and col, and the raster line (0-199) in raster, and the pixel column (0-319 or 0-639) in pixCol — row, col, raster, and pixCol are all of type int.

setPage(page) — Select new active page.

scrUp(n,ulRow,ulCol,lrRow,lrCol,attr) — Scroll up the region with the upper right corner of ulRow and ulCol, and the lower right corner of lrRow and lrCol. Scroll the region n lines, and fill in the newly blank area with the attribute attr. If n is zero, the region is cleared.

scrDn(n,ulRow,ulCol,lrRow,lrCol,page) — Exactly like scrUp( ), but scroll down rather than up.

getACh(page,&ch,&attr) — Read the character and attribute at the current cursor position on the specified page, and store them in ch and attr. The parameters ch and attr are both of type char.

putACh(page,ch,attr,n) — Write the character and attribute ch and attr at the current cursor position on the specified page. Write n of the same character. If this is a graphics display mode, and bit 7 of attr is 1, then the character is exclusive-ored with the current display.

putOCh(page,ch,n) — Write only the character ch at the current cursor position on the specified page. Write n of the same character, but do not change the attribute.

putTty(page,ch,color) — Write the character ch to the screen with the foreground color given, in the page specified. After the character is written to the display, the cursor position is incremented. Several control characters are recognized and interpreted, including:

Character	Meaning
'\n'	Linefeed: set cursor to the same column, next row
'\r'	Carriage return: set cursor to column zero, next row
'\007'	Bell: go "beep"
'\010'	Backspace: set cursor to the previous column

getSt(&mode,&width,&page) — Get the current mode, width of the screen in character columns, and active page — mode, width, and page are all of type int.

The general format of each interface routine—save registers, get input parameters, call BIOS, put output parameters, restore registers—is the same. In fact, we could have had all the routines JMP to a single block of code for restoring registers. This would have saved space, but it would have cost an extra instruction execution time for each call. While this time penalty would have been small, interface libraries are written to be as efficient as possible. Often, the reason for using the ROM BIOS directly is to speed up a program, so we want to keep unnecessary code to an absolute minimum.

Note the usage of pointers to variables, as in the getPos function. It isn't enough simply to move data between the registers and the stack. The value on the stack is, instead, a pointer; and the register values must be written indirectly into memory elsewhere. It is also important to know the size of the variable the pointer points to. If the variable is type int, the top byte must either be set from a register or be zeroed if the register value is only 8 bits in size. Otherwise, the C program will receive results with the upper byte set to an indeterminate value. If the top byte is set to a register or zeroed when it shouldn't be—when the pointer is to a char type variable—a value will be written over the wrong memory location. This sort of "wrong location write" is one of the hardest bugs to track down.

These routines are all one-to-one: each C function calls one and only one ROM BIOS function. These are purely BIOS interface routines. In subsequent chapters we will present some extensions to the library, in which one interface routine calls multiple BIOS functions to present an easier interface for the programmer to use.

Listing 7-5 shows a C program which, like the program in Listing 7-3, displays the configuration of the machine. In this case, however, additional ROM BIOS routines are used to manipulate the display. First, the screen is cleared. Second, the cursor is positioned to the middle of the screen and the memory size is written there. Third, the cursor is repositioned to the top of the screen and the equipment configuration is written. Finally, the cursor is repositioned to its normal place at the bottom of the screen.

The int86 Function

The Microsoft C compiler includes a function called int86 in its run-time library. This function allows you to call the ROM BIOS without having to resort to assembly code. Its basic purpose is to let you call any of the software interrupts, pass data to them through the registers, and read the results that were returned in the registers. To pass register values, a data structure is defined that includes fields for each of the registers. When the int86 function is called, it is passed the number of the interrupt to be invoked, plus pointers to two register structures, one for input and one for output.

For example, the following code will set the cursor position to row 5, column 17:

```
union REGS inregs;                /* Reg structure for input. */
union REGS outregs;               /* Reg structure for output. */
                     .
                     .
                     .
inregs.h.dh = 5;                  /* Set row to 5. */
inregs.h.dl = 17;                 /* Set column to 17. */
inregs.h.bh = 0;                  /* Set page to 0. */
inregs.h.ah = 2;                  /* Function 2: set cursor pos. */
int86(0x10,&inregs,&outregs);     /* Call the ROM BIOS. */
```

This book is written using only assembly language interface routines and not int86. This is done for two reasons. First, after reading this book, a programmer should be comfortable with mixing C and assembly. Therefore, the more examples of assembly called from C, the better. Second, assembly routines are more efficient than the equivalent routine written in C using int86. This is especially true with routines that make multiple ROM BIOS calls. In this book, we are trying to squeeze as much performance as possible out of the program, so we want to avoid any additional execution time cost if at all possible.

On the other hand, there are definitely times when being able to stay entirely in C outweighs the added efficiency of assembly. The programmer should, therefore, be well aware of the int86 function and how to use it. He can then make an informed choice about which technique—assembly language or int86—to use in his program.

Summary

Included with every IBM PC is a set of routines in read-only-memory (ROM), called the ROM BIOS. These routines provide a low-level interface to the hardware of the machine, and also perform the initial self-test and booting of the computer. The hardware interface routines are called using the software interrupt facility of the processor. This is similar to a subroutine call but is easier to make memory location independent.

Unfortunately, software interrupts cannot be invoked directly from C programs, so a small assembly language interface routine is needed to call a ROM BIOS routine from C. The assembly interface routine basically converts from the CALL-instruction-with-parameters-passed-on-the-stack convention used by C, to the INT-instruction-with-parameters-passed-in-processor-registers convention used by the ROM BIOS.

Another technique that can be used to invoke the ROM BIOS from C is the int86 function which comes with the C compiler. The int86 function is somewhat less efficient, but allows the programmer to stay entirely within the C language without resorting to assembly language at all.

To demonstrate these techniques, we presented an example using the ROM BIOS routines that return the amount of memory in the system, as well as the configuration of the attached equipment. We then introduced the more complex set of video display ROM BIOS interface routines. These routines serve as an example for writing future routines to interface to the BIOS. Additional libraries for other parts of the ROM BIOS will be presented in later chapters.

Exercises

1. Write a C program that allows you to select one of the display routines, asks for the values of the parameters to pass to it, calls the routine, and then displays the results, if any. Try calling the BIOS functions and see what the results are.

2. Look through the BIOS code in the IBM *Technical Reference* manual. Look particularly at the display routines, and try to follow a call through execution in the BIOS. Don't worry if you have trouble—these are complex routines, tightly coded. The exercise should give you a better understanding of what actually happens when your program displays a character.

Listing 7-1. "eqlib.asm":

```
;                Equipment Configuration Library

_TEXT    segment byte public 'CODE'      ; Place the code in the code segment
         assume  CS:_TEXT                ; Assume the CS register points to it

; _memSz()
;
; Function: Return the number of 1K blocks of memory in the system.
;
; Algorithm: Just call the ROM BIOS via interrupt 10H.

         public  _memSz                  ; This routine is public (available to
                                         ; other modules)

_memSz   proc near                       ; _memSz is a NEAR type subroutine
         int     12H                     ; Call the ROM BIOS with interrupt 12 (hex)
         ret                             ; Return to the calling program
_memSz   endp                            ; End of subroutine

; _getEq()
;
; Function: Return the current equipment configuration.
;
; Algorithm: Call ROM BIOS interrupt 11H to get the configuration.

         public  _getEq                  ; Routine is available to other modules
_getEq   proc near                       ; NEAR type subroutine
         int     11H                     ; Call the ROM BIOS with interrupt 11 (hex)
         ret                             ; Return to calling program
_getEq   endp                            ; End of subroutine

_TEXT    ends                            ; End of code segment
         end                             ; End of assembly code
```

Listing 7-2. "eqlib.h":

```
/*               Equates for Use with eqlib.asm
 */

/* Masks and shift counts for fields in the return value of getEq: */

#define prtnMask 0xC000          /* Mask for number of printers bits. */
#define prtnShft 14             /* Number of bits to shift. */

#define gioMask 0x1000          /* Mask for game I/O attached bit. */
#define gioShft 12              /* Number of bits to shift it. */

#define RS232Mask 0xE00         /* Mask for number of serial ports bits. */
#define RS232Shft 9             /* Number of bits to shift. */
```

Listing 7-2. "eqlib.h" *(cont.)*:

```
#define dsknMask 0xC0          /* Mask for number of disk drives bits. */
#define dsknShft 6             /* Bits to shift. */

#define vmodeMask 0x30         /* Mask for initial video mode bits. */
#define CO40 0x10              /* Value for 40x25 color. */
#define CO80 0x20              /* Value for 80x25 color. */
#define MONO 0x30              /* Value for 80x25 monochrome. */

#define sbramMask 0xC          /* Mask for system board RAM size (/16K). */
#define sbramShft 2            /* Number of bits to shift. */

#define diskMask 1             /* Diskette drive present bit. */
```

Listing 7-3. "showeq.c":

```c
#include "eqlib.h"

/*      main()

        Function: Get and display the system memory size and the
        equipment configuration.

        Algorithm: Call the ROM BIOS interface routines memSz and
        getEq. Then interpret their replies and display the results.
*/

main()

{
        unsigned theEq; /* The equipment configuration. */
        unsigned i;

        /* Display the memory size. */
        printf("Memory size is %dK.\n\n Equipment present:\n    ",memSz());

        /* Get the equipment configuration. */
        theEq = getEq();
        /* Get the number of printers. */
        i = (theEq & prtnMask) >> prtnShft;
        /* If there are any at all, show how many. */
        if (i != 0) printf("%d printer(s).\n    ",i);
        /* If there's a game I/O interface present, say so. */
        if (theEq & gioMask) printf("1 game I/O.\n    ");
        /* Get the number of serial ports. */
        i = (theEq & RS232Mask) >> RS232Shft;
        /* If there are any, show how many. */
        if (i != 0) printf("%d serial port(s).\n    ",i);
        /* If there are any diskette drives present, show how many. */
        if (theEq & diskMask) printf("%d diskette drive(s).\n    ",
```

Listing 7-3. "showeq.c" *(cont.)*:

```
                                         ((theEq & dsknMask) >> dsknShft)+1);
    /* Show the initial video mode. */
    printf("Initial video mode: ");
    i = theEq & vmodeMask;
    if (i == CO40) printf("40x25 color");
    else if (i == CO80) printf("80x25 color");
    else if (i == MONO) printf("80x25 monochrome");
    /* Show the system board RAM size. */
    printf(".\n    System board RAM size: %dK bytes.\n",
            16*(((theEq & sbramMask) >> sbramShft)+1));
}
```

Listing 7-4. "vlib.asm":

```
;                   Text Video Library

_TEXT    segment byte public 'CODE'      ; Place the code in the code segment
         assume  CS:_TEXT                ; Assume the CS register points to it

; _setMod(mode)
;
; Function: Set the display mode to that specified by mode.
;
; Algorithm: Call the ROM BIOS set mode function; int 10H, AH = 0.

         public  _setMode                ; Routine is available to other modules

         mode = 4                        ; Offset from BP to parameter mode

_setMod proc near                        ; NEAR type subroutine
         push    bp                      ; Save BP register
         mov     bp,sp                   ; Set BP to SP; easier to get parameters
         push    si                      ; Save the SI register
         push    di                      ; Save the DI register
         mov     al,[bp+mode]            ; Set AL to mode
         mov     ah,0                    ; Set AH to 0 (set mode function)
         int     10H                     ; Call ROM BIOS video interrupt
         pop     di                      ; Restore DI
         pop     si                      ; Restore SI
         pop     bp                      ; Restore the BP register
         ret                             ; Return to calling program
_setMod endp                             ; End of subroutine

; _setCTyp(start,end)
;
; Function: Set a new cursor, which starts on scan line start and ends on
; scan line end.
;
; Algorithm: Call the ROM BIOS set cursor type function; int 10H, AH = 1.
```

Listing 7-4. "vlib.asm" *(cont.)*:

```
        public   _setCTyp        ; Routine is available to other modules

        start = 4                ; Offset from BP to parameter start
        end = 6                  ; Offset to parameter end

_setCTyp proc near              ; NEAR type subroutine
        push    bp              ; Save BP register
        mov     bp,sp           ; Set BP to SP; easier to get parameters
        push    si              ; Save the SI register
        push    di              ; Save the DI register
        mov     ch,[bp+start]   ; Set CH to start
        mov     cl,[bp+end]     ; Set CL to end
        mov     ah,1            ; Set AH to 1 (set cursor type function)
        int     10H             ; Call ROM BIOS video interrupt
        pop     di              ; Restore DI
        pop     si              ; Restore SI
        pop     bp              ; Restore the BP register
        ret                     ; Return to calling program
_setCTyp endp                   ; End of subroutine

;  _setPos(page,row,col)
;
; Function: Set the cursor position on the page specified to the row and
; column specified.
;
; Algorithm: Call the ROM BIOS set cursor position function; int 10H, AH = 2.

        public   _setPos         ; Routine is available to other modules

        page = 4                 ; Offset from BP to parameter page
        row = 6                  ; Offset to parameter row
        col = 8                  ; Offset to col

_setPos proc near               ; NEAR type subroutine
        push    bp              ; Save BP register
        mov     bp,sp           ; Set BP to SP; easier to get parameters
        push    si              ; Save the SI register
        push    di              ; Save the DI register
        mov     bh,[bp+page]    ; Set BH to the page
        mov     dh,[bp+row]     ; Set DH to the row
        mov     dl,[bp+col]     ; Set DL to the column
        mov     ah,2            ; Set AH to 2 (set cursor position function)
        int     10H             ; Call ROM BIOS video interrupt
        pop     di              ; Restore DI
        pop     si              ; Restore SI
        pop     bp              ; Restore the BP register
        ret                     ; Return to calling program
_setPos endp                    ; End of subroutine
```

Listing 7-4. "vlib.asm" *(cont.)*:

```
;   _getPos(page,&rowPtr,&colPtr,&startPtr,&endPtr)
;
; Function: Get the current cursor. This includes getting the row and
; column, as well as the start and end scan lines of the cursor. The
; page parameter tells which page's cursor to get.
;
; Algorithm: Call the ROM BIOS get cursor function; int 10H, AH = 3.

        public  _getPos             ; Routine is available to other modules

        page = 4                    ; Offset from BP to parameter page
        rowPtr = 6                  ; Offset to parameter rowPtr
        colPtr = 8                  ; Offset to colPtr
        startPtr = 10               ; Offset to startPtr
        endPtr = 12                 ; Offset to endPtr

_getPos proc near                   ; NEAR type subroutine
        push    bp                  ; Save BP register
        mov     bp,sp               ; Set BP to SP; easier to get parameters
        push    si                  ; Save the SI register
        push    di                  ; Save the DI register
        mov     bh,[bp+page]        ; Set BH to the page
        mov     ah,3                ; Set AH to 3 (get cursor function)
        int     10H                 ; Call ROM BIOS video interrupt
        xor     al,al               ; Zero AL
        mov     bx,[bp+rowPtr]      ; *rowPtr = row number (with top byte zeroed)
        mov     [bx],dh
        mov     [bx+1],al
        mov     bx,[bp+colPtr]      ; *colPtr = column number (with zero top byte)
        mov     [bx],dl
        mov     [bx+1],al
        mov     bx,[bp+startPtr];   *startPtr = cursor scan line start
        mov     [bx],ch
        mov     [bx+1],al
        mov     bx,[bp+endPtr]      ; *endPtr = cursor scan line end
        mov     [bx],cl
        mov     [bx+1],al
        pop     di                  ; Restore DI
        pop     si                  ; Restore SI
        pop     bp                  ; Restore the BP register
        ret                         ; Return to calling program
_getPos endp                        ; End of subroutine

;   _getLite(&rowPtr,&colPtr,&rasterPtr,&pixColPtr)
;
; Function: If the light pen button is not depressed, return FALSE.
; Otherwise, return TRUE and the location of the press in the locations
; pointed to by rowPtr, colPtr, rasterPtr, and pixColPtr.
;
; Algorithm: Call the ROM BIOS get light pen function; int 10H, AH = 4.
```

Listing 7-4. "vlib.asm" *(cont.)*:

```
        public  _getLite          ; Routine is available to other modules

        rowPtr = 4                ; Offset from BP to parameter rowPtr
        colPtr = 6                ; Offset to parameter colPtr
        rasterPtr = 8             ; Offset to rasterPtr
        pixColPtr = 10            ; Offset to pixColPtr

_getLite proc near               ; NEAR type subroutine
        push    bp                ; Save BP register
        mov     bp,sp             ; Set BP to SP; easier to get parameters
        push    si                ; Save the SI register
        push    di                ; Save the DI register
        mov     ah,4              ; Set AH to 4 (get light pen function)
        int     10H               ; Call ROM BIOS video interrupt
        or      ah,ah             ; Is the button down?
        mov     ax,0              ; Assume not (i.e., return FALSE)
        jz      glDone            ; Branch if it indeed wasn't down
        push    bx                ; Save the BX register (the pixel column)
        mov     bx,[bp+rowPtr]    ; *rowPtr = row number, with top byte zeroed
        mov     [bx],dh
        mov     [bx+1],al
        mov     bx,[bp+colPtr]    ; *colPtr = column number
        mov     [bx],dl
        mov     [bx+1],al
        mov     bx,[bp+rasterPtr] ; *rasterPtr = raster line
        mov     [bx],ch
        mov     [bx+1],al
        pop     ax                ; Restore the pixel column into AX
        mov     bx,[bp+pixColPtr] ; *pixColPtr = pixel column
        mov     [bx],ax
        mov     ax,1              ; Return TRUE

glDone: pop     di                ; Restore DI
        pop     si                ; Restore SI
        pop     bp                ; Restore the BP register
        ret                       ; Return to calling program
_getLite endp                     ; End of subroutine

; _setPage(page)
;
; Function: Set the active display page.
;
; Algorithm: Call the ROM BIOS set page function; int 10H, AH = 5.

        public  _setPage          ; Routine is available to other modules

        page = 4                  ; Offset from BP to parameter page

_setPage proc near               ; NEAR type subroutine
```

Listing 7-4. "vlib.asm" *(cont.)*:

```
        push    bp              ; Save BP register
        mov     bp,sp           ; Set BP to SP; easier to get parameters
        push    si              ; Save the SI register
        push    di              ; Save the DI register
        mov     al,[bp+page]    ; Set AL to the page number
        mov     ah,5            ; Set AH to 5 (set active page function)
        int     10H             ; Call ROM BIOS video interrupt
        pop     di              ; Restore DI
        pop     si              ; Restore SI
        pop     bp              ; Restore the BP register
        ret                     ; Return to calling program
_setPage endp                   ; End of subroutine

; _scrUp(n,ulRow,ulCol,lrRow,lrCol,attr)
;
; Function: Scroll a rectangular block of the display up by n lines. The
; block to scroll has an upper left corner of row ulRow and column ulCol,
; and a lower right corner of row lrRow and column lrCol. New lines are
; filled with blanks with attribute attr.
;
; Algorithm: Call the ROM BIOS scroll up function; int 10H, AH = 6.

        public  _scrUp          ; Routine is available to other modules

        n = 4                   ; Offset from BP to parameter n
        ulRow = 6               ; Offset to parameter ulRow
        ulCol = 8               ; Offset to ulCol
        lrRow = 10              ; Offset to lrRow
        lrCol = 12              ; Offset to lrCol
        attr = 14               ; Offset to attr

_scrUp  proc near               ; NEAR type subroutine
        push    bp              ; Save BP register
        mov     bp,sp           ; Set BP to SP; easier to get parameters
        push    si              ; Save the SI register
        push    di              ; Save the DI register
        mov     al,[bp+n]       ; Set AL to the number of lines to scroll
        mov     ch,[bp+ulRow]   ; Set CH to the upper left row
        mov     cl,[bp+ulCol]   ; Set CH to the upper left column
        mov     dh,[bp+lrRow]   ; Set DH to the lower right row
        mov     dl,[bp+lrCol]   ; Set DL to the lower right column
        mov     bh,[bp+attr]    ; Set BH to the attribute to fill with
        mov     ah,6            ; Set AH to 6 (scroll up function)
        int     10H             ; Call ROM BIOS video interrupt
        pop     di              ; Restore DI
        pop     si              ; Restore SI
        pop     bp              ; Restore the BP register
        ret                     ; Return to calling program
_scrUp  endp                    ; End of subroutine
```

Listing 7-4. "vlib.asm" *(cont.)*:

```
;  _scrDn(n,ulRow,ulCol,lrRow,lrCol,attr)
;
;  Function: Scroll a rectangular block of the display down by n lines. The
;  block to scroll has an upper left corner of row ulRow and column ulCol,
;  and a lower right corner of row lrRow and column lrCol. New lines are
;  filled with blanks with attribute attr.
;
;  Algorithm: Call the ROM BIOS scroll up function; int 10H, AH = 6.

            public    _scrDn           ; Routine is available to other modules

            n = 4                      ; Offset from BP to parameter n
            ulRow = 6                  ; Offset to parameter ulRow
            ulCol = 8                  ; Offset to ulCol
            lrRow = 10                 ; Offset to lrRow
            lrCol = 12                 ; Offset to lrCol
            attr = 14                  ; Offset to attr

_scrDn      proc near                  ; NEAR type subroutine
            push      bp               ; Save BP register
            mov       bp,sp            ; Set BP to SP; easier to get parameters
            push      si               ; Save the SI register
            push      di               ; Save the DI register
            mov       al,[bp+n]        ; Set AL to the number of lines to scroll
            mov       ch,[bp+ulRow]    ; Set CH to the upper left row
            mov       cl,[bp+ulCol]    ; Set CH to the upper left column
            mov       dh,[bp+lrRow]    ; Set DH to the lower right row
            mov       dl,[bp+lrCol]    ; Set DL to the lower right column
            mov       bh,[bp+attr]     ; Set BH to the attribute to fill with
            mov       ah,7             ; Set AH to 7 (scroll down function)
            int       10H              ; Call ROM BIOS video interrupt
            pop       di               ; Restore DI
            pop       si               ; Restore SI
            pop       bp               ; Restore the BP register
            ret                        ; Return to calling program
_scrDn      endp                       ; End of subroutine

;  _getACh(page,&chPtr,&attrPtr)
;
;  Function: Get the character and the attributes of the character at the
;  current cursor position in the specified page.
;
;  Algorithm: Call the ROM BIOS get character/attribute function; int 10H,
;  AH = 8.

            public    _getACh          ; Routine is available to other modules

            page = 4                   ; Offset from BP to parameter page
            chPtr = 6                  ; Offset to parameter chPtr
            attrPtr = 8                ; Offset to attrPtr
```

Listing 7-4. "vlib.asm" *(cont.)*:

```
_getACh proc near                ; NEAR type subroutine
        push    bp               ; Save BP register
        mov     bp,sp            ; Set BP to SP; easier to get parameters
        push    si               ; Save the SI register
        push    di               ; Save the DI register
        mov     bh,[bp+page]     ; Set BH to the page number
        mov     ah,8             ; Set AH to 8 (get char/attribute function)
        int     10H              ; Call ROM BIOS video interrupt
        mov     bx,[bp+chPtr]    ; *chPtr = character at cursor
        mov     [bx],al
        mov     bx,[bp+attrPtr]  ; *attrPtr = attribute at cursor
        mov     [bx],ah
        pop     di               ; Restore DI
        pop     si               ; Restore SI
        pop     bp               ; Restore the BP register
        ret                      ; Return to calling program
_getACh endp                     ; End of subroutine

; _putACh(page,char,attr,n)
;
; Function: Put n copies of the character and attribute specified at the
; current cursor position of the specified page.
;
; Algorithm: Call the ROM BIOS put character/attribute function; int 10H,
; AH = 9.

        public  _putACh          ; Routine is available to other modules

        page = 4                 ; Offset from BP to parameter page
        char = 6                 ; Offset to parameter ch
        attr = 8                 ; Offset to attr
        n = 10                   ; Offset to n

_putACh proc near                ; NEAR type subroutine
        push    bp               ; Save BP register
        mov     bp,sp            ; Set BP to SP; easier to get parameters
        push    si               ; Save the SI register
        push    di               ; Save the DI register
        mov     bh,[bp+page]     ; Set BH to the page number
        mov     cx,[bp+n]        ; Set CX to the number of chars to write
        mov     al,[bp+char]     ; Set AL to the character
        mov     bl,[bp+attr]     ; Set BL to the attribute
        mov     ah,9             ; Set AH to 9 (put char/attribute function)
        int     10H              ; Call ROM BIOS video interrupt
        pop     di               ; Restore DI
        pop     si               ; Restore SI
        pop     bp               ; Restore the BP register
        ret                      ; Return to calling program
_putACh endp                     ; End of subroutine
```

Listing 7-4. "vlib.asm" *(cont.)*:

```
;  _putOCh(page,char,n)
;
; Function: Write n copies of the character char to the current cursor
; position on the specified page. Leave the attribute as it was.
;
; Algorithm: Call the ROM BIOS write character function; int 10H, AH = 10.

        public  _putOCh          ; Routine is available to other modules

        page = 4                 ; Offset from BP to parameter page
        char = 6                 ; Offset to parameter ch
        n = 8                    ; Offset to n
_putOCh proc near                ; NEAR type subroutine
        push    bp               ; Save BP register
        mov     bp,sp            ; Set BP to SP; easier to get parameters
        push    si               ; Save the SI register
        push    di               ; Save the DI register
        mov     bh,[bp+page]     ; Set BH to the page number
        mov     cx,[bp+n]        ; Set CX to the number of chars to write
        mov     al,[bp+char]     ; Set AL to the character to write
        mov     ah,10            ; Set AH to 10 (write character function)
        int     10H              ; Call ROM BIOS video interrupt
        pop     di               ; Restore DI
        pop     si               ; Restore SI
        pop     bp               ; Restore the BP register
        ret                      ; Return to calling program
_putOCh endp                     ; End of subroutine

;  _putTty(page,char,color)
;
; Function: Write the character char to the current cursor position of the
; page specified; if in graphics mode, write it in the color given. Unlike
; the putACh and putOCh functions, this function advances the cursor after
; writing, and interprets some control codes such as carriage return, line
; feed, and backspace.
;
; Algorithm: Call the ROM BIOS TTY write character function; int 10H, AH = 13.

        public  _putTty          ; Routine is available to other modules

        page = 4                 ; Offset from BP to parameter page
        char = 6                 ; Offset to parameter ch
        color = 8                ; Offset to color

_putTty proc near                ; NEAR type subroutine
        push    bp               ; Save BP register
        mov     bp,sp            ; Set BP to SP; easier to get parameters
        push    si               ; Save the SI register
        push    di               ; Save the DI register
```

Listing 7-4. "vlib.asm" *(cont.)*:

```
            mov     bh, [bp+page]      ; Set BH to the page number
            mov     al, [bp+char]      ; Set AL to the character to write
            mov     bl, [bp+color]     ; Set BL to the foreground color to use
            mov     ah, 14             ; Set AH to 14 (TTY write char function)
            int     10H                ; Call ROM BIOS video interrupt
            pop     di                 ; Restore DI
            pop     si                 ; Restore SI
            pop     bp                 ; Restore the BP register
            ret                        ; Return to calling program
_putTty endp                           ; End of subroutine

; _getSt(&modePtr,&widthPtr,&pagePtr)
;
; Function: Get the current display mode, display width (in characters),
; and the active page number.
;
; Algorithm: Call the ROM BIOS get video state function; int 10H, AH = 15.

            public  _getSt             ; Routine is available to other modules

            modePtr = 4                ; Offset from BP to parameter modePtr
            widthPtr = 6               ; Offset to parameter widthPtr
            pagePtr = 8                ; Offset to pagePtr

_getSt  proc near                      ; NEAR type subroutine
            push    bp                 ; Save BP register
            mov     bp, sp             ; Set BP to SP; easier to get parameters
            push    si                 ; Save the SI register
            push    di                 ; Save the DI register
            mov     ah, 15             ; Set AH to 15 (get video state function)
            int     10H                ; Call ROM BIOS video interrupt
            mov     dh, bh             ; Save BH in DH
            mov     bx, [bp+modePtr]   ; *modePtr = the current video mode
            mov     [bx], al
            xor     al, al             ; Set AL to zero
            mov     [bx+1], al         ; Zero high byte of *modePtr
            mov     bx, [bp+widthPtr]  ; *widthPtr = ah (with top byte zero)
            mov     [bx], ah
            mov     [bx+1], al
            mov     bx, [bp+pagePtr]   ; *pagePtr = the active page number
            mov     [bx], dh
            mov     [bx+1], al
            pop     di                 ; Restore DI
            pop     si                 ; Restore SI
            pop     bp                 ; Restore the BP register
            ret                        ; Return to calling program
_getSt  endp                           ; End of subroutine

_TEXT   ends                           ; End of code segment

        end                            ; End of assembly code
```

Listing 7-5. "showeq2.c":

```
#include "eqlib.h"

/*      main()

        Function: Get and display the system memory size and the
        equipment configuration.

        Algorithm: Call the ROM BIOS interface routines memSz and
        getEq. Then interpret their replies and display the results.
*/

main()

{
        int theEq;        /* The equipment configuration. */
        int i;

        /* Clear the display. */
        scrUp(0,0,0,24,79,0);

        /* Display the memory size at the bottom of the screen. */
        setPos(0,15,30);
        printf("Memory size is %dK.",memSz());

        /* Display the equipment configuration at the top of the screen. */
        setPos(0,0,0);
        printf("Equipment present:\n    ");
        /* Get the equipment configuration. */
        theEq = getEq();
        /* Get the number of printers. */
        i = (theEq & prtnMask) >> prtnShft;
        /* If there are any at all, show how many. */
        if (i != 0) printf("%d printer(s).\n    ",i);
        /* If there's a game I/O interface present, say so. */
        if (theEq & gioMask) printf("1 game I/O.\n    ");
        /* Get the number of serial ports. */
        i = (theEq & RS232Mask) >> RS232Shft;
        /* If there are any, show how many. */
        if (i != 0) printf("%d serial port(s).\n    ",i);
        /* If there are any diskette drives present, show how many. */
        if (theEq & diskMask) printf("%d diskette drive(s).\n    ",
                            ((theEq & dsknMask) >> dsknShft)+1);
        /* Show the initial video mode. */
        printf("Initial video mode: ");
        i = theEq & vmodeMask;
        if (i == CO40) printf("40x25 color");
        else if (i == CO80) printf("80x25 color");
        else if (i == MONO) printf("80x25 monochrome");
        /* Show the system board RAM size. */
        printf(".\n    System board RAM size: %dK bytes.\n",
                16*(((theEq & sbramMask) >> sbramShft)+1));
```

Listing 7-5. "showeq2.c" *(cont.)*:

```
    /* Return the cursor to the bottom of the page. */
    setPos(0,23,0);
}
```

Chapter 8

Plain, ANSI &
BIOS Screen I/O:
ShowFile

- Three Screen Manipulation Techniques

- Character Input/Output and the Calling Heirarchy

- Keyboard Character Input and Keyboard Scan Codes

- The ShowFile Program: Displaying Text and Scrolling

- Vanilla, ANSI, and ROMBIOS Approaches

I n this chapter, we will develop a program that reads and displays a text file on the screen. It will allow the user to page through the file using the PageUp, PageDown, up arrow, and down arrow keys. We will present three different ways to manipulate the display:

- Using simple TTY-style output.
- Using ANSI.SYS screen controls.
- Using the ROM BIOS screen control routines.

We will compare and measure these three approaches, and in the process of developing the third approach, we will present two new ROM BIOS interface routines. These routines allow the program to manipulate the text display, regardless of the type of display adapter being used. But before we get to the program itself, we need to know about character I/O, which can be used to display data on the screen, and the IBM PC keyboard, which is used to enter commands to the program.

Character Input/Output (I/O)

MS-DOS understands two types of devices: block and character. Block devices are generally disk drives, which deal with data a block at a time and are random access in nature. Character devices — displays, terminals, communications ports, etc. — deal with data a character at a time and are sequential access in nature. Devices in the two classes are treated similarly but not identically.

In the Encrypt example (Chapter Six), we presented the hierarchy of routines and buffers used when accessing block devices. Figure 8-1 shows a similar hierarchy for character devices. As in the case of block devices, the C stream I/O functions are the highest level functions: they present data to the application in useable chunks. Below these are the C file I/O routines, which interface to MS-DOS. These are called "file" routines even though they are sometimes used to access non-file devices. Next is the operating system, MS-DOS, which opens and closes character devices, and calls the appropriate driver. Below MS-DOS is the device driver. Besides interfacing to the device, drivers can add additional functionality—the ANSI.SYS driver is one example of this. Often the drivers call the ROM BIOS to actually control the hardware. And at the bottom of the hierarchy is the hardware itself.

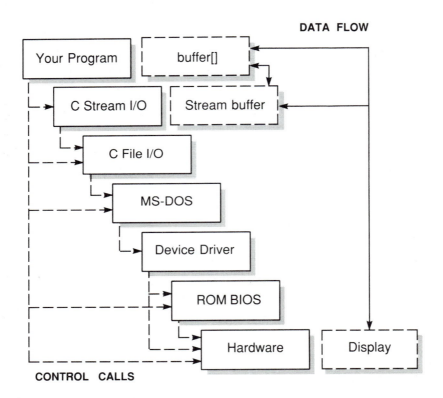

Figure 8-1. Character I/O

It is possible to bypass most or all of this hierarchy by calling the ROM BIOS directly or going directly to the hardware. This reduces the overhead and speeds up the program. But it also puts a burden on the program, since the intermediate layers are not available, and it reduces the portability of the program, since the ROM BIOS and hardware may vary from machine to machine.

Keyboard Character Input

The American Standard Code for Information Interchange, or ASCII, is a standardized correspondence between byte values and symbols. The symbol "a", for example, has an ASCII value of 97. There are ASCII values for all the letters of the alphabet, both upper and lower case; for the digits; and for a number of special symbols. There are also a number of control characters such as "carriage return" and "line feed."

The IBM PC keyboard has 83 keys, including keys for all the normal ASCII characters and a number of non-standard, extended keys. Each key is assigned a number called a "scan code." Scan codes are used internally for communication between the keyboard and the IBM PC. The ROM BIOS converts the scan codes into ASCII, if possible. When a C program reads keyboard input — generally by calling the getch function — it will receive a one character ASCII code, if the key pressed corresponds to an ASCII character. If the key is one of the extended keys, however, there is no corresponding ASCII code, and the program will receive a zero character indicating this. The program should then call getch a second time, and it will receive a scan code character identifying which extended key was pressed. The ASCII, or scan codes generated by each of the keys, are listed in Appendix D.

The ShowFile Program

The ShowFile program displays a text file. When it begins executing, it displays the first screenful of lines in the file. After that, it waits for commands from the user. The page-up, page-down, up-arrow, and down-arrow keys can be used to move through the file one page or one line at a time. The 'u' and 'd' keys serve as alternatives to the page-up and page-down keys, respectively. When the user is finished, he can quit by hitting either the escape key or the 'q' key.

The ShowFile program is presented in the Listing 8-1. It uses two additional assembly language routines that call the ROM BIOS, shown in Listing 8-2.

Displaying a text file according to commands from the keyboard involves two tasks: interpreting the commands, and displaying the file. In making this division, we simplify our job by reducing the size of the functional blocks. We also simplify future modifications to the program. The line number we start displaying from — which is kept in the global variable curLine — is the interface between the two parts. A value of zero in curLine indicates the first line in the file. Given this division of the program, the main loop simply calls each portion of the program repeatedly until the user issues a quit command.

The nextCommand routine implements the command interpretation part of the program. It waits for and executes the next command from the keyboard. As discussed in the previous section, keyboard input is either a single ASCII character or a zero character followed by a scan code. The former is used for all keys that have ASCII equivalents; the latter is used for keys that do not, such as function keys, arrow keys, PgUp and PgDn, and so on.

The function nextCommand reads in the command, decides which type of character it is (ASCII or scan code), and looks it up in one of two tables. One table is used for ASCII commands, and the other for scan codes. If the key is not found in the table, nextCommand does nothing. If the key is found, the table specifies a function to call and a parameter to pass to the function. By supplying a parameter as well as a function, one function can perform several related tasks. For example, the upLines function can scroll up or down, by one line or by a page. The table ends with a zero key value entry (see Figure 8-2). If a quit command is issued, the function from the table, called by nextCommand, returns TRUE. nextCommand simply returns this value to the main program. This table-driven approach to interpreting commands makes it easy to add new commands or to modify existing commands.

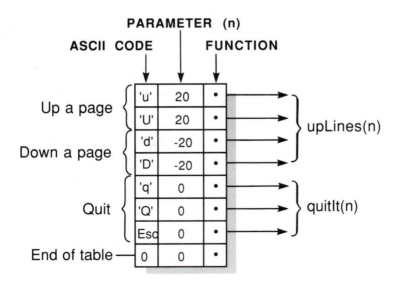

Figure 8-2A. Command Table

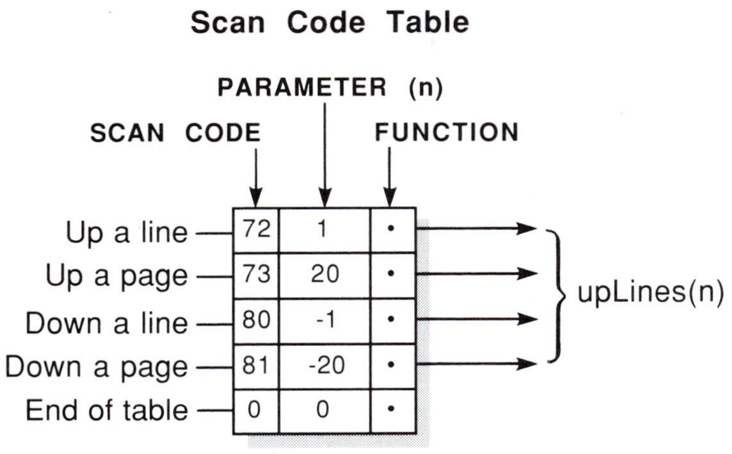

Scan Code Table

PARAMETER (n)

SCAN CODE   **FUNCTION**

	SCAN CODE	PARAMETER (n)	FUNCTION
Up a line —	72	1	•
Up a page —	73	20	•
Down a line —	80	-1	•
Down a page —	81	-20	•
End of table —	0	0	•

upLines(n)

Figure 8-2B. Command Table

Before the text from the file can be displayed, it must be read into memory. In addition—since the file is displayed by lines, and the display starts at a specific line—we will need to find the offset within the file where the lines to be displayed actually start. The simplest way to do this is to read the entire file into memory and then build a table of line start pointers. But this would limit the program to working on files that fit within memory. This is adequate for many applications, but an unfortunate restriction for others. An alternative is to reread the file each time, skipping the lines that are off the top of the screen. This approach accommodates all files, but can be very slow, since it requires a great deal of unnecessary disk I/O if we are displaying lines in the middle of the file.

A compromise approach is to build a table of offsets to the place where each line starts within the file, and then use the fseek function to position the input there when reading. This design is shown in Figure 8-3. It does suffer to some degree from the problems of the previous two approaches: it limits the file size to the number of line offsets that can fit in memory, and it requires disk I/O to access the text to be displayed. But neither of these restrictions is as severe as the restrictions of the other approaches. This sort of compromise is very common in computer algorithm design.

The program could scan the entire file to build the offset array at the start. But very often, the person using the program is only interested in the first few screenfuls of information. Scanning the rest of the file would therefore be a waste of time, so ShowFile builds the offset array as needed. This task is simplified by the fact that lines are almost always accessed sequentially. The function readLine is used to read in a line, given a pointer to its entry in the offset array. It also sets the offset for the following line. The readLine function requires that the offset of the line to be read must be known, but it discovers the offset to the following line. Therefore, if lines are read in sequence, readLine can simply be called repeatedly to read them. Of course, this process must start somewhere: that starting point is the offset for the very first line in the file, since it's known always to be zero. It is conceivable, however, that a command may call for the display to start on a line that has not yet been read into memory. The while statement at the beginning of the showPage function makes sure that all lines up to and including the first line of the display have been read.

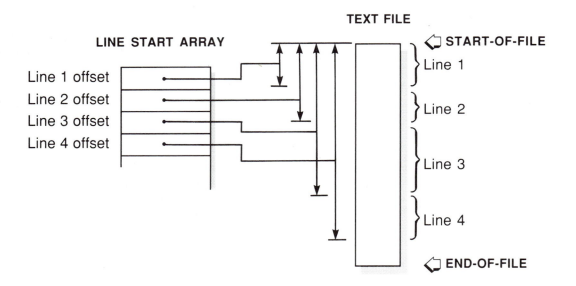

Figure 8-3. Line Start Array

Displaying Text

Each time ShowFile displays a page of text, it first clears the display and then writes the page. There are a number of different ways to clear the screen and write data to it. Three approaches to writing to and/or controlling the display are included in ShowFile. The constants VANILLA, ANSI, and ROM BIOS (only one of which should be defined at a time) select which approach is used. Each approach has its advantages and disadvantages.

VANILLA

This is the simplest approach. In fact, this approach will work on virtually any machine, not just the IBM PC. It uses simple standard output stream I/O. It makes only one assumption: that the screen is 25 lines long and therefore sending 25 newlines will clear it.

ADVANTAGES: Works on any machine.

DISADVANTAGES: Isn't very fast.

ANSI

In this approach, the same output technique is used as in VANILLA, but an ANSI display control sequence is used to clear the screen. It is assumed, therefore, that the receiving display will understand ANSI terminal control sequences. On the IBM PC, this means that the ANSI display driver must be added to the system. This is done by including the line "DEVICE = ANSI.SYS" in the CONFIG.SYS file. ANSI terminals will take certain actions based on control sequences embedded in the text sent to them. In our case, we use only one: the clear screen command "\033]2J".

ADVANTAGES: Works with any ANSI terminal/display.

DISADVANTAGES: Requires ANSI.SYS be included in system,
moderately slow.

ROMBIOS

The final approach is to call the ROM BIOS routines to perform text display and screen control. This could have been accomplished with the ROM BIOS video interface routines presented in the previous chapter. However, it is even simpler with the two new routines here. We will describe these routines in more detail in the following section.

Note that when using these ROM BIOS routines, we must append a carriage return at the end of each line. Normally, the C I/O routines expand the newline (line feed) character into carriage return/line feed for us, but here we're bypassing those routines. The newline itself serves as the line feed, but we must add the carriage return.

ADVANTAGES: Fast, no need for ANSI.SYS.

DISADVANTAGES: Will only work with IBM PC ROM BIOS compatible computers.

Direct Access

An even faster approach is possible: directly accessing the RAM where the display adaptor stores the characters that are being displayed. This approach will be discussed in Chapter Thirteen.

Assembly Routines

The two new ROM BIOS video interface routines are scrClr and scrPuts. Whereas the routines previously presented for accessing the ROM BIOS each called exactly one ROM BIOS routine, these new routines each call more than one. This places more of the functionality of the program in assembly, where it is harder to understand and change. But it also makes a simpler and clearer interface to the calling routines without requiring an intermediate C routine.

The scrClr function uses the scroll up call to clear the screen, finds the currently active page, and then calls the position cursor routine to leave the cursor at the top-left corner. This is what is most often wanted when clearing the display.

The scrPuts routine outputs a null-terminated C string to the display using the TTY write routine. It gets the currently active page, then loops through the string, writing each byte with a call to the TTY write function. This is essentially equivalent to "fputs(s,stdout)" (but is not equivalent to "puts(s)" since it doesn't append a newline).

As should always be done when writing a function, we designed these routines to be more general than their specific application here. They can be reused in the next application that needs direct display access.

Performance

As we said in Part I of the book, when you try to improve the performance of a program, you should always measure the program's performance before and after any changes are made. Otherwise, it is impossible to tell whether you've been successful and to what degree. In this chapter, we are comparing the three ways to clear the display and write characters to it. In order to measure the time involved, we have included a CALIBRATE option in the ShowFile source code. When enabled, this option causes the program to display each screenful twenty times. Twenty displays take long enough that we can time them with a stopwatch and compare the different versions of the program. The following table summarizes these times:

Version	Time for 20 Screens	Time for 1 Screen (computed)
VANILLA	64 seconds	3.2
ANSI	44 seconds	2.2
ROMBIOS	31 seconds	1.5

By using the ANSI control codes to clear the screen, we realized a performance improvement of 31%. And by using the ROM BIOS to both clear the display and write the characters to be displayed, we realized an improvement of 52% over the original program. For a program that may be used frequently, this improvement is very much worth the effort spent to achieve it. In Part III of the book, we will present an even faster version of the ShowFile program, one that directly writes into the display memory, bypassing even the ROM BIOS.

Summary

Displaying a file consists of two major functional blocks: getting commands from the user and displaying the part of the file that was requested. In order to get and process user input, the program must read the keyboard, must understand and process both ASCII input and extended scan codes as well. Once the program knows which lines in the file should be displayed, it must find those lines in the file itself. This is accomplished in ShowFile by building a table of offsets into the file. The job of actually displaying the data on the screen can then be accomplished in one of several ways. The method we choose depends upon how the data is sent to the display adapter, and how functions such as clearing the screen are handled. ShowFile includes code to implement three of the possible alternatives: simple, vanilla output; using the ANSI.SYS driver; and directly calling the ROM BIOS. Each of these alternatives represents a different trade-off between speed and limitations as to the machines the program will be able to run on.

In the process of developing the ROM BIOS version of ShowFile, two new video interface library routines were also presented. Finally, we measured the difference in performance of the three approaches.

Exercises

Note: ShowFile is a very handy program to have around. It's even handier when you have access to the sources and can tailor it to your own needs and desires.

It is worth spending some time adding features, such as those suggested in the following exercises.

1. Although ShowFile will not allow curLine to be decremented past the beginning of the file, it will allow it to be incremented past the end. Lines beyond the end are displayed as blank. Change the program to stop at the end of the file and to display a positive EOF (end-of-file) indication on the screen.

2. Add Home and End functions to go to the beginning and end of the file.

3. Add Left Arrow and Right Arrow functions to move the text to the left or right. This involves adding a curColumn global.

4. Add an optional parameter after the file name that specifies the attributes/color to be used when displaying the file.

5. Change the display algorithm so that it does not clear the screen entirely, but uses as much text already on the screen as possible. This will be especially noticeable when scrolling up or down by a single line. Note that the ROM BIOS provides scroll up and scroll down routines that can be used here.

6. Add a line caching scheme that keeps the last 50 lines in an array, and does not read from the file if these lines are present.

7. [very advanced] Change the line caching scheme to use all available memory outside the program code/data space.

Listing 8-1. "show.c":

```
/*                      Show Text File Utility

        This program displays a text file on the screen and redisplays
        it according to the user's use of the page-up, page-down,
        up-arrow, down-arrow, 'u', and 'd' keys. It exits when the user
        types either 'q' or ESC.
*/

#include <stdio.h>

#define CALIBRATE           /* If defined, display pages 21 times for timing. */

#define VANILLA             /* Define for vanilla, TTY style output. */
/*#define ANSI*/            /* Define for ANSI.SYS style output. */
/*#define ROMBIOS*/         /* Define for ROM BIOS style output. */

#define MAXLINES 10000      /* Maximum number of lines in file. */

#define LINESIZE 200        /* Maximum number of characters in a line. */

FILE *inFile;               /* File identifier for file to be displayed. */

int curLine;                /* Where to start displaying from. */

struct cmdType {            /* Command table entry form. */
 char cmdKey;               /* The key code or ASCII value. */
 int (*cmdFunc)();          /* The function to call. */
 int cmdParm;               /* The parameter to pass to it. */
};

int upLines(), quitIt();

struct cmdType keyTab[] = {         /* Normal key table. */
        'u', upLines, 20,           /* 'u' key: scroll backward 20 lines. */
        'U', upLines, 20,           /* 'U' key: scroll backward 20 lines. */
        'd', upLines, -20,          /* 'd' key: scroll forward 20 lines. */
        'D', upLines, -20,          /* 'D' key: scroll forward 20 lines. */
        'q', quitIt, 0,             /* 'q' key: quit. */
        'Q', quitIt, 0,             /* 'Q' key: quit. */
        033, quitIt, 0,             /* ESC key: quit. */
        0, quitIt, 0                /* End-of-table. */
};

struct cmdType zKeyTab[] = {        /* Zero-prefix key table. */
        72, upLines, 1,             /* Up-arrow key: scroll backward 1 line. */
        73, upLines, 20,            /* Up-page key: scroll backward 20 lines. */
        80, upLines, -1,            /* Down-arrow key: scroll forward 1 line. */
        81, upLines, -20,           /* Down-page key: scroll forward 20 lines. */
        0, quitIt, 0                /* End-of-table. */
};
```

Listing 8-1. "show.c" *(cont.)*:

```
long lineStart[MAXLINES];        /* Offsets from start of file to lines. */
long *nextStart;                 /* Pointer to next available line start. */

#define TRUE 1
#define FALSE 0

/*      main(argc,argv)

        Function: Display a text file on the screen.

        Algorithm: Start at the beginning of the file. Display a page,
        reading the file as needed. Then repeatedly wait for keyboard
        input, and take the appropriate action based on it.
*/

main(argc,argv)

int argc;
char *argv[];

{
        int i;

        /* Check that the user gave us the right number of command
           line parameters. */
        if (argc != 2) {
                /* If not, tell him what's wrong and exit. */
                puts("Usage: show <filename>\n");
                exit(1);
        };

        /* Open the input file, if possible. */
        if ((inFile = fopen(argv[1],"r")) == NULL) {
                /* If it wouldn't open, let the user know and exit. */
                puts("Couldn't open input file.\n");
                exit(1);
        };

        /* Start at the first line in the file. */
        curLine = 0;
        /* Set the file offset for that line in the line start array. */
        lineStart[0] = 0L;
        /* Set nextStart to indicate that this is the only entry we've
           filled in in lineStart so far. */
        nextStart = &lineStart[1];

        /* Repeatedly display a page, and then get and execute commands. */
        do {
```

Listing 8-1. "show.c" *(cont.)*:

```
#ifdef CALIBRATE
                /* If we're going to calibrate, repeat the following page
                   display 20 times. */
                for (i = 20; i > 0; i--)
#endif CALIBRATE

                        showPage();
        } while (!nextCommand());
}

/*      nextCommand()

        Function: Get and execute the next keyboard command. Return
        TRUE if it's time to quit.

        Algorithm: Get the keyboard input using getch. It then looks
        the character up in the keyTab or zKeyTab tables and executes
        the function found there (if any). Finally, it returns the value
        returned by the executed function.
*/

nextCommand()

{
        char c;                  /* The input from the user. */
        struct cmdType *cPtr;    /* A pointer into the command table. */

        /* Get the command from the user. */
        c = getch();
        /* If it isn't an extended code, use the ASCII command table. */
        if (c != 0) cPtr = keyTab;
        /* Otherwise, get the second character (the scan code), and use
           the scan code command table. */
        else {
                c = getch();
                cPtr = zKeyTab;
        };

        /* Search thru the command table for the user input value. */
        for (; cPtr->cmdKey != 0; cPtr++)
                if (cPtr->cmdKey == c)
                        /* If we found it, execute it. */
                        return((*cPtr->cmdFunc)(cPtr->cmdParm));

        /* If we didn't find it in the table, don't do anything at all. */
        return(FALSE);
}

/*      quitIt(dummy)
```

Listing 8-1. "show.c" *(cont.)*:

```
        Function: Quit command.

        Algorithm: Just return TRUE.
*/

quitIt (dummy)

int dummy;

{
        return (TRUE);
}

/*      upLines (num)

        Function: Move the window up by num lines (may be negative).

        Algorithm: Just adjust curLine.

        Comments: The actual change in the display will be done by
        the showPage function.
*/

upLines (num)

int num;

{
        /* Adjust the curLine global. */
        curLine -= num;
        /* But make sure we don't move back past the beginning of the file. */
        if (curLine < 0) curLine = 0;
        /* Return FALSE -- i.e., don't quit. */
        return (FALSE);
}

/*      showPage ()

        Function: Display the page starting at curLine.

        Algorithm: First, clear the screen. Second, make sure that
        the line start array has the first line to be displayed.
        Then, starting at the first line on the screen, read and
        display each visible line.
*/

showPage ()

{
```

Listing 8-1. "show.c" *(cont.)*:

```
        int i,j;
        long *lineStPtr;        /* Pointer into the line start array. */
        char line[LINESIZE];    /* Buffer into which to read lines. */

        /* Clear the screen. */
        clrScreen();

        /* Make sure the first line offset is in the line start array. */
        while (&lineStart[curLine] >= nextStart)
                readLine(nextStart,line);

        /* For each line to be displayed... */
        for (lineStPtr = &lineStart[curLine], i = 24; i; i--, lineStPtr++) {
                /* Read the line in. */
                readLine(lineStPtr,line);
                /* And display it. */
                dispLine(line);
        };
}

/*      readLine(lStPtr,lBuf)

        Function: Read the line whose line start array entry is pointed
        to by lStPtr into the buffer pointed to by lBuf.

        Algorithm: Use fseek to position the file to the line requested,
        then read it in with fgets. Finally, set the next entry in the
        line start array to the file position after the read.

        Comments: The line start array entry pointed to by lStPtr must
        have been filled in already or the results of calling this
        function are undefined.
*/

readLine(lStPtr,lBuf)

long *lStPtr;
char *lBuf;

{
        /* Position the file to the line requested. */
        fseek(inFile,*lStPtr,0);
        /* Read in the line. */
        fgets(lBuf,LINESIZE,inFile);
        /* Record the offset to the next line in the file. */
        if (lStPtr == (nextStart-1)) *nextStart++ = ftell(inFile);
}

/*      clrScreen(), dispLine(lBuf)
```

Listing 8-1. "show.c" *(cont.)*:

        Function: Clear the screen (clrScreen()) or display a line
(dispLine())

        Algorithm: The algorithm depends on which of VANILLA, ANSI, and
        ROMBIOS are defined. See the main text of the chapter for more
        details.
*/

```c
clrScreen()

{
#ifdef VANILLA
        int i;

        /* Write blank lines to scroll everything off the screen. */
        for (i = 0; i < 25; i++) dispLine("\n");
#endif VANILLA

#ifdef ANSI
        /* Send the ANSI clear screen sequence. */
        fputs("\033[2J",stdout);
#endif ANSI

#ifdef ROMBIOS
        /* Call the ROM BIOS to clear the screen for us. */
        scrClr();
#endif ROMBIOS
}

dispLine(lBuf)

char *lBuf;

{
#ifdef VANILLA
        /* Use the regular standard output routines. */
        fputs(lBuf,stdout);
#endif VANILLA

#ifdef ANSI
        /* Use the regular standard output routine. */
        fputs(lBuf,stdout);
#endif ANSI

#ifdef ROMBIOS
        /* Call the ROM BIOS. */
        scrPuts(lBuf); scrPuts("\r");
#endif ROMBIOS
}
```

Listing 8-2. "v2lib.asm":

```
;                   Video Display Library (part 2)

_TEXT    segment byte public 'CODE'        ; Place the code in the code segment
         assume  CS:_TEXT                  ; Assume the CS register points to it

; _scrClr()
;
; Function: Clear the screen.
;
; Algorithm: Call the ROM BIOS scroll up function to do the actual clearing.

         public  _scrClr              ; This routine is public (available to
                                      ; other modules)

_scrClr proc near                     ; This is a NEAR type subroutine
         push    bp                   ; Save the BP resgister
         push    si                   ; And SI
         push    di                   ; And DI
         xor     al,al                ; Set the number of lines to scroll to zero
         mov     ch,al                ; Set the upper left corner row to 0
         mov     cl,al                ; Set the upper left corner column to 0
         mov     dh,24                ; Set the lower right corner row to 24
         mov     dl,79                ; Set the lower right corner column to 79
         mov     bh,7                 ; Set the attribute to white-on-black
         mov     ah,6                 ; Video function 6: scroll up
         int     10H                  ; Call the ROM BIOS video interrupt
         mov     ah,15                ; Do a get state interrupt to get the
                                      ; page # into bh
         int     10H                  ; Video BIOS interrupt
         mov     dx,0                 ; Set the row and column to 0
         mov     ah,2                 ; Do a set cursor position interrupt
         int     10H                  ; Video interrupt
         pop     di                   ; Restore the DI register
         pop     si                   ; And SI
         pop     bp                   ; And BP
         ret                          ; Return to the calling program
_scrClr endp                          ; End of subroutine

; _scrPuts(s)
;
; Function: Do a TTY style write of the null-terminated string pointed
; to by s.
;
; Algorithm: Repeatedly call the ROM BIOS TTY style write character
; function for each character in the string.

         public  _scrPuts             ; Routine is available to other modules

         s = 4                        ; The offset to the s parameter
```

Listing 8-2. "v2lib.asm" *(cont.)*:

```
_scrPuts proc near              ; NEAR type subroutine
        push    bp              ; Save the BP register
        mov     bp,sp           ; Set BP to SP, so we can access the
                                  parameters
        push    si              ; Save the SI register
        push    di              ; And DI
        mov     si,[bp+s]       ; Set SI to the string pointer

sLoop:  lods    byte ptr [si]   ; AL = *SI++ (get the next byte in the string)
        or      al,al           ; Is it zero (end-of-string)?
        jz      sExit           ; If it is, exit the loop
        mov     bl,3            ; Set foreground color to white
        mov     ah,14           ; Do a TTY style write using the BIOS
        int     10H             ; ROM BIOS video interrupt
        jmp     sLoop           ; Go get the next character

sExit:  pop     di              ; Restore the DI register
        pop     si              ; Restore the SI register
        pop     bp              ; Restore the BP register
        ret                     ; Return to calling program
_scrPuts endp                   ; End of subroutine
_TEXT   ends                    ; End of code segment
        end                     ; End of assembly code
```

Chapter 9

Display and Direct Keyboard I/O: *Border*

- Display Colors and Attributes and Setting the Palette

- Three ROM BIOS Keyboard Functions

- The Attrib Program: Full Color Display Control

S ome functions on the IBM PC cannot be accomplished using only MS-DOS. One example of this is setting the attributes of the display. In this chapter, we present three programs that illustrate how to perform this function. We also present a library of routines that interface to the keyboard functions of the ROM BIOS, plus another routine that interfaces to the video portion of the ROM BIOS. The programs developed in this chapter are excellent vehicles for exploring the capabilities of the keyboard for input and the range of attributes available with the display.

Display Colors and Attributes

Two bytes are associated with each character displayed on the screen of the IBM PC. One byte is, of course, the ASCII value of the character; the other byte is known as the "attribute" of the displayed character. The attribute causes a character to be displayed underlined, flashing, or in a different color. Both the monochrome adapter (MA) and the color graphics adapter (CGA) have attribute bytes associated with each character in text display mode, but the meaning of the attributes is different. Figure 9-1 shows the attributes available with the CGA. As an example, an attribute of 00000111 (binary) is normal white on black, while an attribute of 11000001 is blinking blue on red.

The attribute byte available with the monochrome adapter has the same format, but it recognizes only a limited number of colors: black (red, green, and blue all off), white (all three on), and one special case: underline (red and green off, blue on), which means that underlined characters displayed on a color graphics adapter will be blue with no underlines. The blinking and intensity bits still work the way they do on the CGA.

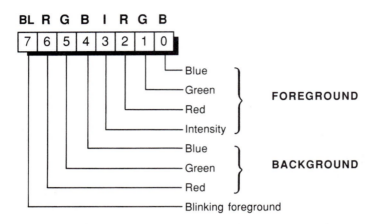

Figure 9-1. CGA Character Attributes

In addition to the character attribute bytes, the color graphics adapter also allows the program to set the border color. The border is the area on the display surrounding the character display positions. It can be set to any of sixteen colors. The color specification is identical to the bottom four bits of the color character attribute: an intensity bit, a red bit, a green bit, and a blue bit. The ROM BIOS set palette function sets the border color of the display when the CGA is used. If the display is in a graphics mode rather than a text mode, the same color will also be used for the background in the main portion of the screen—i.e., it redefines "black." The set palette function will also select between two color sets when CGA or EGA multi-color graphics are used. An interface routine to the set palette function is given in Listing 9-1. When used from C, it has the following format:

Function

setPal(colrID,colrVal)—Set palette color colrID to colrVal. Color ID 0 sets the
    background or border color; color ID 1 sets the palette to be used for graphics: 0
    for black/green/red/ yellow, or 1 for black/cyan/magenta/white.

The Border program shown in Listing 9-2 is an example of how to use the setPal function. It takes a number from the command line and sets the border to the corresponding color. Border will run only, of course, on the CGA or EGA.

Note: To see the full range of possible colors, you need to issue a "mode co40" command before running the Border program.

ROM BIOS Keyboard Functions

Before presenting a variation on the Border program that allows the user to select the border color more easily, we need to develop routines to access the ROM BIOS keyboard facilities. The ROM BIOS offers the program much greater access to the keyboard than is available through MS-DOS. It allows the program to monitor the current state of the shift, control, and alt keys. It is this facility that the new Border program will use to set the border color. Listing 9-3 provides the following three C-callable routines:

Function

---

keyRd( )—Returns the next keyboard character and its scan code. The low byte of the returned word contains the ASCII value, and the high byte contains the scan code. If this is a non-ASCII key, the low byte will be zero.

keyChk(&key)—Returns FALSE if there is no keyboard input waiting. It returns TRUE if there is keyboard input waiting. It sets the variable "key" to the character (as described in keyRd), but does not read the character. A subsequent call to keyRd is needed to remove the character from the input queue.

keyShf( )—Returns the current keyboard shift status, as shown in Figure 9-2.

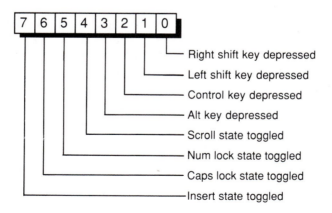

Figure 9-2. keyShf Return Values

A simple variation on the Border program allows you to explore the range of possible colors with the IBM PC. Rather than setting one color and exiting, this program watches for changes in the shift, control, and alt keys, and changes the border color accordingly. It stops when any other key is hit. Since the shift, control, and alt states are in the bottom four bits of the value returned from keyShf, that value can be passed directly to setPal. There is, of course, no preplanned connection between the functions keyShf and setPal; it just fortuitously happens that both deal with four bit values. The keyChk function is used to test for the exit condition. Listing 9-4 shows the final program. The following table shows how to figure out which color number you've selected by a given combination of shift keys:

If this key is depressed	Add this into the color #
Right-hand shift	1
Left-hand shift	2
Control	4
Alt	8

The Attrib Program

Now that we have a program to set the border color, we would like a complimentary program to set the attributes of the characters on the screen. Setting the character attributes involves more than four bits. We need a program to do more than read the shift keys and pass their values to the ROM BIOS. Our approach will use the current shift key states to set the bottom four bits—the foreground intensity and red, green, and blue bits—but if the user hits the space bar, the same shift keys will set the top four bits—the foreground blinking, and the background color. Listing 9-5 contains the program. Each time the attribute changes, the program uses the getACh and putACh functions from Chapter Seven to read and rewrite each of the character/attribute pairs on the display.

Summary

Both the monochrome and color graphics displays of the IBM PC have attribute bytes associated with each character displayed. These bytes indicate which color or attribute to use to display the character and whether or not the character should be displayed blinking. The color graphics display also allows the program to set the border color of the display. We presented a simple program that sets the color of the border by using the setPal function. Then we developed an easier-to-use version of the same program, which uses the shift, control, and alt keys to select the color for the border. This version of the program used a library of routines for accessing the keyboard facilities of the ROM BIOS, these routines allowed the program to monitor the shift, control, and alt keys. Finally, we presented a program to change the character attributes of all the characters on the current display.

Exercises

1. Change Border to accept a parameter containing any combination of the letters "r", "g", "b", and "i" (and the upper case equivalents). For each letter present in the parameter, set the corresponding bit in the border: bit zero for "b", bit one for "g", bit two for "r", and bit three for "i".

2. Similarly, modify Bord2 so that the "r", "g", "b", and "i" keys are used to toggle the corresponding bits in the current border color. Also have the "z" key clear all the color bits. The shift keys should momentarily toggle the bits as long as the shift, control, or alt key is held down.

Listing 9-1. "v3lib.asm":

```
;                    Equipment Configuration Library

_TEXT   segment byte public 'CODE'     ; Place the code in the code segment
        assume  CS:_TEXT               ; Assume the CS register points to it

; _setPal(colorID,color)
;
; Function: Set the palette color ID to the color given.
;
; Algorithm: Call ROM BIOS set palette video function.

        public  _setPal               ; Routine is available to other modules

        colorID = 4                   ; The offset to the color ID parameter
        color = 6                     ; The offset to the color parameter

_setPal proc near                     ; NEAR type subroutine
        push    bp                    ; Save the BP register
        mov     bp,sp                 ; Set BP to SP, so we can access parameters
        push    si                    ; Save the SI register
        push    di                    ; Save the DI register
        mov     bh,[bp+colorID]       ; Set BH to the color ID
        mov     bl,[bp+color]         ; Set BL to the color
        mov     ah,11                 ; Function 11: set palette
        int     10H                   ; Call the ROM BIOS with interrupt 10 (video)
        pop     di                    ; Restore the DI register
        pop     si                    ; Restore the SI register
        pop     bp                    ; Restore BP
        ret                           ; Return to calling program
_setPal endp                          ; End of subroutine

_TEXT   ends                          ; End of code segment
        end                           ; End of assembly code
```

Listing 9-2. "border.c":

```
/*                   Change Border Color

        This program changes the background color/attributes.
*/

/*      main(argc,argv)

        Function: Change the color of the border of the display to that
        given as a command line parameter.

        Algorithm: Check the number of parameters. If there is one, then
        convert it to a number using atoi, and pass that to the setPal
        function to actually set the border color.

        Comments: This program will do nothing with a non-color display
        adapter.
*/
```

Listing 9-2. "border.c" *(cont.)*:

```
main(argc,argv)

int argc;
char *argv[];

{
        /* Check for the right number of parameters. */
        if (argc != 2) {
                /* If wrong, tell the user and exit. */
                puts("Usage: border <border color>");
                exit(1);
        };

        /* Convert the parameter to a number and pass it to setPal. */
        setPal(0,atoi(argv[1]));
}
```

Listing 9-3. "klib.asm":

```
;                       Equipment Configuration Library

_TEXT    segment byte public 'CODE'      ; Place the code in the code segment
         assume  CS:_TEXT                ; Assume the CS register points to it

; _keyRd()
;
; Function: Return the next key pressed. The ASCII value (if any) is in the
; lower byte; the scan code is in the upper byte. If the key doesn't have
; an ASCII value, the lower byte is zero.
;
; Algorithm: Call ROM BIOS read key function of the keyboard interrupt.

         public  _keyRd               ; Routine is available to other modules

_keyRd   proc near                    ; NEAR type subroutine
         mov     ah,0                 ; Function 0: read key
         int     16H                  ; Call the ROM BIOS with interrupt 16 (keybd)
         ret                          ; Return to calling program
_keyRd   endp                         ; End of subroutine

; _keyChk(&keyPtr)
;
; Function: Return TRUE if there is a key press waiting, and if so, return
; the key in the location pointed to by keyPtr; if there is no key waiting,
; return FALSE. *keyPtr is set to the same value that would be returned
; from keyRd, but the key press is not actually read; keyRd must be called
; to remove it from the queue.
;
; Algorithm: Call ROM BIOS key check function of the keyboard interrupt.

         public  _keyChk              ; Routine is available to other modules

         keyPtr = 4                   ; The offset to the keyPtr parameter
```

Listing 9-3. "klib.asm" *(cont.)*:

```
_keyChk  proc  near            ; NEAR type subroutine
         push  bp              ; Save the BP register
         mov   bp,sp           ; Set BP to SP, to get at the parameters
         mov   ah,1            ; Function 1: check for key press
         int   16H             ; Call the ROM BIOS with interrupt 16 (keybd)
         mov   bx,[bp+keyPtr]  ; Save the key, if there is any
         mov   [bx],ax
         mov   ax,0            ; Assume not key (i.e., return FALSE)
         jz    noKey           ; Branch if no key
         mov   ax,1            ; Otherwise return TRUE
noKey:   pop   bp              ; Restore the BP register
         ret                   ; Return to calling program
_keyChk  endp                  ; End of subroutine

;  _keyShf()
;
;  Function: Return the current state of the shift keys and toggled modes.
;  See the main text of the chapter for details on the format of the word
;  returned.
;
;  Algorithm: Call ROM BIOS get keyboard state function of the keyboard
;  interrupt.

         public  _keyShf       ; Routine is available to other modules

_keyShf  proc  near            ; NEAR type subroutine
         mov   ah,2            ; Function 2: get keyboard state
         int   16H             ; Call the ROM BIOS with interrupt 16 (keybd)
         ret                   ; Return to calling program
_keyShf  endp                  ; End of subroutine

_TEXT    ends                  ; End of code segment
         end                   ; End of assembly code
```

Listing 9-4. "border2.c":

```
/*            Change Border Color from Keyboard

         This program changes the background color/attributes.
*/

/*       main(argc,argv)

         Function: Watch the keyboard and change the border color of the
         display based on the current state of the shift, control and
         alt keys. Exit when any other key is pressed.

         Algorithm: Repeatedly call keyChk to see if something other than
         shift keys are pressed. If not, call keyShf to get the current
         state of the shift keys, and pass that on to setPal to actually
         set the color of the border.
*/
```

Listing 9-4. "border2.c" *(cont.)*:

```
main(argc,argv)

int argc;
char *argv[];

{
        int key;

        /* Repeatedly call keyChk to see if anything non-shift was pressed. */
        while (!keyChk(&key))
                /* If not, set the border to the current shift state. */
                setPal(0,keyShf());
}
```

Listing 9-5. "attrib.c":

```
/*              Change character attributes from Keyboard

        This program changes the attributes of all characters on the screen.
*/

#define TRUE 1
#define FALSE 0

/*      main(argc,argv)

        Function: Watch the keyboard and change the attributes of each
        character on the display based on the current state of the shift,
        control and alt keys. The low four bits of the attributes are to
        be set to the current shift state; the upper four bits are set from
        the shift state when the space bar is pressed. Exit when any key
        other than the space bar is pressed.

        Algorithm: Repeatedly call keyChk to see if something other than
        shift keys are pressed. If not, call keyShf to get the current
        state of the shift keys; if they've changed, call getACh/putACh
        for each character on the display.
*/

main(argc,argv)

int argc;
char *argv[];

{
        int key;                        /* Key pressed. */
        char curAttr, lastAttr;         /* Current and last attribute. */
        char ch, attr;                  /* Char and attribute from display. */
        int i,j;                        /* Row and column indices. */

        /* Set the attribute to white on black. */
        lastAttr = 7;
```

Listing 9-5. "attrib.c" *(cont.)*:

```
    /* Repeatedly call keyChk to see if anything non-shift was pressed. */
    while (TRUE) {
            /* Assume the top bits stay the same as they were. */
            curAttr = lastAttr & 0xF0;
            /* Check for a key press. */
            if (keyChk(&key)) {
                    /* If yes, check for the space bar. */
                    if ((key & 0xFF) == ' ') {
                            /* If yes, clear the key from the queue. */
                            keyRd();
                            /* Set the new top of the attribute. */
                            curAttr = (keyShf() << 4) & 0xF0;
                    /* Otherwise, exit the loop. */
                    } else break;
            };
            curAttr |= keyShf() & 0xF;
            /* If we've got a new attribute, set all the characters
               to it. */
            if (curAttr != lastAttr)
                    for (i = 0; i < 24; i++)
                            for (j = 0; j < 79; j++) {
                                    /* Position the cursor. */
                                    setPos(0,i,j);
                                    /* Get the old character/attribute. */
                                    getACh(0,&ch,&attr);
                                    /* Put the new character/attribute. */
                                    putACh(0,ch,curAttr,1);
                                    /* Remember the new attribute. */
                                    lastAttr = curAttr;
                            };
    };
}
```

Chapter 10

CGA & EGA ROM BIOS Graphics: *Fractal*

- Introduction to Fractals: Folded Surfaces and Strange Attractors

- A Fractional Number of Dimensions

- ROM BIOS Graphic Display Routines: CGA, EGA and ECD

- Two Dot Routines: All Modes

- The Fract Program: rdlu Sequences

I n this chapter we will present a program that uses the graphics facilities of the ROM BIOS to draw fractals. Versions of this program will work on either the color graphics adapter (CGA) or the enhanced graphics adapter (EGA). In developing this program, we will present routines to read and write dots on the screen using the ROM BIOS graphics display facilities and we will discuss the various graphics modes of the CGA and EGA.

Fractals

A fractal is not a single thing or simple class of things. Rather, it is a more general attribute shared by many objects, both natural and man-made. You may have already seen programs that produce pictures of fractals on the IBM PC. Each program, however, displays only a few of the wide range of possible types of fractals. Our program will draw a fractal involving wiggly line segments. Another type of fractal involving folded surfaces creates special effects for science fiction movies. Still another type displays a mathematical phenomenon called "strange attractors."

These are the best known examples of fractals, but there are many more kinds of fractals and many more ways to see, explore, and display them. For more information you may want to read The Fractal Geometry of Nature by Benoit Mandelbrot. Mandelbrot—generally recognized as the leading expert on fractals, and the person who coined the term—argues that fractals are common in nature, and are not a man-made curiosity.

A fractal, by the simplest definition, is something that possesses a fractional number of dimensions. How can something possess a fractional number of dimensions? Let's examine one type of fractal which involves wiggly line segments. We start with a line segment, as shown in Figure 10-1A. This line segment has one dimension and is finite in length. Next, we replace the line segment with a sequence of line segments, as shown in Figure 10-1B. Then we replace each of those segments with the same sequence, as shown in Figure

10-1C. If we continue this process ad infinitum, i.e., using ever smaller segments, we get a curious result: according to the principles of traditional topology, the resulting line segment is one-dimensional but infinite in length. If we use a more complicated sequence, such as in Figure 10-2, the line segment seems to be longer, but is also infinite in length. According to traditional topology, we cannot differentiate the length of the two line segments. In fractal mathematics, however, we use a slightly different definition of "dimension," allowing for fractional dimensions. Each line segment is between one and two dimensions, with the second segment having a higher dimensionality. You do not need to understand the mathematics involved to make pretty pictures with fractals— all you need is the program in this chapter.

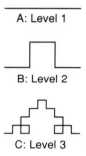

Figure 10-1. A Fractal Pattern

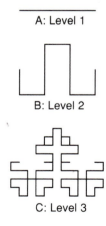

Figure 10-2. Another Fractal Pattern

One way of looking at a fractal line segment is in terms of "wiggliness." The more wiggly, the higher the dimension. Lines with finite wiggliness have one dimension. Lines with infinite wiggliness, like those described above, have more than one dimension. A sufficiently wiggly line graduates from being a line and becomes a two-dimensional surface.

The program we'll develop in this chapter will approximate a line segment fractal. We won't be able to draw all of it: since it's infinitely long, drawing it would take an infinite amount of time and would require a display with infinitely high resolution. The IBM PC is good, but it's not that good! Instead, we will design the program so you can limit the number of line segment subdivisions. You can play with the amount of detail and see where the time and display limitations start getting in the way. First, though, we'll need to develop a means of accessing the graphics display of the IBM PC.

ROM BIOS Graphic Display Routines

There are two different graphics display adapters and two different graphic displays available from IBM for the PC. The adapter is the board that goes inside the IBM PC, while the display is the TV-set-like box that generally sits on top of the PC. The adapters contain the information to be displayed and determine the characteristics of the display, including the numbers of dots on the screen and the number of colors available for each dot. The two graphics adapters are the Color Graphics Adapter (CGA) and the Enhanced Graphics Adapter (EGA); the EGA allows more dots and colors than the CGA. The displays simply display the image. The two displays are the Color Display (CD) and the Enhanced Color Display (ECD); the Enhanced Color Display is required for some of the higher resolution modes (more dots) available with the EGA. IBM also offers a Monochrome Adapter and a Monochrome Display, but these do not support graphics, except in a very limited manner. The following table illustrates the graphics capabilities of each of these display adapters:

Resolution	Simultaneous colors	CGA	EGA	ECD required
320x200	4	Yes	Yes	No
640x200	2 (B&W)	Yes	Yes	No
320x200	16	No	Yes	No
640x200	16	No	Yes	No
640x350	2 (B&W)	No	Yes	Yes
640x350	16	No	Yes	Yes

The resolution column shows the number of dots the adapter can display. For example, 640x200 means 640 dots across the screen (columns) by 200 dots from top to bottom (rows). The simultaneous colors column shows the number of colors that a single screen can contain at one time. For instance, in the case of the four-color mode, one of two sets of four colors must be chosen, so that while there are more than four possible colors available, only four can be displayed at one time. Most of the display resolutions are supported by the IBM Color Display monitor, but the highest resolution displays (640x350) require the ECD.

The ROM BIOS provides facilities for writing dots to the screen and for reading the current value of the dots already on the screen. Before the dots can be manipulated, however, one of the graphics modes must be selected using the ROM BIOS set mode call, which was discussed in Chapter Seven. The following table shows the modes for the various types of graphic displays (the modes are in decimal):

Mode	Resolution & colors	Supported by
4	320x200, 4 colors	CGA & EGA
6	640x200, B&W	CGA & EGA
13	320x200, 16 colors	EGA only
14	640x200, 16 colors	EGA only
15	640x350, B&W	EGA only
16	640x350, 16 colors	EGA only

Once the mode has been set, two ROM BIOS interface routines are available, one to put a dot on the screen at a specified row and column, and the other to get the current value of a dot:

putDot(page,row,column,color) — Set the dot at the specified row and column on the specified display page to the color given. If bit 7 of the color is 1, exclusive-or the color with the one already on the display. Note that the page specification is meaningful only when using the EGA; the CGA has only one graphics page. Also, the range of valid colors depends on the adapter being used and the mode the adapter is in.

getDot(page,row,column) — Return the value of the dot at the row and column given, on the display page specified. As in putDot, the page parameter is meaningful only when used with the EGA, and the range of values returned by getDot depends upon the current display adapter and mode.

Rows (display lines) are numbered from zero to either 199 or 349, depending on the resolution. The top row on the screen is row number zero, the second is row one, the third is row two, etc. This is backwards from normal coordinate numbering, where zero is at the bottom. The columns are numbered from zero to 319 or 639. They start at zero on the left side of the display and increase going to the right, just as normal coordinates do.

Depending upon the number of colors involved, the color parameter to putDot and the value returned from getDot can have one of three different formats: For black and white, it is either 0 for black or 1 for white. For four-color mode, it ranges from 0 to 3; the specific colors selected depend upon the palette setting discussed in Chapter Nine, but are one of the following two possibilities:

Value	Color (palette 0)	Color (palette 1)
0	Black	Black
1	Green	Cyan
2	Red	Magenta
3	Brown	White

In four-color mode, the color for value 0, also known as the background color, can be changed to a color other than the default black. This is also discussed in Chapter Nine.

Finally, sixteen-color mode allows a value from zero to fifteen:

Value	Color
0	Black
1	Blue
2	Green
3	Cyan
4	Red
5	Magenta
6	Brown
7	White
8	Dark gray
9	Light blue
10	Light green
11	Light cyan
12	Light red
13	Light magenta
14	Yellow
15	Intensified white

Another way to interpret the color value is shown in Figure 10-3, with each bit contributing a component to the displayed color if it's on.

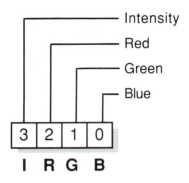

Figure 10-3. Color Dots

Listing 10-1 contains the assembly language interface routines for the ROM BIOS putDot and getDot functions.

The Fract Program

Listing 10-2 contains the Fract program. The program consists of three functions: getPatt reads in the line sequence patterns from the user; doPatt draws the fractal from the patterns; and main coordinates the operation. In addition, there are three tables and a number of other global variables used by the program.

The main function reads in a fractal from the user and draws it; then it asks if it should draw another, and if so, it repeats the process. Before querying the user, however, the program calls setMode, a function that accomplishes two goals. First, it sets the graphic display mode. In Listing 10-2, mode 14 is used, which requires an Enhanced Graphics Adapter, but will operate with either the Color Display or the Enhanced Color Display. You can change this to mode 16 to make use of the full facilities of the Enhanced Color Adapter and Enhanced Color Display (EGA/ECD); but then it will no longer work on a Color Display. The second function that setMode performs is to clear the display—that is, it sets all dots to zero (black).

We can simplify the job of reading line sequences considerably by constraining the line segments to be either vertical or horizontal. Then a sequence can be specified by a series of movement commands, "up," "down," "left," and "right." These can be further reduced to the letters, "u", "d", "l", and "r". For example, "rdlu" is a simple box, "rurdr" is the sequence in Figure 10-1B, and "druurddru" is the sequence in Figure 10-2B. Within the program itself, these four directions will be stored numerically to simplify computations: 0 for up, 1 for down, 2 for left, and 3 for right.

The program uses line segment sequences for two purposes. The first provides a starting pattern for the fractal. In the example shown in Figure 10-1, a simple single line segment was used as the starting pattern. But it's much more interesting to use a more complex pattern, one example of which is a closed box—Figure 10-4 shows how a box pattern develops using the pattern from Figure 10-1B. The shape of this initial line sequence is one of the things specified by the user. The other line sequence the program uses is the one which is repeatedly and recursively substituted for line segments in order to form the fractal. Note that this sequence is valid only if it ends at the same up/down level at which it began—that is, if we're going to replace a line segment with this sequence, then it had better have starting and ending points at the same vertical level. Both these line sequence patterns are read in via calls to getPatt from main.

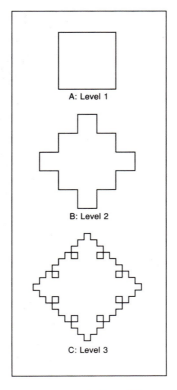

Figure 10-4. A Box Fractal

The function getPatt consists of a do...while statement which repeatedly attempts to get a valid pattern from the user. It prompts the user for a line sequence and reads it in using the standard I/O gets function. Then it translates each component direction from ASCII into direction numbers, accepting either upper or lower case. While getPatt is doing this, it keeps track of the up/down and left/right level. The up/down level is used to check whether this sequence is valid if it's a replacement sequence rather than an overall pattern, and the left/right level is returned by the function—this is the length of the sequence in units of "right" steps. The line segment sequences or patterns are stored in the global variables boxPatt and linePatt—boxPatt is named based on the assumption that most overall patterns will be boxes. The length of these patterns are stored in boxPSz and linePSz. And the left/right length of the line pattern is stored in lineLen.

The recursive function doPatt draws the lines. For each line in the sequence, doPatt is called to draw the recursively repeated line sequence in its place. To start the process, doPatt is called with the overall sequence. It cycles through each segment in that sequence, and for each one, it calls itself with the repeating line sequence to draw the sub-sequence, and the sub-sub-sequence, and so on. If we were drawing a true fractal, this would continue forever, with doPatt calling itself calling itself calling itself.... If we want to see any actual drawing, however, we'll need to stop this infinite process. We stop it by using the lev parameter to doPatt, which is incremented on each subcall to doPatt. The lev parameter tells what level of recursion doPatt is currently processing. When the level of recursion reaches the level stored in the global variable named level—which was read from the user—the recursion stops and a real line segment is drawn. The bulk of doPatt is, in fact, involved with drawing those real line segments.

The global variables x and y indicate where a conceptual pen is currently located on the screen. It's important that these variables be floating point, not integers, because if the level of recursion is very deep, the line segment sizes will be very small, possibly less than 1. Each time a segment is actually drawn, the x and y variables are updated to indicate the new pen position. Note that x and y are initially set to 270 for x and 50 for y. This is a reasonable starting point, since patterns are generally drawn toward the right and downward, and since the user input is displayed on the left side of the display. If you are using an Enhanced Color Display and have changed setMode to use mode 16, you might want to increase the value of y to 100, but it isn't strictly necessary. The other global drawing parameter is the color parameter, which tells what color dots to use when drawing. This is initially set to 7, and then is decremented for each segment in the overall pattern. If you want to use the Color Graphics Adapter rather than the EGA, this value will need to be set to 1 (white) and then not be changed, since the CGA has only two colors available at the 640x200 resolution. The display mode must also be set to 6, rather than 14, to work with the CGA.

One of the challenges in drawing a line segment is knowing which way to draw it. The patterns tell whether it should be drawn up, down, left, or right. Given this direction, the tables xDir and yDir show which way to draw it in terms of direction changes in the x and y axis. But remember that the segment being drawn is part of a replacement for another segment, and that other segment may be in any direction. The sub-segment direction is relative to that of the original segment being replaced. For example, if we're replacing a segment going up, and one of the component sub-segments goes left, we actually want to draw a segment going down on the screen. Or, if we're replacing a segment going left (the opposite of the "normal" right facing drawing), and the sub-segment is going up, then we actually want to draw a segment going down.

This sounds very confusing and it is. But we can concentrate this confusion into one table, called dirDir. This table contains the direction to be drawn on the screen when indexed by the direction of the segment being replaced and the direction of the sub-segment. Thus, if we wanted to draw a replacement sub-segment going right for an original segment going up, we'd draw it going in the direction indicated by dirDir[UP][RIGHT]. Once this translation has been made, we can work entirely with coordinate directions on the screen, which are much less confusing.

Running the Fract Program

Once started, the Fract program asks for a box sequence, the length in screen dots of the component line segments, a line segment sequence with which to replace the line segments, and a maximum level of recursion. Most of the time a box sequence of "rdlu" or "rrdllu" (a square box or an oblong box), and a length of 50 or 100 is best. The line sequence can be anything you like. Some interesting examples are given in Figure 10-5. The level is usually best set to 3 or 4, though sometimes values as high as 6 are interesting. Higher levels, however, take considerably longer to draw and usually exceed the display resolution of both the CGA and EGA. The following table lists some interesting input values to try. Figure 10-5 shows the line sequences that correspond to the values in the table.

Box sequence	Line length	Line sequence	Level
rrdllu	50	druurd	3
rdlu	100	rdur	4
rdlu	100	rdurudr	3
rrdllu	50	ruuddrdur	3
rrdllu	100	rdruurdr	3
rdlu	100	urrrrd	3
rrdllu	50	ruudddur	3
rdlu	50	urdurd	3
rrdllu	100	urdrr	3 or 4
rrdllu	50	uurddrurdr	3
rdlu	100	rdruudr	3

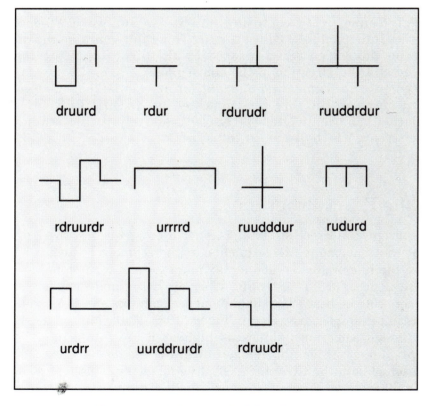

Figure 10-5. Example Line Patterns

Summary

The fractal program presented in this chapter makes use of the graphics capabilities of the IBM PC, using either the Color Graphics Adapter (CGA) or the Enhanced Graphics Adapter (EGA). The flexibility and simplicity of the interface to the display (the two functions setMode and putDot) is made possible by using the ROM BIOS, which provides the interface to both adapters through a single set of function calls.

The Fract program allows the user to enter a pair of patterns (line sequences) which are used to build and draw an approximation to a fractal line segment.

Exercises

1. Change Fract to draw lines in three dimensions. In addition to "up," "down," "left," and "right," also allow "forward" and "backward." Display the third dimension as a color.

2. Change Fract to accept up to five line patterns, then have doPatt pick one of the five at random each time. This is a random fractal.

3. [advanced] Change Fract to allow arbitrary directions for lines, other than strictly horizontal or vertical.

Listing 10-1. "v4lib.asm":

```
;                      Video Library (part 4)

_TEXT    segment byte public 'CODE'        ; Place the code in the code segment
         assume   CS:_TEXT                 ; Assume the CS register points to it

; _putDot(page,row,col,color)
;
; Function: Write a dot to the screen on the page, row, and column specified.
; Write it in color. Note that page is only used with the EGA, and
; the range of valid colors depends on the adapter and mode being used.
;
; Algorithm: Call the ROM BIOS put dot function; int 10H, AH = 12.

         public   _putDot               ; Routine is available to other modules

         page = 4                        ; Offset from BP to parameter page
         row = 6                         ; Offset to parameter row
         col = 8                         ; Offset to col
         color = 10                      ; Offset to color

_putDot  proc near                       ; NEAR type subroutine
         push     bp                     ; Save BP register
         mov      bp,sp                  ; Set BP to SP; easier to get parameters
         push     si                     ; Save SI
         push     di                     ; Save DI
         mov      bh,[bp+page]           ; Set BH to the page
         mov      dx,[bp+row]            ; Set DX to the row
         mov      cx,[bp+col]            ; Set CX to the column
         mov      al,[bp+color]          ; Set AL to the color
         mov      ah,12                  ; Set AH to 12 (put dot function)
         int      10H                    ; Call ROM BIOS video interrupt
         pop      di                     ; Restore the DI register
         pop      si                     ; Restore the SI register
         pop      bp                     ; Restore the BP register
         ret                             ; Return to calling program
_putDot  endp                            ; End of subroutine

; _getDot(page,row,col)
;
; Function: Return the color of the dot at the page, row, and column given.
; Note: The page specification is only meaningful when using the EGA, and
; the color returned will be constrained to a range that depends on the
; display adapter and mode being used.
;
; Algorithm: Call the ROM BIOS get dot function; int 10H, AH = 13.

         public   _getDot               ; Routine is available to other modules

         page = 4                        ; Offset from BP to parameter page
         row = 6                         ; Offset to parameter row
         col = 8                         ; Offset to col

_getDot  proc near                       ; NEAR type subroutine
         push     bp                     ; Save BP register
         mov      bp,sp                  ; Set BP to SP; easier to get parameters
         push     si                     ; Save SI
```

Listing 10-1. "v4lib.asm" *(cont.)*:

```asm
        push    di              ; Save DI
        mov     bh,[bp+page]    ; Set BH to the page
        mov     dx,[bp+row]     ; Set DX to the row
        mov     cx,[bp+col]     ; Set CX to the column
        mov     ah,13           ; Set AH to 13 (get dot function)
        int     10H             ; Call ROM BIOS video interrupt
        xor     ah,ah           ; Zero the top byte of the return value
        pop     di              ; Restore the DI register
        pop     si              ; Restore the SI register
        pop     bp              ; Restore the BP register
        ret                     ; Return to calling program
_getDot endp                    ; End of subroutine

_TEXT   ends                    ; End of code segment

        end                     ; End of assembly code
```

Listing 10-2. "fract.c":

```c
/*                      Fractal Generation Program
*/

#include <stdio.h>
#include <math.h>

#define FALSE 0
#define TRUE 1

/* Movement directions: */

#define UP 0
#define DOWN 1
#define LEFT 2
#define RIGHT 3

/* Table to convert from the direction of a segment being drawn (first
   index) and the direction of a subsegment (second index) to absolute
   screen up/down/left/right: */

int dirDir[4][4] = {
        LEFT, RIGHT, DOWN, UP,   /* Line up. */
        RIGHT, LEFT, UP, DOWN,   /* Line down. */
        DOWN, UP, RIGHT, LEFT,   /* Line left. */
        UP, DOWN, LEFT, RIGHT    /* Line right. */
};

/* X-axis multiplier for up/down/left/right movement: */

int xDir[4] = {
        0, 0, -1, 1     /* Line right. */
};

/* Y-axis multiplier for up/down/left/right movement: */

int yDir[4] = {
```

Listing 10-2. "fract.c" *(cont.)*:

```
        -1, 1, 0, 0      /* Line right. */
};

int boxPatt[100];        /* The box pattern. */
int boxPSz;              /* It's size. */

int linePatt[100];       /* The line pattern. */
int linePSz;             /* It's size. */
int lineLen;             /* Width of line pattern in line segments. */

int level;               /* The level of detail to go to. */

float x, y;              /* The current pen position. */

int color;               /* The current pen color. */

/*      main()

        Function: Get box and line patterns, the line size, and the
        level to draw to from the user. Then draw the fractal. When
        done, ask if another one should be drawn. Repeat the sequence
        as long as the user wants.

        Algorithm: Use getPatt to read in the patterns for the box and
        the line pattern. Use gets/atoi for the other, numeric input.
        Then call doPatt to actually draw the fractal.
*/

main()

{
        char str[100];  /* Input buffer for user responses. */
        int side;       /* Size of line in screen dots. */

        /* Repeat while the user wants more. */
        do {
                /* Set the display mode; use 6 for CGA, 14 for EGA with
                    color display, or 16 for EGA with enhanced color disp. */
                setMod(14);
                /* Get the box pattern. */
                getPatt("box",boxPatt,&boxPSz,TRUE,TRUE);
                /* Get the size of the box line. */
                printf("Side size: ");
                gets(str);
                side = atoi(str);
                /* Get the line pattern. */
                lineLen = getPatt("line",linePatt,&linePSz,TRUE,FALSE);
                /* Get the level to display to. */
                printf("Level: ");
                gets(str);
                level = atoi(str);
                /* Set the pen position and color to start with. */
                x = 270; y = 50; color = 7;
                /* Draw the fractal. */
                doPatt(boxPatt,boxPSz,RIGHT,(float) side,0);
                /* Ask if the user wants to do another one. */
```

Listing 10-2. "fract.c" *(cont.)*:

```
                printf("Do another one? ");
                gets(str);
        } while ((str[0] == 'y') || (str[0] == 'Y'));
}

/*      getPatt(prmpt,patt,size,noUp,noLeft)

        Function: Get a pattern from the user. Issue the prompt
        string pointed to by prmpt. Then read the pattern into
        the pattern array pointed to by patt, and set the size
        pointed to by size. If noUp is TRUE, don't allow patterns
        that end at a different up/down level than they began.
        If noLeft is TRUE, don't allow patterns that end at a
        different left/right level than they started. getPatt
        returns the number of segments to the right the pattern
        ends at from its starting position.

        Algorithm: Prompt the user and then read in the pattern
        string. Scan through it, converting from 'u'/'d'/'l'/'r'
        to UP/DOWN/LEFT/RIGHT. When done, check it for validity.
        If it fails, tell the user and do it all over again.
*/

getPatt(prmpt,patt,size,noUp,noLeft)

char *prmpt;
int *patt;
int *size;
int noUp;
int noLeft;

{
        char str[100];          /* Input buffer for user input. */
        char *cp;               /* Char pointer to scan buffer with. */
        int *pPtr;              /* Pattern array pointer. */
        int upCnt, rightCnt;    /* Up/down and left/right offsets. */
        int badPatt;            /* TRUE if pattern is bad. */

        /* Repeat until he gets it right. */
        do {
                /* Prompt him for a pattern string. */
                printf("Enter %s pattern: ",prmpt); gets(str);
                /* Assume the pattern's OK. */
                badPatt = FALSE;
                /* Scan through the pattern string. */
                for (cp = str, pPtr = patt, upCnt = rightCnt = 0, *size = 0;
                        *cp != 0; cp++, pPtr++, (*size)++) {
                        switch (*cp) {
                                case 'u':
                                case 'U':
                                        /* Up one. */
                                        *pPtr = UP;
                                        upCnt++;
                                        break;
                                case 'd':
```

Listing 10-2. "fract.c" *(cont.)*:

```
                        case 'D':
                                /* Down one. */
                                *pPtr = DOWN;
                                upCnt--;
                                break;
                        case 'l':
                        case 'L':
                                /* Left one. */
                                *pPtr = LEFT;
                                rightCnt--;
                                break;
                        case 'r':
                        case 'R':
                                *pPtr = RIGHT;
                                rightCnt++;
                                break;
                        default:
                                badPatt = TRUE;
                                break;
                };
                if (badPatt) {
                        printf("Only U, D, L, or R allowed!\n");
                        break;
                };
        };
        if (noUp && (upCnt != 0)) {
                printf("Pattern must end at the same up/down level ");
                printf("it began at.\n");
                badPatt = TRUE;
        };
        if (noLeft && (rightCnt != 0)) {
                printf("Pattern must end at the same right/left ");
                printf("level it began at.\n");
                badPatt = TRUE;
        };
    } while (badPatt);
    return(rightCnt);
}

/*      doPatt(patt,pattSize,dir,size,lev)

        Function: Draw the pattern pointed to by patt, of size pattSize,
        in the direction dir (UP, DOWN, LEFT, or RIGHT), with each line
        segment of size size; this will be level lev. If lev doesn't yet
        match the global variable level, then recursively call doPatt to
        draw each segment as a series of segments from the line pattern.

        Algorithm: For each segment in the pattern, if we're at the drawing
        level (lev == level), then figure out the proper direction to
        draw and draw the segment; otherwise, call doPatt to draw the
        sub-pattern.
*/

doPatt(patt,pattSize,dir,size,lev)

int *patt;
```

Listing 10-2. "fract.c" *(cont.)*:

```c
int pattSize;
int dir;
float size;
int lev;

{
        int *pPtr;                         /* A pointer into the pattern. */
        int pCnt;                          /* Count of pattern segments left. */
        int xPlusMinus, yPlusMinus;        /* The x and y drawing increments. */
        register int i, j;                 /* Row and column drawing indices. */
        int iEnd, jEnd;                    /* Where to stop drawing. */
        int temp;
        int subDir;                        /* The absolute up/down/left/right. */
        int dotVal;                        /* Color to draw. */

        /* For each segment in the pattern... */
        for (pPtr = patt, pCnt = 0; pCnt++ < pattSize; pPtr++) {
                /* If we're at drawing level... */
                if (lev == level) {
                        /* Find the absolute direction. */
                        subDir = dirDir[dir][*pPtr];
                        /* Convert the pen position to row/column ints. */
                        i = x; j = y;
                        /* Get the pen increment for drawing. */
                        xPlusMinus = xDir[subDir];
                        yPlusMinus = yDir[subDir];
                        /* Compute the new pen position after drawing. */
                        x += xPlusMinus*size; y += yPlusMinus*size;
                        /* Convert the end point to row/column ints. */
                        iEnd = x; jEnd = y;
                        /* We always want to draw in ascending coordinates.
                           Therefore, we must swap i/iEnd and j/jEnd if
                           we'd be drawing descending. */
                        if (iEnd < i) {
                                temp = i; i = iEnd; iEnd = temp;
                        };
                        if (jEnd < j) {
                                temp = j; j = jEnd; jEnd = temp;
                        };
                        /* Similarly, we need the abs of the increments. */
                        xPlusMinus = abs(xPlusMinus);
                        yPlusMinus = abs(yPlusMinus);
                        /* Set the color to draw. For the EGA, this should
                           be the global variable color; for CGA, it should
                           be 1. */
                        dotVal = color;
                        /* Decide whether we're drawing a vertical or
                           horizontal line. */
                        if (xPlusMinus == 0) {
                                /* If vertical, draw it. */
                                do putDot(0,j++,i,dotVal); while (j < jEnd);
                        } else {
                                /* If horizontal, draw it. */
                                do putDot(0,j,i++,dotVal); while (i < iEnd);
                        };
```

Listing 10-2. "fract.c" *(cont.)*:

```
        /* If we're not down to drawing level yet, call doPatt to
           draw the next level down. */
        } else doPatt(linePatt,linePSz,dirDir[dir][*pPtr],
                        size/((float) lineLen),lev+1);

        /* If this is the top level, switch to the next color for
           drawing the next segment. */
        if (lev == 0) {
                color--;
                if (color == 0) color = 15;
        };
    };
}
```

Chapter 11

Serial Port—
Keyboard/Display I/O:
Term

I n this chapter, we will develop a terminal program that transfers data between the keyboard/display and the serial port, as shown in Figure 11-1. We will then present a second version of the program which allows the data to be both displayed and printed as it is received. To build these two programs, we will need to access the serial and printer port functions of the ROM BIOS. We will show assembly language interface libraries to these two parts of the BIOS. Due to the technique used to interface to the serial port, these programs will be limited to serial data rates of 300 bits per second or lower. In Chapter Fifteen, we will present another technique that works at higher data rates; that chapter will, however, build upon the material presented here.

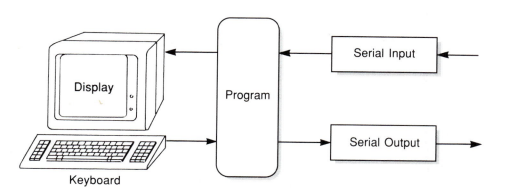

Figure 11-1. The Term Program

The terminal program consists of a loop that continually checks the keyboard and the serial port for data. If it finds data available from the keyboard—i.e., the user struck a key—then it sends the data out the serial port. On the other hand, if it finds data available from the serial port—i.e., a new character was received by the hardware—it displays that character on the screen.

As in the last two chapters, the programs presented here could not have been written relying on the facilities provided by MS-DOS alone. In this case, there is no MS-DOS facility for checking whether the serial port has incoming data waiting. The MS-DOS serial port input call suspends the program until data is available, making it impossible to continue to check for keyboard input.

Serial Input/Output (I/O)

Before we can write the Term program, we need some background information on what serial ports are and how they work. Generally, when data is transferred within a computer, several bits are transferred simultaneously. This is called transferring data in parallel. In the IBM PC and IBM PC/XT, for example, data is moved between the processor and memory in 8-bit chunks known as bytes. When data is sent to the printer via the printer port, it is also moved in 8-bit chunks because the printer port is a parallel interface. This type of parallel transfer of data requires eight separate wires on which to send the data, plus several more for controlling the transfer. Serial transfers reduce the number of wires by transferring the data one bit at a time, or "serially." Figure 11-2 illustrates this difference between parallel and serial data transfers. Serial input/output (I/O) is most often used for transferring data between two computers, or between a computer and a terminal (a simple keyboard and display), possibly using a modem.

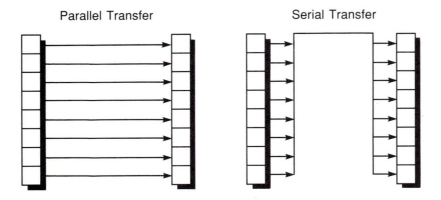

Figure 11-2. Parallel and Serial Data Transfers

There are several different types of serial interfaces. We will discuss what is known as "asynchronous" serial. The name "asynchronous" comes from the fact that the interface does not include a clock to synchronize the transfer. This is the most common form of serial interface used with personal computers. When data is converted from parallel to asynchronous serial, some additional bits are tacked on to help the transfer process. And the topmost bit of the byte may be discarded because when sending ASCII data, this top bit doesn't contain useful information. Figure 11-3 shows the complete format of a byte being sent serially. Bytes can be sent immediately following each other, or there can be a pause between bytes, during which time the line is always set to 1. Since each byte begins with a 0 bit, called the start bit, it's easy to find the start of the byte even if the line has been idle, sending 1s for some time. The line always goes from 1 to 0 when the start bit arrives.

This process is also aided by the stop bit(s): it ensures that the line is 1 at the end of the byte, ensuring a transition from 1 to 0 when the start bit of the next byte arrives, even if there was no idle time between bytes.

A parity bit helps to verify that the data arrives at the destination without errors: the sender sets the parity bit to 0 or 1 to make the total number of 1 bits in the byte either even or odd. The receiver can then check whether the number he received has the same evenness or oddness (parity) that it had before it left the sender, and therefore can tell if it was garbled along the way. This is not a perfect error check, but it helps. The presence of the parity bit is optional.

The serial data, then, has the following parts:

Name	Use
Start bit	This bit helps the receiver find the start of the byte, since it is always 0.
Stop bit(s)	These bit(s) also help the receiver find the start. They are always 1, so that there is always a transition from 1 to 0 at the start of each byte—when no data is being sent, the line is held at 1.
Data bits	This is the data itself, which can consist of any combination of 0s or 1s.
Parity bit	This allows the receiver to determine if the data was received without errors—serial data is often sent through noisy, error-prone environments. The transmitter sets the parity bit so that the count of the number of bits that are on is either even for "even parity" or odd for "odd parity."

The hardware in the IBM PC constructs this asynchronous serial form of a byte. The program need only specify the number of data bits, the number of stop bits, and the parity, and then pass bytes to the hardware by calling the ROM BIOS. All the rest is done automatically. Similarly, the hardware automatically detects and reports several possible errors associated with incoming data: First, the parity of each byte is checked on received bytes; if it's wrong, a "parity error" has occurred. Second, if the received data doesn't look proper—for example, the stop bit(s) are not 1—then a "framing error" has occurred. And finally, since the hardware can only handle one byte at a time, if a new byte arrives before the program has read the previous one, an "overrun error" occurs. When this happens, one of the bytes is lost forever.

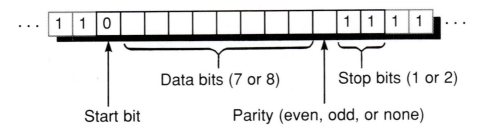

Figure 11-3. Serial Data Format

In addition to the variety of data formats available, serial data can be sent at any of a number of speeds, called bit rates or baud rates. (Note: This is actually an incorrect use of the term "baud rate," but it's a very common one. If you want to be technically correct, use "bit rate" instead.) The most common bit rates are 300, 1200, 2400, and 9600 bits per second. In order to determine the byte transfer rate, divide the bit rate by the total number of data, parity, start, and stop bits. Since at these data rates, most machines use one start bit, one stop bit, and either eight data bits with no parity or seven data bits with parity, you can simply divide the bit rate by ten to get the byte rate. Therefore, 9600 bits per second is 960 bytes per second—NOT 9600/8 = 1200 bytes per second, as one might naively assume.

To communicate successfully, the sending and receiving machines must be using the same bit rate, the same number of data bits, the same number of start and stop bits, and the same parity. If they use different settings, the data will be garbled, or the receiver will continually detect parity or framing errors.

The serial port hardware of the IBM PC takes parallel format data from the processor, converts it to serial format data, and turns it into changes in voltage levels on wires connected to the back of the PC. The voltage levels, what they mean, and to which pins on the 25-pin connector (called a DB-25) they are connected, all have been standardized, so you can easily connect those wires to other computers or devices. The standard is called RS-232. There are two wires used for exchanging data, known as "transmit data" or TD and "receive data" or RD, and a "signal ground" wire, required for electrical reasons. These three wires are the minimum that is necessary for sending and receiving data with another computer or device. You can talk to another IBM PC by connecting the two PC's ground wires, and connecting one PC's transmit wire to the receive wire on the other and vice versa.

Sometimes the two computers are connected directly with only a cable. Sometimes the connected computers use modems to transfer the data. A modem is a device that takes the serial data voltage levels and converts them into sounds that can be sent over the telephone network. When the sounds arrive at a second modem at the destination, they are converted back into voltage levels. With this additional piece of equipment involved, the operation becomes more complex. For example, the computer would like to know when the modem is powered on and ready to go, when a connection has been made to another modem, and when that connection has been broken. Also, it would be nice to be able to tell the modem when the computer is ready to accept incoming calls. Therefore, in addition to the transmit and receive data lines described above, RS-232 defines several more lines to help control the modem. These include:

Name	Abbreviation	Meaning
Data terminal ready	DTR	Computer is ready
Data set ready	DSR	Modem is ready
Ring indicator	RI	Phone is ringing
Received line signal detect or Carrier detect	CD	Modem hears the other modem
Request to send	RTS	Computer wants to transmit
Clear to send	CTS	OK for computer to transmit

The DTR/DSR wires indicate when the computer and modem are ready. The DTR line is also very often used to hang up the modem, by telling it that the computer is no longer ready. The RI line indicates that the incoming phone line is ringing—it is on while there is actual ringing on the line, and off between rings. The CD line indicates when the two modems can hear each other—i.e., the phone connection is established and data transfer can begin. RTS and CTS are used for the computer to request a chance to transmit, and for the modem to let the computer know when it can transmit. These lines are generally used with half-duplex modems, where only one side can transmit at any given time. These modem control signals can be of great help in building an application, and sometimes are even irreplaceable. More often, however, the programmer can ignore them, and can concentrate solely on the transmit and receive data lines.

There are a tremendous number of variations on how RS-232 signals and data are used and misused. Covering all of them would consume a book in itself, and would be more confusing than helpful. This section is intended to serve as a very basic introduction to serial I/O. So don't be surprised if you run into a variation not discussed here.

Term

Listing 11-1 contains the first program, Term. The program uses the ROM BIOS serial port interface library, shown in Listing 11-2. Term is a basic terminal emulation program that performs two functions: first, every time the user strikes an ASCII key on the keyboard, Term passes the character to the ROM BIOS serial port send routine, which transmits it through the serial port. And second, every time a character is received by the serial port hardware, Term displays that character on the screen. This main program loop is diagramed in Figure 11-4.

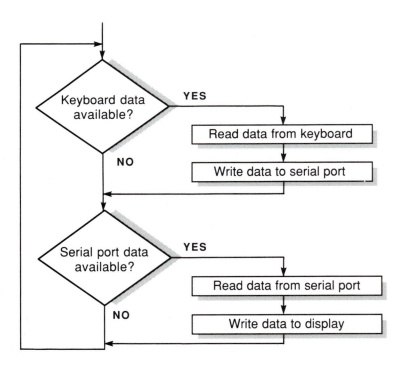

Figure 11-4. Term Main Loop Flowchart

First, the program initializes the serial port by composing an initialization word and passing it to the serInit function. For this program, we use 300 bits per second, 8 data bits, 1 stop bit, and no parity. Later in this chapter, we will explain how this description is translated into the value 0x83. The main loop of the program begins next. The ROM BIOS keyboard library, presented in the last chapter, checks for keyboard input. If it finds anything, the program checks the input to see whether it is an ASCII character or an IBM PC special function character. If it is a special function key, the program exits. If an ASCII character was entered, that character is sent to the serial port using the ROM BIOS serial port send function. Next, the serial port is checked for input via the ROM BIOS serial port status function. If this function indicates that an input character is waiting, the program reads that character, again using a BIOS function. It then calls the BIOS display interface library to display the character on the screen, using the TTY write function. This function will also take the appropriate action if the character is a carriage return, line feed, backspace, or bell. The TTY write function can take a long time to complete, particularly if it has to scroll the screen up a line. Because of this, Term is limited to 300 bits per second maximum data rate. In Chapter Fifteen, we'll develop a program that does not have this limitation. In all cases, Term uses COM1, and therefore passes a 0 as the first parameter to each of the serial port routines.

The Serial Port BIOS Functions

The serial port ROM BIOS interface routines are shown in Listing 11-2. Listing 11-3 presents an include file with constants defined for use with the serInit and serStat functions. These routines allow the program to manipulate the serial port(s) of the machine. The first parameter of each routine is the port number to which the function call is to be applied: 0 specifies COM1 and 1 specifies COM2. The following routines are available:

Function

serInit(port,config) — Configure and initialize the port. The parameter config specifies the baud rate, number of data and stop bits, and the parity. Figure 11-5 shows the bits used to specify each part of the configuration, and Listing 11-3 includes constants that can be added to produce the desired configuration. We could, for instance, substitute "B300 + DB8 + SB1 + PNONE" for SERCONFIG in Listing 11-1.

serSend(port,ch) — Send the character ch out the specified port. serSend returns a word with ch in the low byte, and a status indication in the high byte. If the BIOS was unable to send the character, serSend returns a value with bit 15 set (i.e., (serSend(...) & 0x8000) != 0); if bit 15 is not set, then the top byte of the returned value is the status of the line, using the same format as the top byte returned by serStat below.

serRecv(port) — Wait for and receive a character from the serial port. serRecv returns the received character in the low byte of the returned value, and a status indication in the high byte. The status byte is zero if there were no errors; otherwise it indicates an error as shown in the corresponding byte of serStat.

serStat(port) — Return the status of the serial port. Figure 11-6 shows the meanings of the bits, and Listing 11-3 contains constant bit masks that can be used in the program to test specific bits.

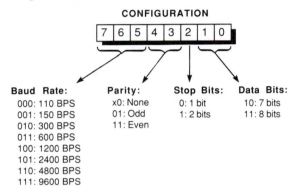

CONFIGURATION

| 7 | 6 | 5 | 4 | 3 | 2 | 1 | 0 |

Baud Rate:
000: 110 BPS
001: 150 BPS
010: 300 BPS
011: 600 BPS
100: 1200 BPS
101: 2400 BPS
110: 4800 BPS
111: 9600 BPS

Parity:
x0: None
01: Odd
11: Even

Stop Bits:
0: 1 bit
1: 2 bits

Data Bits:
10: 7 bits
11: 8 bits

Figure 11-5. serInit Configuration Format

SERIAL PORT STATUS

Line Status | Modem Status

| 15 | 14 | 13 | 12 | 11 | 10 | 9 | 8 | 7 | 6 | 5 | 4 | 3 | 2 | 1 | 0 |

— Delta clear to send
— Delta data set ready
— Trailing edge ring
— Delta receive line signal detect
— Clear to send
— Data set ready
— Ring
— Receive line signal detect
— Receive data ready
— Overrun error
— Parity error
— Framing error
— Break detect
— Transmit holding register empty
— Transmit shift register empty
— Time out

Figure 11-6. serStat Return Value Format

TermPrint

We now have a working terminal program, which we can use to talk to other computers and devices such as modems attached to the serial port. But our communications are very transitory—once the displayed characters have scrolled off the top of the screen, they're gone forever. In this section, we will develop a variation on the original terminal program, which will optionally send the serial port input to the printer as well as the display, as shown in Figure 11-7. It will use the printer port ROM BIOS interface functions to accomplish this.

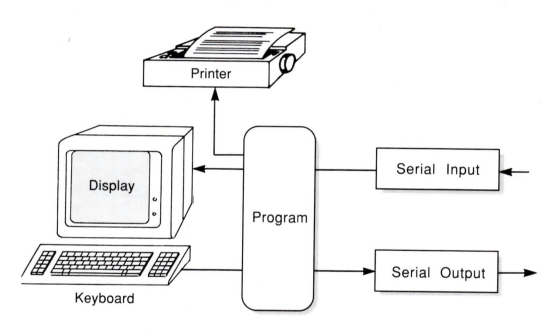

Figure 11-7. The TermPrint Program

The TermPrint program is shown in Listing 11-4. It is identical to the Term program, except in three places: first, it initializes the printer as well as the serial port. Second, if the user presses the F1 key, it toggles a flag that tells whether to send characters to the printer as well as the display. This flag is initially "off," so that no printing takes place. When the user hits the F1 key, it changes modes and prints everything that comes in. When the user hits the F1 key again, it turns it back off so no printing occurs. And third, when a character is received from the serial port, TermPrint sends the character to the printer port as well as to the display, but only if printing is currently enabled. Figure 11-8 shows the corresponding flow chart. TermPrint also uses the serial.h include file, rather than the custom constants used in Term.

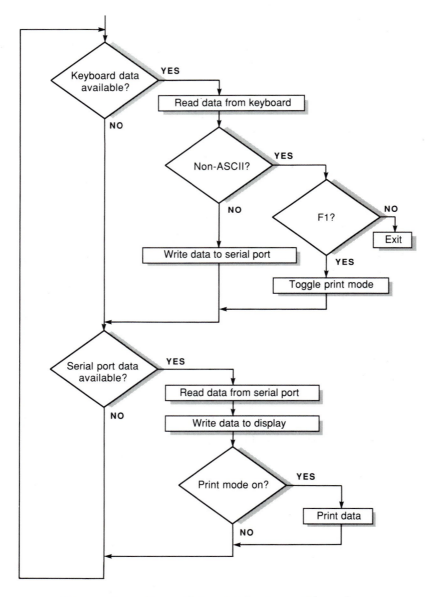

Figure 11-8. TermPrint Main Loop Flowchart

TermPrint uses the printer port ROM BIOS interface library, which is described below.

The Printer Port BIOS Functions

The printer port functions in the ROM BIOS allow the user to communicate directly with the printer ports. Listing 11-5 shows the assembly language interface routines which can be used to call the printer port functions of the BIOS, and Listing 11-6 shows an include file which contains some related constants. The first parameter of each routine is the port number, which is 0 for LPT1, 1 for LPT2, or 2 for LPT3 (serious programmers must get used to counting from 0 rather than from 1 as normal people do). The following routines are available:

Function

---

prtInit(port)—Initialize the printer port specified. prtInit returns the current status of the printer, as given for prtStat below.

prtPrint(port,ch)—Print the character ch on the port specified. Returns with bit 0 set if the character could not be printed (e.g., (prtPrint( ) & 1) != 0); the other bits in the returned value indicate the status as specified in prtStat.

prtStat(port)—Return the status of the serial port. Figure 11-9 shows the meanings of the bits, and Listing 11-6 contains constant bit masks which can be used in the program to test specific bits.

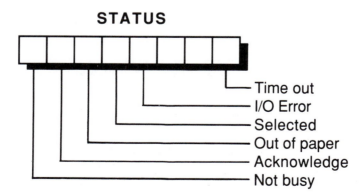

STATUS

- Time out
- I/O Error
- Selected
- Out of paper
- Acknowledge
- Not busy

Figure 11-9. prtStat Return Value Format

Summary

Two basic types of data transfer are used in computer data communication: parallel and serial. Parallel transfers send all the bits at once over multiple wires. Serial transfers take the bits to be transferred and send them one after the other over a single wire. One type of serial interface, known as asynchronous serial, is commonly used to connect personal computers to other computers and to modems. In addition to the data to be sent, several other bits are included with each asynchronous serial byte to aide the transfer process. The serial data is physically sent over wires which conform to the RS-232 standard. This standard determines which wires and what voltage levels to use. In many circumstances, only the transmit and receive signals are necessary to use serial communication. If, on the other hand, a modem is involved, additional signals are often used to control the modem and to discover its current status.

Facilities for handling all these aspects of serial communication are available in the hardware and ROM BIOS of the IBM PC. Using these facilities, we have developed Term—a simple, low-data-rate terminal program. We used ROM BIOS routines to send data to the printer (parallel) port to develop a second version of the program that can optionally print as well as display the data coming from the serial port.

Exercises

1. Change TermPrint to accept command line parameters which specify (a) which serial port; (b) the baud rate; (c) the number of data bits; (d) the number of stop bits; and (e) the parity.

2. Change TermPrint to respond to the F3 key by asking the user for the communications parameters given in 1. This will allow him to change them on-the-fly.

3. Have the F5 key cause the program to ask for a file name, and then put all incoming characters into that file as well as on the display.

4. Have the F6 key get the current status of the serial port and display it in an easy to read format for the user.

5. Have the F4 key save the current configuration, as generated in 2. Change TermPrint to accept a file name with a configuration as an optional parameter. If no name is present, try a default name. If the default file is not present either, use a default set of parameters.

6. [advanced] Have alt-shift-‹letter› ask for a string of characters. Store the string associated with the ‹letter›. Have alt-‹letter› send the associated string out the

serial port, if any has been defined. Have the F7 and F8 keys store and retrieve a file of such ‹letter›/string combinations. (This is a macro facility.)

7. [very advanced] Find the definition of the XModem error-free file transfer protocol, which allows transmission of file over a serial line without errors (both the protocol and the definition are available on many BBSs and timesharing services). Have F9 implement an XModem file transmit, and F10 implement an XModem file receive.

If you finish all the exercises above, you will have a very complete communications program, with a function-key layout as follows.

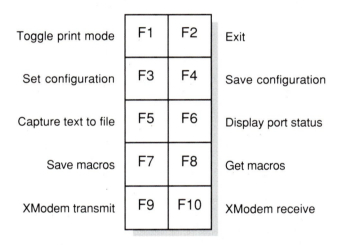

Figure 11-10. Final Function Key Layout

Listing 11-1. "term.c":

```
/*                       Terminal Emulator Program
*/

#define SERCONFIG 0x43   /* 300 baud, 8 bits, 1 stop bit, no parity. */

#define SERDRDY 0x100    /* Serial receiver data ready bit mask. */

#define TRUE 1
#define FALSE 0

/*      main()

        Function: Display data coming from COM1 on the screen, and send
        keystrokes from the keyboard out to COM1.

        Algorithm: Loop, waiting for data from either side to appear.
        Use keyChk to see if there's anything from the keyboard; if
        there is, send it using serSend. Use serRecv to check if
        there's anything from the serial port; if there is, display
        it using putTty.
*/

main()

{
        int ch; /* Character to transfer. */

        /* Initialize the port. */
        serInit(0,SERCONFIG);

        /* Main loop. */
        while (TRUE) {
                /* Check for keyboard input. */
                if (keyChk(&ch)) {
                        /* If yes, clear the character from the queue. */
                        keyRd();
                        /* Check for non-ASCII. */
                        if ((ch & 0xFF) == 0) {
                                break;
                        };
                        /* Send the character out the serial port. */
                        serSend(0,ch);
                };
                /* Anything available from the serial port? */
                if (serStat(0) & SERDRDY) {
                        /* If so, read it in. */
                        ch = serRecv(0);
                        /* And put it on the screen. */
                        putTty(0,ch,3);
                };
        };
}
```

Listing 11-2. "slib.asm":

```
;                    Serial Port ROM BIOS Interface Library

_TEXT     segment byte public 'CODE'        ; Place the code in the code segment
          assume  CS:_TEXT                  ; Assume the CS register points to it

; _serInit(port,config)
;
; Function: Initialize and configure serial port port (0 for COM1, 1 for
; COM2). See the main text of the chapter for details on the format of the
; config parameter.
;
; Algorithm: Call the ROM BIOS config function; int 14H, AH = 0.

          public  _serInit             ; Routine is available to other modules

          port = 4                     ; Offset from BP to parameter port
          config = 6                   ; Offset to parameter config

_serInit proc near                     ; NEAR type subroutine
          push    bp                   ; Save BP register
          mov     bp,sp                ; Set BP to SP; easier to get parameters
          mov     dx,[bp+port]         ; Set DX to the port number
          mov     al,[bp+config]       ; Set AL to the configuration
          mov     ah,0                 ; Set AH to 0 (configure port function)
          int     14H                  ; Call ROM BIOS serial port interrupt
          pop     bp                   ; Restore the BP register
          ret                          ; Return to calling program
_serInit endp                          ; End of subroutine

; _serSend(port,char)
;
; Function: Send the character char out over serial port port. Return the
; completion code/status.
;
; Algorithm: Call the ROM BIOS put char function; int 14H, AH = 1.

          public  _serSend             ; Routine is available to other modules

          port = 4                     ; Offset from BP to parameter port
          char = 6                     ; Offset to parameter char

_serSend proc near                     ; NEAR type subroutine
          push    bp                   ; Save BP register
          mov     bp,sp                ; Set BP to SP; easier to get parameters
          mov     dx,[bp+port]         ; Set DX to the port number
          mov     al,[bp+char]         ; Set AL to the character
          mov     ah,1                 ; Set AH to 1 (send char function)
          int     14H                  ; Call ROM BIOS serial port interrupt
          pop     bp                   ; Restore the BP register
          ret                          ; Return to calling program
_serSend endp                          ; End of subroutine
```

Listing 11-2. "slib.asm" *(cont.)*:

```asm
; _serRecv(port)
;
; Function: Wait for and receive a character from the serial port.
; Return the character in the low byte of the return value, and the
; status in the high byte.
;
; Algorithm: Call the ROM BIOS receive char function; int 14H, AH = 2.

        public  _serRecv         ; Routine is available to other modules

        port = 4                 ; Offset from BP to parameter port

_serRecv proc near               ; NEAR type subroutine
        push    bp               ; Save BP register
        mov     bp,sp            ; Set BP to SP; easier to get parameters
        mov     dx,[bp+port]     ; Set DX to the port number
        mov     ah,2             ; Set AH to 2 (receive char function)
        int     14H              ; Call ROM BIOS serial port interrupt
        pop     bp               ; Restore the BP register
        ret                      ; Return to calling program
_serRecv endp                    ; End of subroutine

; _serStat(port)
;
; Function: Return the status of the serial port specified.
;
; Algorithm: Call the ROM BIOS serial status function; int 14H, AH = 3.

        public  _serStat         ; Routine is available to other modules

        port = 4                 ; Offset from BP to parameter port

_serStat proc near               ; NEAR type subroutine
        push    bp               ; Save BP register
        mov     bp,sp            ; Set BP to SP; easier to get parameters
        mov     dx,[bp+port]     ; Set DX to the port number
        mov     ah,3             ; Set AH to 3 (serial status function)
        int     14H              ; Call ROM BIOS serial port interrupt
        pop     bp               ; Restore the BP register
        ret                      ; Return to calling program
_serStat endp                    ; End of subroutine

_TEXT   ends                     ; End of code segment

        end                      ; End of assembly code
```

Listing 11-3. "slib.h":

```c
/*              ROM BIOS Serial Port Interface Constants
*/
```

```c
/* Configuration constants -- the bit rate, parity, stop bits, and
    word length constants can be added together to form a configuration
    that can be passed to serInit.
```

Listing 11-3. "slib.h" *(cont.)*:

```
*/

/* Bit rates: */

#define B110 0x00        /* 110 bits/second. */
#define B150 0x20        /* 150 bits/second. */
#define B300 0x40        /* 300 bits/second. */
#define B600 0x60        /* 600 bits/second. */
#define B1200 0x80       /* 1200 bits/second. */
#define B2400 0xA0       /* 2400 bits/second. */
#define B4800 0xC0       /* 4800 bits/second. */
#define B9600 0xE0       /* 9600 bits/second. */

/* Parity: */

#define PNONE 0          /* No parity. */
#define PODD 8           /* Odd parity. */
#define PEVEN 0x18       /* Even parity. */

/* Stop bits: */

#define SB1 0            /* 1 stop bit. */
#define SB2 4            /* 2 stop bits. */

/* Data bits: */

#define DB7 2            /* 7 data bits. */
#define DB8 3            /* 8 data bits. */

/* Status bit masks -- these constants can be used to test bits in the
   line and modem status bytes.
*/

/* Line status: */

#define TIMEOUT 0x8000   /* Time-out. */
#define TSRE 0x4000      /* Transmit shift register empty. */
#define THRE 0x2000      /* Transmit holding register empty. */
#define BREAKDET 0x1000  /* Break detect. */
#define FRAMERR 0x800    /* Framing error. */
#define PARERR 0x400     /* Parity error. */
#define OVERERR 0x200    /* Overrun error. */
#define RCVDRDY 0x100    /* Receiver data ready. */

/* Modem status: */

#define RLSD 0x80        /* Receive line signal detect (carrier detect). */
#define RI 0x40          /* Ring indicator. */
#define DSR 0x20         /* Data set ready. */
#define CTS 0x10         /* Clear to send. */
#define DRLST 8          /* Delta receive line signal detect. */
#define TERD 4           /* Trailing edge ring detect. */
#define DDSR 2           /* Delta data set ready. */
#define DCTS 1           /* Delta clear to send. */
```

Listing 11-4. "termp.c":

```
/*                 Terminal Emulator Program with Printing
*/

#include "slib.h"

#define TRUE 1
#define FALSE 0

/*      main()

        Function: Display data coming from COM1 on the screen, and send
        keystrokes from the keyboard out to COM1. If F1 is pressed,
        toggle into print-also mode, where each input is also sent to
        the printer port.

        Algorithm: Loop, waiting for data from either side to appear.
        Use keyChk to see if there's anything from the keyboard; if
        there is, send it using serSend. Use serRecv to check if
        there's anything from the serial port; if there is, display
        it using putTty, and if we're in print mode, also print it
        using prtPrint.
*/

main()

{
        int ch;           /* Character to transfer. */
        int printOn;      /* TRUE if printing is toggled on. */

        /* Initialize the printer. */
        prtInit(0);
        printOn = FALSE;

        /* Initialize the serial port. */
        serInit(0,B1200+DB8+SB1+PNONE);

        /* Main loop. */
        while (TRUE) {
                /* Check for keyboard input. */
                if (keyChk(&ch)) {
                        /* If yes, clear the character from the queue. */
                        keyRd();
                        /* Check for non-ASCII. */
                        if ((ch & 0xFF) == 0) {
                                /* Check for F1 key. */
                                if (((ch>>8) & 0xFF) == 59)
                                        /* If F1, toggle print mode. */
                                        printOn = !printOn;
                                else break;
                        };
                        /* Send the character out the serial port. */
                        serSend(0,ch);
                };
                /* Anything available from the serial port? */
                if (serStat(0) & RCVDRDY) {
                        /* If so, read it in. */
```

Listing 11-4. "termp.c" *(cont.)*:

```
                        ch = serRecv(0);
                        /* And put it on the screen. */
                        putTty(0,ch,3);
                        /* If we're in print mode, print it as well. */
                        if (printOn) prtPrint(0,ch);
                };
        };
}
```

Listing 11-5. "plib.asm":

```
;                       Printer Port ROM BIOS Interface Library

_TEXT   segment byte public 'CODE'     ; Place the code in the code segment
        assume  CS:_TEXT               ; Assume the CS register points to it

; _prtInit(port)
;
; Function: Initialize the printer port specified. Returns the port status.
;
; Algorithm: Call the ROM BIOS printer init function; int 17H, AH = 0.

        public  _prtInit               ; Routine is available to other modules

        port = 4                       ; Offset from BP to parameter port

_prtInit proc near                     ; NEAR type subroutine
        push    bp                     ; Save BP register
        mov     bp,sp                  ; Set BP to SP; easier to get parameters
        mov     dx,[bp+port]           ; Set DX to the port number
        mov     ah,1                   ; Set AH to 1 (init port function)
        int     17H                    ; Call ROM BIOS printer port interrupt
        mov     al,ah                  ; Return status in AX
        xor     ah,ah                  ; With high byte zero
        pop     bp                     ; Restore the BP register
        ret                            ; Return to calling program
_prtInit endp                          ; End of subroutine

; _prtPrint(port,char)
;
; Function: Print the character char on port port. Return the port status.
;
; Algorithm: Call the ROM BIOS print char function; int 17H, AH = 0.

        public  _prtPrint              ; Routine is available to other modules

        port = 4                       ; Offset from BP to parameter port
        char = 6                       ; Offset to parameter char

_prtPrint proc near                    ; NEAR type subroutine
        push    bp                     ; Save BP register
        mov     bp,sp                  ; Set BP to SP; easier to get parameters
        mov     dx,[bp+port]           ; Set DX to the port number
        mov     al,[bp+char]           ; Set AL to the character
        mov     ah,0                   ; Set AH to 0 (print char function)
```

Listing 11-5. "plib.asm" *(cont.)*:

```
        int     17H             ; Call ROM BIOS printer port interrupt
        mov     al,ah           ; Return the status in AX
        xor     ah,ah           ; With the top byte zero
        pop     bp              ; Restore the BP register
        ret                     ; Return to calling program
_prtPrint endp                  ; End of subroutine

; _prtStat(port)
;
; Function: Return the status of the printer port specified.
;
; Algorithm: Call the ROM BIOS printer status function; int 17H, AH = 2.

        public  _prtStat        ; Routine is available to other modules

        port = 4                ; Offset from BP to parameter port

_prtStat proc near              ; NEAR type subroutine
        push    bp              ; Save BP register
        mov     bp,sp           ; Set BP to SP; easier to get parameters
        mov     dx,[bp+port]    ; Set DX to the port number
        mov     ah,2            ; Set AH to 2 (printer status function)
        int     17H             ; Call ROM BIOS printer port interrupt
        mov     al,ah           ; Return status in AX
        xor     ah,ah           ; With the top byte zero
        pop     bp              ; Restore the BP register
        ret                     ; Return to calling program
_prtStat endp                   ; End of subroutine

_TEXT   ends                    ; End of code segment

        end                     ; End of assembly code
```

Listing 11-6. "plib.h":

```
/*              ROM BIOS Printer Port Interface Constants
*/

/* Status bit masks -- these constants can be used to test bits in the
   printer status byte.
*/

#define NOTBUSY 0x80    /* Not busy. */
#define ACK 0x40        /* Acknowledge. */
#define NOPAPER 0x20    /* Out of paper. */
#define SELECTED 0x10   /* Selected. */
#define IOERROR 8       /* I/O error. */
#define PRTTIMEOUT 1    /* Time-out. */
```

Part III

Accessing the Hardware Directly

Chapter 12

How to Access the Hardware Directly

- Good and Bad of Writing Directly to Hardware

- Interacting with Hardware: Shared Memory, IN/OUT, Interrupts

- IBM PC Open Architecture Hardware Overview: PC vs. XT vs. AT

- Physical Address Space, I/O Address Space, Interrupts

- Accessing Memory Outside the Program Address Space: FAR Pointers

- Using the IN and OUT Instructions

- Four Step Process for Using Interrupts

In order for your program actually to do anything, it must make use of the hardware of the computer. This is true whatever your program does, however you write it, in whatever language, using whatever run-time library. First of all, the memory of the PC is used to store the program. Second, the processor interprets the instructions stored in memory. These two kinds of hardware utilization are the absolute minimum required to run a program in any kind of machine. But when the program outputs something to be displayed on the screen, it must also make use of the display adapter hardware, which contains its own memory together with hardware to take data stored in that memory and display it on the screen. When the program writes a block of data to a disk, it must use the disk controller hardware to instruct the disk to spin, the read/write head to move, and data to be transferred from memory onto the disk itself. And when the program prints something on the printer, it must transfer data to the printer interface, the data to be sent is converted to electrical signals on the wires in the printer cable. In short, whenever the PC executes a program, it uses the processor and memory hardware; whenever that program wants to effect anything outside the processor and memory, it must use other hardware as well.

Most of the time, the application program you've written doesn't need to interact directly with the hardware. The detailed work of interfacing to the bottom level hardware is handled by the ROM BIOS, MS-DOS, or a run-time library supplied with the compiler. It's generally a good thing, in fact, that the program isn't directly aware of the details of the hardware. The routines in the ROM BIOS, MS-DOS, and run-time libraries that handle the hardware interface protect the program from being tied to the details of the hardware being used. If the hardware is changed, the interface routines need to be changed, but changes are not also required in the entire set of application programs that have been written to use the hardware.

Sometimes there are good reasons for an application to access the hardware directly. The interface routines may not allow access to some capability that's available in the hardware, and is needed by the application. Or perhaps the general purpose interface routines are not as fast and efficient as less general, special purpose routines. If a given hardware feature is needed, or speed is important to the application, it may be worth bypassing the normal interface in favor of one that is application specific.

In this chapter, we will discuss the various ways that a program can directly control the hardware of the PC. The examples that follow will use these techniques, and will show the specific details of interacting with various parts of the hardware.

A program interacts with the hardware of the machine in three ways:

1. Shared memory. For some devices, a block of memory is shared between the processor and the attached hardware. This is particularly true of display memory, which can be simultaneously accessed by the processor and by the hardware which displays its contents on the screen.

2. Input/output (I/O) instructions. The IN and OUT instructions provide for communication between the processor and attached hardware. They read data from and write data to a hardware device. In a sense, they use a second address space, independent from the memory address space. Rather than memory bytes, this space contains I/O ports.

3. Hardware interrupts. The hardware can also "interrupt" the processor when a specific event happens or some condition changes. These interrupts are like the software interrupts discussed in an earlier chapter, but they are generated by the hardware and can occur at virtually any time while the program is executing.

IBM PC Hardware Overview

The IBM PC is called an "open architecture" machine. It is "open" both because more hardware can be added on by plugging additional cards into the hardware slots provided, and because IBM has published all the details of how to interface that additional hardware to the main IBM PC board. The parts of the PC hardware that are on the main board are always present, always available to the application program that's running. The parts of the PC hardware that are added on using the slots can vary—one PC may have a monochrome adapter and no serial interface, while another may have a color graphics adapter and two serial interfaces. And, of course, you may find even more exotic and unusual hardware, such as a speech synthesizer or mouse interface. This means that not every program will run on every IBM PC; many require specific hardware to be present in the machine. It also means that if at all possible, programs should be written to find out what hardware is present and to use it—this especially applies to display adapters.

Figure 12-1 shows the layout of the main board of the IBM PC:

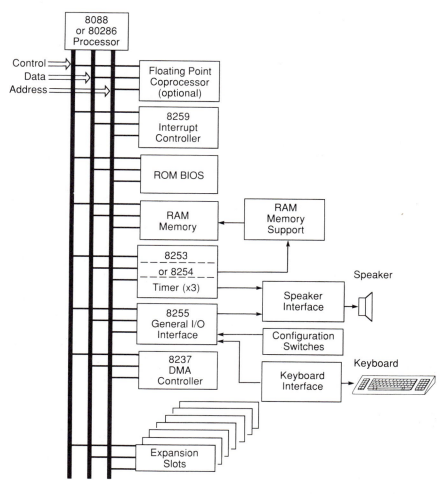

Figure 12-1. IBM PC System Board

The main board of the PC contains either an 8088 or an 80286 processor, a preset program in ROM (read-only memory) called the ROM BIOS, a block of RAM (random access memory), an interface to the keyboard, and a speaker. It also includes hardware to keep track of time, handle hardware interrupts efficiently, and interface to the add-on hardware in the slots. The add-on hardware interface also has the ability to transfer data to and from the slots while the processor is busy with other tasks—this is called direct memory access (DMA), since it goes directly from the I/O device to memory, bypassing the processor. The main board of the PC does not include any hardware to display data on a screen or to interface to a printer or serial port—but each of these facilities and more can be provided by add-on hardware installed in slots.

At this level there are very few differences between the IBM PC, IBM PC/XT, and IBM PC/AT. The PC and PC/XT differ only in the amount of RAM on the system board. The PC/AT differs in the amount of memory on the board, and it also uses a different timer, the 8254 rather than the 8253 (but these two devices are very similar). In addition, the AT has two 8259 interrupt controllers, as opposed to one for the PC and PC/XT, and it has two DMA controllers as well. When writing programs intended to run on any of the PC family machines, though, we intentionally avoid using these additional facilities. Another big difference between the PC or PC/XT and the PC/AT is the width of the data line connecting the processor and the attached devices: in the PC/AT it's twice as big. The AT can transfer data to the processor in 16-bit chunks, while the PC and PC/XT are limited to 8 bits at a time. This makes for a dramatic increase in processing speed, an increase made even larger by the faster clock rate of the processor.

The fact that the PC, PC/XT, and PC/AT are all so similar is a major advantage: it means that we can easily write programs that will run on any of these models. In fact, although the AT processor has capabilities beyond those available in the earlier models, these capabilities are seldom used, precisely because programs that use the extended features cannot run on the other models. This applies also to the available memory space: most applications limit themselves to the one megabyte available to both the 8088/8086 and the 80286 operating in "real mode." In this book, we will avoid the AT-specific features and concentrate on those aspects of the machines that are consistent across the entire family.

The following three sets of address assignments are fundamental to any complete description of the hardware of the IBM PC. The first is the physical address space usage—where the various ROM, RAM, and display memory components are to be found. The second is which I/O port addresses are used for which devices. And the third is which interrupt vectors are assigned to which purpose or device. These three sets of assignments include the memory and devices on the main board, but also cover other devices that can be added using the expansion slots.

The processor has a physical memory address space of 1M bytes, with addresses ranging from 0 to FFFFF (hex); however, it can access this large potential memory only in segments of 64K bytes, as discussed in Chapter Seven. (Note: The AT has the ability to address more than 1MB of memory, but not when operating in "real" mode, which limits it to that of the older 8088/8086 type processor.) Memory usage falls into five categories:

1. ROM BIOS. This is the preprogrammed set of routines that comes with every IBM PC, and that are present even before the machine is booted.

[Note: ROM Basic is also included in this class, but is not present on non-IBM machines.]

2. ROM BIOS extensions. This includes any additional ROM BIOS functions that are included on add-on cards in the expansion slots. The ROM BIOS extensions for the fixed disk and enhanced graphics adapter are the most common examples.

3. Main board RAM. This is the read/write memory on the main board of the IBM PC, up to 256K bytes of it (512K for the AT).

4. Expansion RAM. This is additional read/write memory provided on add-on cards plugged into the expansion slots.

5. Display memory. This is the memory shared by the display hardware. Data placed in this memory appears on the screen, either as characters or as dots.

Figure 12-2 shows the assigned usage of the physical memory addresses.

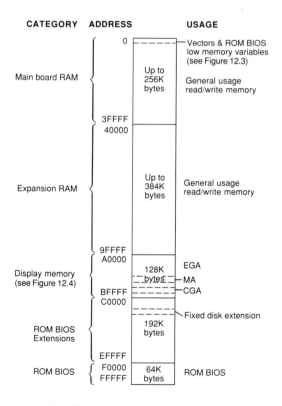

Figure 12-2. Memory Address Assignments

The low memory vectors and variables are shown in Figure 12-3.

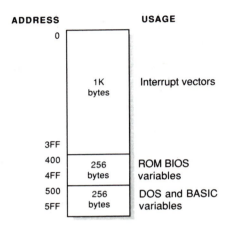

Figure 12-3. Low Memory

The display memory area is shown in Figure 12-4.

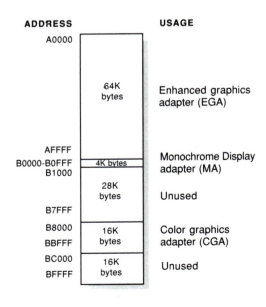

Figure 12-4. Display Memory

The I/O space of the processor is entirely separate from the memory space. The processor has 65,536 individual I/O port addresses, not all of which are used in the IBM PC. They are read and written using the IN and OUT instructions respectively. Most languages, including C, have run-time library routines to allow the program to use the IN and OUT instructions without requiring assembly language. The following I/O addresses are reserved by IBM for the following uses:

Address (hex)	Use
0-1F	8237 DMA controller
20-3F	8259 interrupt controller
40-5F	8253 or 8254 timer
60-6F	8255 parallel interface or 8042 keyboard interface and data latches (AT)
70-7F	Real-time clock (AT)
80-9F	DMA page register
A0-BF	NMI mask register or second 8259 interrupt controller (AT)
C0-DF	Second 8237 DMA controller (AT)
E0-EF	Reserved
FO-FF	Math co-processor (AT)
1F0-1F8	Fixed disk (AT)
200-20F	Game controller
210-217	Expansion unit
220-24F	Reserved
278-27F	Second parallel printer port
2F0-2F7	Reserved
2F8-2FF	Second serial port
300-31F	Prototype card
320-32F	Fixed disk
360-36F	Reserved
378-37F	Parallel printer port
380-38C	SDLC communications
380-389	Second bi-sync communications
3A0-3A9	Bi-sync communications
3B0-3BF	Monochrome display/printer adapter (MA)
3C0-3CF	Reserved
3D0-3DF	Color graphics adapter (CGA)
3E0-3E7	Reserved
3F0-3F7	Diskette
3F8-3FF	Serial port

Of these I/O ports, we will be concerned only with the serial communications interfaces, also known as the asynchronous communications interfaces, the timer, and the interrupt controller—addresses 2F8-2FF/3F8-3FF, 40-5F, and 20-3F (hex).

Only very advanced applications will need to directly interact with the other devices, since the ROM BIOS provides fully adequate interfaces for these other devices.

Interrupts are used for four purposes in the 8086/8088/80286. First, to let the hardware inform the processor that an event has occurred or a condition has changed. Second, to handle processor error conditions such as divide-by-zero. Third, to call the ROM BIOS and MS-DOS. And fourth, to store pointers to tables used by the ROM BIOS or MS-DOS. In Chapter Eight, we gave a general table of interrupt number assignments. The following table lists the interrupts used specifically for signalling events from the hardware to the processor, giving their number and address—note that the address of a vector can be derived from its number by multiplying the number by four:

Number (hex)	Vector Address (hex)	Usage
2	8-B	(NMI) Parity error
8	20-23	System timer (IRQ0)
9	24-27	Keyboard (IRQ1)
A	28-2B	Reserved (IRQ2)
B	2C-2F	Second serial port (IRQ3)
C	30-33	First serial port (IRQ4)
D	34-37	Fixed disk or second printer (AT) (IRQ5)
E	38-3B	Diskette (IRQ6)
F	3C-3F	Printer (IRQ7)
70	1C0-1C3	Real-time clock (AT) (IRQ8)
71	1C4-1C7	Reserved (AT) (IRQ9)
72	1C8-1CB	Reserved (AT) (IRQ10)
73	1CC-1CF	Reserved (AT) (IRQ11)
74	1D0-1D3	Reserved (AT) (IRQ12)
75	1D4-1D7	Reserved (AT) (IRQ13)
76	1D8-1DB	Fixed disk (AT) (IRQ14)
77	1DC-1DF	Reserved (AT) (IRQ15)

Of these interrupt vectors, we will be concerned only with the serial port and timer vectors.

Accessing Memory Outside the Program Address Space

We often want access to memory beyond that which directly belongs to the program. From our discussion of segments and groups in Chapter Five, recall that the processor deals with memory in 64K byte chunks, and that these chunks are known as "segments." Four segments are available at any given time: instructions are taken from the code segment, data is taken from the data segment, the stack is kept in the stack segment, and the extra segment is used to access data not in one of the other three segments.

The processor has four registers that contain the address of the start of each segment, divided by 16 — i.e., each register has an implied additional four zero bits which are added onto the right end of the address. When a program presents the processor with an address within a segment, the processor takes the appropriate segment register, multiplies it by 16, and adds the program supplied offset within the segment, thus producing the actual physical memory address. The four registers are CS, DS, SS, and ES, for the code segment, data segment, stack segment, and extra segment respectively. When a C program runs, using the small memory model, the DS and SS segment registers both point at the same place, the start of the DGROUP group, which contains all the constant and variable storage used by the program. The CS segment register points at the segment containing the code to be executed, called _TEXT.

It is possible to escape the bounds of the preset segment registers either in C or in assembly. In C, the program can use "far" pointers, which are 32 bits rather than 16 bits, and which can point to an address anywhere in the physical memory space. Using this technique, the C program can access any memory location it desires. In assembly, the most common technique is to save the contents of the ES register, then load it with the base address of the memory area the program wishes to access. Most instructions allow you to optionally use the ES rather than the normal DS segment register, and the STOS and MOVS instructions automatically use the ES register for the destination address. If it is changed by the assembly routine, it is important, of course, to restore the ES register to its original value before returning to the C program.

There are three reasons for wanting to access memory locations outside the program's normal address space. First, to access the display memory directly; second, to read or manipulate ROM BIOS variables in low memory; and third, to read and modify interrupt vectors, which are also stored in low memory.

The application can write directly to the display memory, bypassing the ROM BIOS. This can be used to speed up the display process, particularly with a graphic display, but also with character-only applications. The address of the display memory, its size, and the format of the data contained in it vary depending on which display adapter is used and which mode it's in. The program must be ready to adjust to the particular display in use at the moment.

Later, we will present a revised version of the ShowFile program which directly accesses the display memory to display characters on the screen. We will also present a general purpose graphics display interface routine, which we'll use to implement a Pong game. Both of these programs will execute much faster because they directly access the display memory.

The ROM BIOS keeps information about the current state of the system in low memory at addresses 400-4FF (hex). Some of this information is accessible only by direct access, and not by using ROM BIOS interrupt calls. A number of the low memory variables are concerned with the state of the display, including the mode it's in, how many columns of characters are on the screen in this mode, and where the current display page starts relative to the beginning of the display memory. Another large chunk of variables are used in connection with the disk drive interface; but we recommend you don't modify the way the ROM BIOS uses the disk — it's too easy to make mistakes and lose data. Finally, there are a number of variables associated with various other parts of the system, from the timer to the serial ports. The following table lists the most useful low memory variables:

Address	Contents
I/O Addresses	
400-407	I/O address of serial ports
400-401	COM1 address
402-403	COM2 address
404-407	Unused
408-40F	I/O address of printer ports
408-409	LPT1 address
40A-40B	LPT2 address
40C-40D	LPT3 address
40E-40F	Unused
Hardware Configuration	
410-411	Installed hardware flags (as returned from ROM BIOS interrupt 11 (hex))
413-414	Memory size in K bytes
Keyboard Data	
417	Shift state flags (as returned from ROM BIOS interrupt 16 (hex), AH = 2)
418	Second byte of shift state flags (see Figure 12-5)
419	Storage for alternate keypad entry
41A-43D	Keyboard type-ahead buffer and control information
Diskette Data	
43E-448	Diskette drive control information
Video Display Data	
449-466	See Chapter 13 for details of this area.
POST Data	
467-46B	Power-On-Self-Test data area

Address *(cont.)*	Contents

Timer Data

46C-46D	Low word of timer count (incremented 18.2 time every second, reset to zero when it reached midnight)
46E-46F	High word of timer count
470	Timer has passed midnight since last read

System Data

47	Bit 7 is set to 1 when a keyboard break occurs
472-473	Set to 1234 (hex) during keyboard reboot

Fixed Disk Data

474-477	Used by the fixed disk ROM BIOS extension

Port Time-outs

478-47B	Printer port time-outs: how long to try before timing out the I/O request
478	LPT1 time-out
479	LPT2 time-out
47A	LPT3 time-out
47B	Unused
47C-47F	Serial port time-outs: how long to try before timing out the I/O request
47C	COM1 time-out
47D	COM2 time-out
47E-47F	Unused

Additional Keyboard Data

480-481	Start of type-ahead buffer
482-483	End of type-ahead buffer

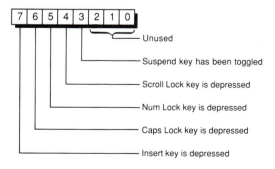

Figure 12-5. Second Byte of Shift Flags (Location 418)

The interrupt vectors are also stored in low memory. If the program wishes to use a device's interrupts, or to change the operation of existing interrupts, it must first change the value of the appropriate interrupt vector. Each vector is composed of two words: the first word is the new instruction pointer (IP); the second word is the new code segment register (CS) value. Figure 12-6 illustrates this arrangement.

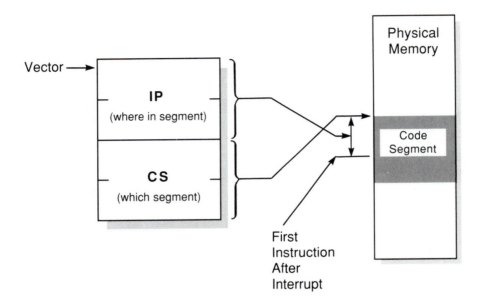

Figure 12-6. Interrupt Vector Format

When the interrupt occurs, the processor's instruction pointer (IP), code segment register (CS), and flags are pushed onto the stack, and the new IP and CS are loaded from the vector. A flag is also set in the processor FLAGS register that disables further interrupts. Execution then begins at offset IP in segment CS, which should be the interrupt service routine for this interrupt. When the service routine is finished, it executes an IRET instruction, which pops the old FLAGS, IP, and CS off the stack and back into the appropriate registers. By restoring the old flag register, the old state of the processor interrupt enable flag is also restored, presumably reenabling interrupts. Assuming that the interrupt service routine has been careful not to change any of the other registers without first saving and later restoring them, the original program then continues execution without ever being aware that it was interrupted. This process is illustrated in Figure 12-7 which shows the state of the registers and stack before, during, and after the interrupt.

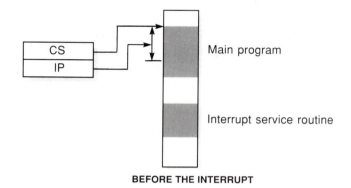

BEFORE THE INTERRUPT

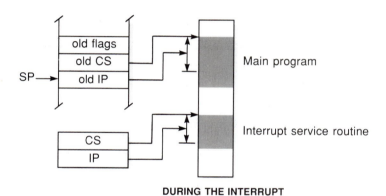

DURING THE INTERRUPT

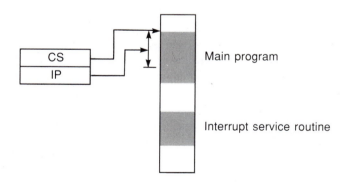

AFTER THE INTERRUPT

Figure 12-7. Interrupt Service

Using the IN and OUT Instructions

The IN and OUT instructions transfer data between the processor and the I/O devices. In one sense, the I/O ports form a separate address space from that of the main memory space. These ports can be accessed only by using the IN and OUT instructions. While the main address space tends to have large chunks of memory set aside for each separate function or device, the I/O space is broken into much smaller chunks. Hardware devices seldom use more than 16 addresses, and most of the time the number is more like 3 or 4. Each port allows access to one byte of data in the attached hardware device. These bytes are often called "registers." Every device has a different set of registers, in a different layout, with different bit assignments. It is difficult to generalize very much about what I/O devices will look like.

With today's technology, I/O devices are generally implemented using VLSI (very large scale integration) chips. For example, the IBM PC uses the following VLSI chips on the main board and some common add-on boards:

Chip	Function
8088 or 80286	Processor
8259	Interrupt controller
8253 or 8254	Timer
8255	General input/output for keyboard, speaker, and configuration switch
8237	DMA controller
MC6845	Graphics display controller (used in both the monochrome and color graphics adapter)
8250	Serial interface (for serial ports)

In order to understand the operation of the IBM PC hardware fully, you need copies of the technical reference manuals for all the hardware being used, from each hardware manufacturer—usually IBM. These will include hardware schematics showing how the various component devices are connected. You'll also need the technical reference manual for each of the component chips, which may be included with the documentation of the hardware, but can always be obtained from the manufacturer of the chip. All of the chips listed above, except the MC6845, are made by Intel; the MC6845 is made by Motorola.

Fortunately, most IBM PC programmers don't need to wade through and understand all of the information in every manual. Generally, you will find that the important part of documentation can be broken down to a few addresses and descriptions of how those addresses are used. In addition, the ROM BIOS can usually handle the details of setting up the chips, and you need concentrate only on the one or two functions we want to implement differently. We will supply some of the details of how the serial port, timer, and interrupt controller chips operate; but mostly, we'll let the ROM BIOS handle the dirty work—that's what it's there for.

Using Interrupts

When the machine is first turned on, all interrupts are disabled and they remain disabled until explicitly enabled by the software. If they weren't disabled, they could cause the program to branch off to an interrupt vector before the program was ready and perhaps even before the interrupt vector was initialized to point at a meaningful interrupt service routine. This would cause the machine to execute random code and crash. Even after the machine has been booted and MS-DOS is running, few interrupts are used. The software interrupts, of course, are used to call the ROM BIOS and MS-DOS, and the processor interrupts occur in cases like divide-by-zero. But the only hardware interrupt that happens routinely is the timer interrupt. An application program, however, can use other interrupts as well.

Interrupts originate in attached I/O devices and eventually reach the processor, where they cause it to execute an interrupt service routine. But before they can get to the processor, a series of gates must be opened that otherwise protect the processor from unexpected interrupts. Some parts of the path that an interrupt takes vary from device to device, but a general picture is given in Figure 12-8:

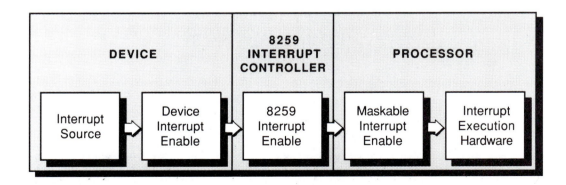

Figure 12-8. Interrupt Enables

The interrupt request starts in the device. Before it can get out, though, it must make its way past the device interrupt enable. The device interrupt enable varies from device to device, and sometimes there's even more than one enable in the device. Once past this point, the interrupt request must get through the 8259 interrupt controller. The 8259 controls and coordinates interrupts coming from all the different devices in the PC. It acts as an intermediary between the processor and the devices. We will discuss the 8259 in some detail later. Finally, the request must get past the processor's own interrupt enable, which is capable of disabling all maskable hardware interrupts, IRQ0-IRQ7 (IRQ0-IRQ15 on the AT). The processor's enable cannot disable the non-maskable interrupt, which takes its name from exactly that fact, that the processor cannot mask it out. This interrupt occurs when there's a memory parity error. Maskable interrupts are enabled when the processor interrupt flag (IF) is set to 1. Therefore, the CLI (clear IF) instruction disables maskable interrupts, and the STI (set IF) instruction enables them.

Using an interrupt is a four-step process:

1. Initialize the interrupt vector to point at the appropriate interrupt service routine.

2. Enable interrupts in the hardware, both at the device itself, and in the 8259 interrupt controller chip—the processor interrupt enable is normally left enabled all the time, except while actually servicing an interrupt.

3. When the interrupt(s) occur, process them in the interrupt service routine.

4. After the application is finished, disable interrupts in the hardware and restore the original interrupt vector.

The format of the interrupt vector and its location in low memory was discussed earlier. The following assembly language code can be used to set the vector:

```
_TEXT     segment byte public 'CODE'

          vector = address of interrupt vector to be set

          .
          .
          .

          push    es                      ; Save ES
          xor     ax,ax                   ; ES = 0
          mov     es,ax
          mov     ax,OFFSET intServ       ; AX = address of routine
          mov     es:vector,ax            ; Set vector IP value
          mov     ax,_TEXT                ; AX = segment address
          mov     es:vector+2,ax          ; Set vector CS value
          pop     es                      ; Restore ES
```

(listing continued)

```
                    .
                    .
                    .
    intServ proc near                       ; The service routine
                    .
                    .
                    .
            iret                            ; Return from interrupt
    intServ endp

    _TEXT   ends

            end
```

Turning on interrupts involves two tasks. First, the hardware device which is going to generate the interrupt must be initialized and its interrupts enabled. How this is done, and in fact, what interrupt(s) the device is capable of generating, varies from device to device. Generally, interrupts are available to signal when new data has arrived, when old data has left, and when some significant change has occurred in the state of the device or the external world. Second, the 8259 interrupt controller must be enabled for the particular type of interrupt the program is expecting.

The 8259 interrupt controller allows up to 8 devices to be attached and generate interrupts—on the AT, two 8259s allow up to 15 devices. The 8259 prioritizes the interrupts, and informs the processor when one has occurred. When it finishes processing, the processor must notify the interrupt controller, so that it will accept the next interrupt. The first 8 hardware interrupts that are handled by the 8259 are numbers 8-F (hex), from the timer, keyboard, first and second serial ports, fixed disk, diskette, and printer (one is reserved). They are referred to as IRQ0-IRQ7. On the AT, another set of interrupts, numbers 70-77 (hex) are handled by a second 8259; these are known as IRQ8-IRQ15. The 8259 is a complex device —we could easily spend a chapter or two explaining its full capabilities. Fortunately, the ROM BIOS takes care of the 8259's most complex operations. We need to know only how to enable and disable one of the interrupts, and how to acknowledge when we're done processing it. Everything else is set up for us by the ROM BIOS. We will concentrate on the first 8259, because it is present in the entire IBM PC family, and because all the interrupts we will want to manipulate are on that 8259.

We communicate with the first 8259 using I/O addresses 20-21 (hex). Within the 8259 is a register that determines which interrupts can occur. It is called the interrupt mask register. Each bit in the register corresponds to one of the eight interrupts—bit 0 for IRQ0, bit 1 for IRQ1,..., bit 7 for IRQ7. If the bit is set to 0, the interrupt is enabled; if the bit is set to 1, the interrupt is disabled. This register can be read by doing an IN operation from I/O address 21 (hex). It can then be rewritten by doing an OUT instruction to the same address. It is important, however, that none of the other interrupt mask bits be changed, since doing so could either disable an interrupt that was in use or enable an interrupt that the PC is not prepared to handle. The way to enable an interrupt, therefore, is to read the mask register, zero the one bit we're interested in, then write the new value. To disable an interrupt, the same I/O address is read (using IN), the appropriate bit is set to one, and the mask value is then written (using OUT). The following code illustrates this, using IRQ0, the timer interrupt:

```
        .
        .
        .

; Enable interrupt:

        in      al,21H          ; Read the mask register
        and     al,0FEH         ; Zero the IRQ0 mask bit
        out     21H,al          ; Output the result

        .
        .
        .

; Disable interrupt:

        in      al,21H          ; Read in the old mask value
        or      al,1            ; Set the IRQ0 bit
        out     21H,al          ; Write it back out

        .
        .
        .
```

In order to acknowledge that we've finished with the interrupt, we must write a special command to the interrupt controller. If we don't do this, it will continue to present the current interrupt and never allow subsequent interrupts to occur. This command is just one of many commands that can be sent to the 8259, but it's the only one we need to know to use interrupts; the rest of the commands are used by the ROM BIOS to initialize and control the 8259. This interrupt acknowledge command, also known as "end of interrupt" or EOI, is invoked by sending 20 (hex) to I/O port 20 (hex):

```
        .
        .
        .

; Acknowledge interrupt:

        mov     al,20H          ; Output 20H to port 20H
```

(listing continued)

```
        out       20H,al

        .
        .
        .
```

The last step in using interrupts is to turn them off before the program finishes. This is extremely important! If the interrupts are not turned off, one may occur while the MS-DOS command interpreter or the next application is running. This would cause the processor to branch off to the vector you set up, which will generally point at a totally meaningless location, the new application having been loaded over your interrupt service routine. This will, of course, cause the machine to crash. But it will not necessarily crash while your application is running; rather, it will crash when some other program is running. This can hide the fact that there is a bug in your program and can cause no end of confusion and lost time and work. So it's *very* important to remember to turn the interrupts off when you're finished. In addition, it's a good idea to keep the original interrupt vector contents and restore it when you're done. It's sort of like cleaning up after yourself, leaving the place in the same shape you found it for the next person.

Now you know enough to write an interrupt service routine. We will present an example in Chapter Fifteen.

Summary

We have described how to interact with the low level hardware of the IBM PC. Normally, application programs are separated from this level of the machine by the ROM BIOS, MS-DOS, and various run-time libraries. Sometimes, though, the program needs to access this level of the system, either because it cannot accomplish its purpose any other way, or because it can accomplish it much more efficiently in this way. There are three main areas of interactions with the hardware. The first is the main address space, which allows access to the read/write memory of the machine, including a number of variables maintained by the ROM BIOS in low memory and the interrupt vectors, also stored in low memory; and to the display memory supplied with the video display cards. The second is the I/O instructions IN and OUT, which allow access to the registers within the hardware devices. These are the primary means of controlling devices from the processor. And the third is interrupts, which are used to allow an attached device to signal the processor that some event has occurred.

We will be using this information to implement a number of applications, including ones that display a file using direct access to the character display memory; play the game Pong by directly modifying the graphics display memory; act as a terminal emulator using interrupts to inform the processor when a new character has arrived; and generate noise by directly controlling the sound generation hardware.

Exercises

1. If you have access to the IBM technical reference material, read the parts of it that cover the material discussed in this chapter.

2. Look through the ROM BIOS listing of the IBM Technical Reference Manual. See how the BIOS manipulates the hardware devices. Particularly pay attention to how the timer interrupts are set up and used.

Chapter 13

Direct Access Screen I/O: *ShowFile II*

- Revisited ShowFile Writing Directly to the Screen

- Display Memory: CGA and EGA Addressing

- Low Memory Display Information

- Improved Assembly Language scrPuts Function

- 50% Speed Improvement Over ROM BIOS Approach

I

n Chapter Eight, we presented the ShowFile program, which shows
a text file on the display. We discussed three different ways of accessing the display:
using plain vanilla character output, using ANSI.SYS, and using ROM BIOS calls.
In this chapter, we will present a fourth and final means of displaying text: direct
access to the display memory. Direct display access is the fastest possible way to
get information from the program to the display. We will develop a replacement
for the scrPuts function which, instead of calling the ROM BIOS to display the
characters, places the characters directly in the display buffer. As we create this
routine, we will take a closer look at the way the display hardware operates.

Display Memory

The display memory is part of the display adapter being used. It contains the data,
either text or graphics, to be displayed on the screen. In addition to being accessed
by the hardware driving the display, it is also accessible to the PC's processor, just
like regular RAM. This means that programs can be written to read and write the
contents of the display directly, which is potentially far more efficient than using
the ROM BIOS to do so. But, as always, there is a trade-off: programs that access
the hardware directly are less portable than programs that use the ROM BIOS. In
this case, a program that directly accesses the display memory will not operate
properly on a machine with a non-standard display adapter.

Depending on which adapter is being used and which mode it's in, the
information in the display memory can correspond to dots on the screen (graphics
mode) or to characters on the screen (text mode). The different adapters and modes
also select the number of dots or characters on the screen, and the number of colors
possible for each dot. This chapter will discuss the text modes of the monochrome
adapter (MA) and the color graphics adapter (CGA). The next chapter will discuss
the graphics modes of the CGA. The EGA can also operate in each of these modes,
as well as the higher resolution modes covered in Chapter Ten.

In the text display modes of the CGA (modes 0-3), the display is composed of
an array of text characters. There are always 25 rows, but there can be either 40

or 80 columns, and color may be enabled or disabled. The CGA also has multiple "pages" of text display, only one of which is actually displayed at any given moment. It is possible to write to one of the pages not being displayed, then to make that the current display, giving the illusion of instantaneous updates. When 40 columns are displayed, there are eight pages; when 80 columns are displayed, there are four pages. The monochrome adapter, on the other hand, has only one mode: 25 rows, 80 columns, black and white. And it has only one page—the one being displayed.

For each character position on the display, there are two bytes in the display memory. The first one selects the character to be displayed, and the second selects the attributes it will have. Figure 13-1 shows the meaning of the bits in the attribute byte:

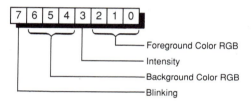

Figure 13-1. The Attribute Byte

The blink bit causes the character to flash on and off. The color bits, for both foreground and background, are called R, G, and B, in that order, since they select red (R), green (G), and blue (B) color components used with the color graphics adapter. The following table shows the colors produced by various combinations of R, G, B, and the intensity bit:

Color RGB	Intensity	Color produced
000	0	Black
001	0	Blue
010	0	Green
011	0	Cyan
100	0	Red
101	0	Magenta
110	0	Brown
111	0	White
000	1	Gray
001	1	Light Blue
010	1	Light Green
011	1	Light Cyan
100	1	Light Red
101	1	Light Magenta
110	1	Yellow
111	1	High Intensity White

The same format is used for both the CGA and the MA. The blink and intensity bits work exactly the same way. With the MA, however, only four foreground/background color combinations are meaningful:

Background RGB	Foreground RGB	Meaning
000	000	Non-display (black on black)
000	001	Underline
000	111	Normal (white on black)
111	000	Reverse (black on white)

The display memory for the CGA starts at physical memory location B8000 (hex). The first two bytes of the display memory correspond to the character and attributes for the first character position of the first display page (see Figure 13-2). The second pair of bytes corresponds to the second character position, etc. The pair of bytes at B809E and B809F corresponds to the last character position on the first line — 1st row, 80th column. The first character and attribute of the second line are stored at B80A0 and B80A1. Characters and attributes are stored in that order: character first, then attribute.

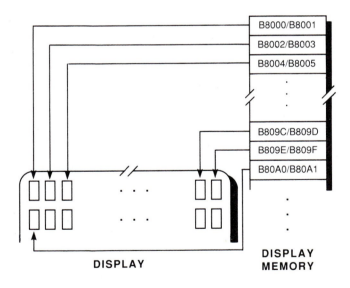

Figure 13-2. CGA Memory Layout

The starting address of subsequent pages can be found by dividing the number of bytes in the display memory by the number of current pages. The CGA has either four or eight pages, so each one has either 2K or 4K bytes. The following table lists the starting address of each of the pages in the CGA:

Page #	40 Column Starting Address	80 Column Starting Address
0	B8000	B8000
1	B8800	B9000
2	B9000	BA000
3	B9800	BB000
4	BA000	None
5	BA800	None
6	BB000	None
7	BB800	None

The monochrome adapter has the same display memory arrangement of characters and attributes, but it has only one page, starting at B0000.

Display Information from Low Memory

There are also several bytes of useful information about the display available in low memory locations maintained by the ROM BIOS. These are generally concerned with the current state of the display, the mode it's in, the page being displayed, etc. The following table lists these locations and describes their contents:

Address	Size (in bytes)	Contents
449	1	Current display mode (can also be obtained with ROM BIOS video call 15)
44A	2	Number of screen columns (40 or 80)
44C	2	Size in bytes of one page of display memory
44E	2	Offset from start of display memory to the start of the current display page
450	16	Cursor position for each page (up to eight byte pairs)
460	2	Current cursor mode setting (can also be obtained with ROM BIOS video call 3)
462	1	Number of currently active page (can also be obtained with BIOS video call 15)
463	2	Port address of active display card (this is only used for very advanced access to the display)
465	1	Current value of the hardware mode select register (not the same as the current display mode; used for advanced access to the display)
466	1	Current color palette setting

Many of these values could be computed, given some basic information such as the type of display and the mode that it's in. By using these "pre-computed" values, however, we can often greatly simplify many tasks involving the display. For example, in order to find the location in memory of a particular character on the display, we must multiply the character's row number by the number of columns in each row (40 or 80). The number of columns could be obtained by table look-up from the display mode, but it's much simpler to just read the value from location 44A.

The New scrPuts Function

In order to change ShowFile to access the display memory directly, we will use an assembly language function. The simplest function, from ShowFile's point of view, would be an exact copy of the scrPuts function, which called the ROM BIOS TTY-style write function. This is a natural function for ShowFile to use, as we explained in Chapter Eight; and it will let us implement the display memory direct access version of ShowFile without making any changes at all to the C code in show.c. All changes will be made in the assembly language library routine scrPuts.

Listing 13-1 shows the new scrPuts function. First, note that there is more involved than simply copying the characters to the display. We must also catch certain characters with special meanings and interpret them. In addition to this, we want to leave the display in good order, placing the cursor position at the end of the newly written characters, just as the original scrPuts did. Then other programs can intermix calls to the new scrPuts and to the ROM BIOS in whatever way they like.

The program has three main parts. The first includes preparing to process the input string, saving the registers which will be modified, getting the current cursor position, and finding the location of the display and the offset within it where we'll be placing the characters. The second is the main loop, which reads and processes the input string, copying the characters and handling the special ones. And the third involves cleaning up, which includes resetting the cursor position and restoring the registers.

A ROM BIOS call is used to get the active display page and the current mode. We could have directly accessed these values in low memory, as we will do later for other values, but here it's more convenient to make one BIOS call than it is to set up a segment register to point to low memory. Next, by checking the mode, we can decide where the display memory is located: modes 0-6 are used by the CGA, while mode 7 is used only by the MA. We will use the ES segment register to access this memory area. All display memory references, therefore, will be relative to the first byte of the display memory. A second ROM BIOS call provides the initial cursor position.

The next step is to find the offset within the display memory location of the current cursor position. This is done by multiplying the row number by the number of columns per screen line (a number available from low memory); adding in the cursor column number; then multiplying by 2 since each display character occupies two bytes in display memory. This code to calculate the display memory position from the cursor row and column will be used later as well.

The main loop then cycles through each byte in the input string, until a zero byte (end-of-string) is reached. Each byte is checked for the special cases of carriage return (hex 0D) or line feed (hex 0A). With a carriage return, the current column number is zeroed, the cursor is placed in the first column of the line; and the code to recalculate the display memory address from the row and column number is invoked. With a line feed, the cursor position is changed to the same column of the next row, and the display memory offset is recalculated. If it doesn't match one of those, but is a control character, it's discarded. It's also discarded if it's a normal, displayable character but we're past the last column of the display. And finally, if it's a normal, displayable character and it's on the screen, it's displayed and the cursor column is incremented. Note that we leave the attribute byte untouched when we write the new character.

After the string is exhausted, the cursor position is reset to its new position using a ROM BIOS call. Then the registers are restored to their previous values and the function exits.

This new scrPuts function is not a perfect copy of the ROM BIOS TTY-style output function. It does not handle the "bell" or backspace control characters. Even more importantly, it will not scroll the display when it reaches the bottom. None of these functions are needed for the ShowFile program, but they are essential for a truly complete replacement for the scrPuts function. Adding the rest of this functionality is left as an exercise for the reader.

ShowFile Revisited

To produce the new version of ShowFile we need only replace the old assembly language scrPuts with the new one and then relink the program. If we run the program with calibration enabled, we can compare the performance to the other approaches in Chapter Eight. The following table shows the times for all of the techniques we've developed:

Version	Time for 20 Screens	Time for 1 Screen (computed)
VANILLA	64 seconds	3.2
ANSI	44 seconds	2.2
ROMBIOS	31 seconds	1.5
DIRECT	16 seconds	0.8

The direct display access approach is four times faster than the original, vanilla approach! And it's almost twice as fast as using the ROM BIOS. It may be possible to optimize the scrPuts function even further, but there is no better general approach: if you can't achieve the speed you need using direct access, you can't achieve it at all in software.

The disadvantage of this approach to updating the display is that it's very specific to the hardware used—even though we did make it independent of whether the MA or CGA is used; or the EGA in MA or CGA emulation mode. As we explained in an earlier chapter, the closer you get to the hardware, the more specific the code becomes to the hardware being used, and the less likely it is to work with new hardware. Because of the enhanced speed, however, a great number of programs do directly access the display memory just the way that we have done here.

Summary

A fourth means of getting data from the program to the display has been presented: going directly to the display memory of the display adapter. This is definitely the fastest of the four ways to display text. It is also the most specific to the hardware being used. We have developed a new version of the function scrPuts, which provides much of the functionality that the old, ROM BIOS based scrPuts provided, but which uses direct access to the display memory to display characters. Using this replacement function, it is possible to change the display access technique without making any changes at all to show.c. The result is a much faster version of ShowFile—twice as fast as the previous best version and almost four times as fast as the original.

This ability to change the implementation of one part of the program—the display access—without having to change any other parts is a result of making the program modular. Modular programming is not just a matter of breaking the program into chunks; it also means carefully choosing the lines along which those breaks are made. The scrPuts function is a good example of a separate module: it has a simple interface to the rest of the program, it's a self-contained function, and it's general enough to be used by other programs in the future.

Exercises

1. Change scrPuts to accept a second parameter, specifying the attributes for each character written to the display.

2. Change ShowFile to make use of the new facility provided in Step 1.

3. Change ShowFile to find the file size from MS-DOS. Display the total size of

the file and the percentage of the way through it of the line at the top of the display.

4. [advanced] Change ShowFile to write to a different display page and then switch the display. Note that the monochrome adapter is now a special case, since it has only one page.

5. [advanced] Add bell, backspace, and scroll processing to the scrPuts function, as described in the text of this chapter. The scroll processing can be implemented using either the ROM BIOS scroll up function or with the MOVS instruction of the processor. Implement it each way and compare the results.

Listing 13-1. "scrPuts.asm":

```
;               Video_Display Library (part 5)

_TEXT     segment byte public 'CODE'        ; Place the code in the code segment
          assume CS:_TEXT                   ; Assume the CS register points to it

; _scrPuts(s)
;
; Function: Do a TTY style write of the null-terminated string pointed
; to by s.
;
; Algorithm: Directly write the characters to the display, then update
; the cursor to the end of the string written.
;
; Comments: This function does not implement full TTY style output; most
; importantly, it will not scroll the display when the end is reached.

          public  _scrPuts               ; Routine is available to other modules

          s = 4                          ; The offset to the s parameter

_scrPuts proc near                       ; NEAR type subroutine
          push    bp                     ; Save the BP register
          mov     bp,sp                  ; Set BP to SP, so we can access the parameters
          push    di                     ; Save the DI register
          push    si                     ; Save the SI register
          push    es                     ; Save the ES register
          mov     ah,15                  ; Get mode & active page number by calling
          int     10H                    ;   the ROM BIOS
          mov     cx,0B000H              ; Assume monochrome adapter base address
          cmp     al,7                   ; Check it by checking the display mode
          je      setma                  ; If it is monochrome, branch
          mov     cx,0B800H              ; Otherwise, set the base address to CGA
setma:    mov     es,cx                  ; ES = adapter base address
          mov     si,[bp+s]              ; SI = start of string to write
          mov     ah,3                   ; Get cursor position into DH/DL by calling
          int     10H                    ;   the ROM BIOS
;
; Calculate the character position offset:
;
calcCh:   push    es                     ; Save display memory ES
          xor     ax,ax                  ; Point ES to low memory (i.e., zero it)
          mov     es,ax
          mov     al,dh                  ; AL = row of cursor
          mov     bl,es:44AH             ; BL = screen width in characters
          mul     bl                     ; AX = row # times columns per row
          mov     cl,dl                  ; CX = column of cursor
          xor     ch,ch
          add     ax,cx                  ; Add the column number to AX
          shl     ax,1                   ; Adjust for char/attribute (multiply by 2)
          add     ax,es:44EH             ; Add in the page start address (from low mem)
          mov     di,ax                  ; Point DI at next display byte
          pop     es                     ; Restore ES to the screen memory base
;
; Main character copying loop:
;
loop:     lods    byte ptr [si]          ; Get the next character in the string
```

Listing 13-1. "scrPuts.asm" *(cont.)*:

```
            or      al,al               ; Check for end-of-string
            jz      exit                ; If end-of-string, exit
            cmp     al,0DH              ; Check for carriage return
            jne     notCR               ; If not carriage return, branch
            xor     dl,dl               ; Go to the first column, this line
            jmp     calcCh              ; Go recalc display pointer
notCR:      cmp     al,0AH              ; Check for line feed
            jne     notLF               ; If not line feed, branch
            inc     dh                  ; Go to the next line, this column
            jmp     calcCh              ; Go recalc display pointer
notLF:      cmp     al,' '              ; Check for other control characters
            jl      loop                ; If it is a control character, skip it
            cmp     dl,bl               ; Are we off the right edge of the screen?
            je      loop                ; If yes, don't display this one
            stos    byte ptr es:[di];   Store the character into display memory
            inc     di                  ; Skip over display attribute
            inc     dl                  ; Next column
            jmp     loop                ; Go do the next one

exit:       mov     ah,2                ; Set the new cursor position by calling
            int     10H                 ;   the ROM BIOS
            pop     es                  ; Restore the ES register
            pop     si                  ; Restore the SI register
            pop     di                  ; Restore the DI register
            pop     bp                  ; Restore the BP register
            ret                         ; Return to calling program
_scrPuts    endp                        ; End of subroutine

_TEXT       ends                        ; End of code segment
            end                         ; End of assembly code
```

Chapter 14

High Speed Object Animation: *Pong*

I n this chapter, we will develop a Pong game for the color graphics adapter (CGA). But even if you're not interested in games, keep reading. Along the way, we will introduce a very powerful routine for drawing graphics on the screen. This routine will be useful any time you want to manipulate the graphics display, for whatever application. In fact, the Pong program itself will be fairly simple once we have the display routine developed. The graphic routine will be implemented in assembly language and will directly manipulate the graphic display memory. Consequently, it will be very fast.

The game of Pong looks like the display in Figure 14-1. The ball moves just like a normal, real-world ball, bouncing off the wall or paddle. The paddle can be moved up and down by the player, using the up and down arrow keys. The object of the game is to not let the ball get past the paddle and off the screen. This version of the program will not keep track of how many times the user lets the ball get by, but score-keeping is an obvious extension for the reader to add.

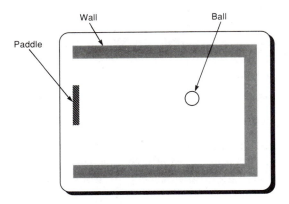

Figure 14-1. Pong

A program that implements Pong must do the following:

- Watch the keyboard for user commands to move the paddle or exit the program.
- Simulate the motion of the ball.
- Update the display to reflect the changes due to the two activities above.

Of these three, the third step is the most technically challenging. It is worth spending some time to develop a general routine to handle the graphics display in a powerful and efficient manner. This routine will be useful whenever we are manipulating a graphics display. We will develop it first, and then use it in the Pong program. Because this is going to be a widely used routine, and because manipulating a graphics display is a very processor-intensive and time-consuming process, we will develop the routine in assembly language. We will, of course, take care to make the routine modular and general enough so that it can be used over and over again without having to be rewritten. Thus the development overhead needed to implement the routine in assembly rather than C will be incurred only once; but the efficiency benefits of using assembly language will be reaped many times.

Display Memory

Before we can discuss how to manipulate the display, we need to talk about how the display works, particularly the display memory. In our previous uses of the display, we've approached it as an abstract array of characters or dots. The details of how the display is actually implemented and manipulated from the processor have been left to the ROM BIOS. But in order to attain our current goals, we now need to deal directly with the graphics adapter.

The color graphics adapter (CGA) hardware takes bits from the display memory and displays them on the screen. Depending upon the display mode, more than one bit may be used to specify the color of one dot on the display. In order to keep things simple, we will discuss mode 6, which is 640x200 black and white dots, one bit per dot. Then we'll extend this to the use of color, with more than one bit per dot.

The display memory is accessible directly from the processor, allowing the processor to efficiently modify the picture on the display. The display memory for the CGA is located at physical memory location B8000 (hex). (Note that the monochrome adapter is at a different location, B0000.) When in mode 6, the highest order bit of the first byte at B8000 is displayed on the screen as the dot at the upper-left corner. If the bit is 1, the dot is white; if the bit is 0, the dot is black. The next highest bit is the next dot, and so on. This arrangement is shown in Figure 14-2.

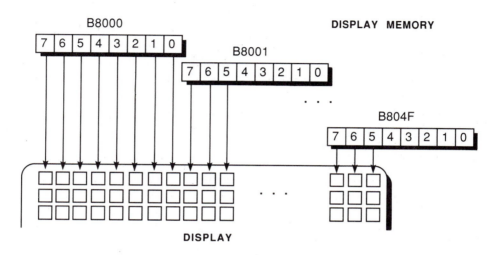

Figure 14-2. Color Graphics Display Memory

Since there are 640 dots across the screen, and there are eight dots in each byte, there are 80 bytes for each line of dots across the screen. The first line extends from B8000 to B804F. Now, you would think that location B8050 would be the first eight dots of the second line. But instead, B8050 contains the first eight dots of the *third* display line, and locations BA000-BA04F contain the dots of the second display line. More generally, the memory at B8000 contains the 1st, 3rd, 5th, etc. lines, while the memory at BA000 contains the 2nd, 4th, 6th, etc. lines. The reason for this has to do with the way the hardware display works: it actually displays the lines in that order, showing half of them first and then returning to show the second half. In fact, your TV operates this way as well.

When the CGA is in 320x200 color mode, it works exactly the same way, except that more than one bit is used to specify the value of each dot on the screen. In this case, pairs of bits are used to select one of four possible colors (including black) for each dot. Because a byte contains four bit pairs, each byte specifies the colors of four dots on the screen. Because there are half as many dots across the screen in this mode, the same number of bytes are used to display one line.

In either case, manipulating the display is really a matter of manipulating the memory located at B8000. Every time the program stores something different at one of those locations, the display changes. The tricky part of using the display is translating between the conceptual view of the display (an array of dots) and the reality (a block of bytes in memory), doing it with half of the bytes at a different address than the rest, and doing it efficiently.

The rect Function

The ROM BIOS includes a routine to draw a dot on the screen. But calling this routine enough times to build the wall or even the paddle in Figure 14-1 would take a long time. And in order to produce the smooth animation that we want for the ball in Pong, the drawing speed must be especially high. We would much rather have a routine that could draw a whole rectangle all at once, rather than a single dot. This would take care of the wall and paddle nicely; and with one extension, it would also take care of the ball. This extension allows us to specify a "pattern" with which to fill the rectangle. The pattern can be used to "texture" the wall; and it can also be used to draw the ball, so long as the ball is smaller than the pattern size.

The pattern is an array of dots that is repeated indefinitely in both the vertical and horizontal directions. We will use a 16x16 dot pattern. A pattern much larger than this becomes cumbersome to use; much smaller, it's too small to produce objects like the ball in Pong. We'll store the pattern as 16 integers, each one 16 bits in size. Figures 14-3 and 14-4 show the patterns for a gray wall and for the ball. The rect function will allow us to draw rectangles that are larger or smaller than the pattern. If the rectangle is larger, the pattern is repeated to fill the area; if it is smaller, then only a part of the pattern is used.

The pattern in C: The pattern blown up as pixels: The pattern (actual size):

```
0xAAAA, 0x5555, 0xAAAA, 0x5555,
0xAAAA, 0x5555, 0xAAAA, 0x5555,
0xAAAA, 0x5555, 0xAAAA, 0x5555,
0xAAAA, 0x5555, 0xAAAA, 0x5555
```

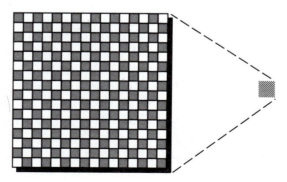

Figure 14-3. A Gray (Half Filled) Pattern

The pattern in C:

```
0x0180, 0x03C0, 0x07E0, 0x0FF0,
0x1FF8, 0x3FFC, 0x7FFE, 0xFFFF,
0xFFFF, 0x7FFE, 0x3FFC, 0x1FF8,
0x0FF0, 0x07E0, 0x03C0, 0x0180
```

The pattern blown up as dots: The pattern (actual size):

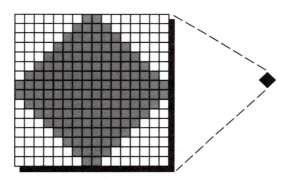

Figure 14-4. A Ball (Diamond) Pattern

There are two ways to interpret patterns. The first is a background that is "uncovered" by the drawing process—that is, the pattern is locked to an absolute grid. The second is as a pattern that starts at the upper-left corner of the rectangle being drawn, wherever the rectangle happens to start. The advantage of the first approach is that, if you draw two overlapping or adjacent rectangles, the patterns will align to form one continuous texture. But the second approach allows you to draw objects like the ball, since the pattern is relative to the rectangle being drawn. We want to provide both of these capabilities in our drawing routine.

The final consideration in designing the drawing routine is what to do with the dots that are on the screen before the routine is called, or more precisely, how to combine the new dots with the old dots. Visually, this combining process means that the the new rectangle replaces the existing display, adds to it, or affects it in some other way. There are several ways in which the old display dot and the new pattern dot can be combined to form a new display dot. In fact, there are sixteen possible functions of two input bits. Four of these functions cover virtually everything we will ever want to do:

Function	Description
Copy	Ignore the old bits; simply copy the pattern bits. The old display is erased and replaced with the new display.
Xor	Exclusive-or the old bits with the pattern bits. The old display dots are toggled (black goes to white, white goes to black) wherever there is a white dot in the pattern.
Bit-set	Set the bits that are 1 in the pattern; leave the other bits as they were. The pattern is "added" to the display.
Bit-clear	Zero the bits that are 1 in the pattern; leave the others bits as they were. The pattern is "subtracted" from the display.

The exclusive-or function deserves a more detailed discussion, especially since it gets used a great deal in graphics, particularly animated graphics. For each bit in the pattern that's 1, this operation "toggles" the corresponding dot on the display (if the existing display dot was black, it becomes white; if it was white, it becomes black). This becomes valuable when you realize that doing the operation twice returns the display to its original state, regardless of what was on the display initially. You can draw something and then erase it, without knowing what was on the display beforehand, and without keeping a copy of the original display. In fact, if a series of exclusive-or operations is done twice, in any order, intermixing different rectangles between the pairs, when all of the rectangles have been exclusive-ored twice, the display will be back in its original state. We will use exclusive-or to draw the ball and the paddle when we write Pong. Note, however, that while this approach works very well when done properly, if the display were to get out of synch—perhaps because the second exclusive-or is missed—it would remain out of synch for the rest of the time the program is executing. A "clear" operation of some sort would be required to restore the display to the proper state.

Putting all of these elements together, we get the following desired rectangle drawing function:

rect(left,top,right,bottom,pattern,globalPatt,drawMode)—Draw a rectangle consisting of the dots from (left,top) up to but not including (right,bottom), using the drawing mode indicated by drawMode: 0 for copy, 1 for exclusive-or, 2 for bit-set, or 3 for bit-clear. The parameter pattern points to an array of 16 words, which is the pattern to use; alternatively, the pattern pointer can be zero, in which case a pattern of all 1s is used. The globalPatt parameter is TRUE if the pattern should be locked to start repeating from (0,0); otherwise it starts repeating from (left,top).

That's a pretty big chunk of functionality, and it will take a moment to sink in. Some examples may help: Figure 14-5 shows what the display will look like after each of two calls to rect. The first call fills the entire screen with a gray pattern, using the copy mode; and the second call clears a rectangle out of the bottom portion using the bit-clear mode. Figure 14-6 illustrates how exclusive-or mode can be used to move objects. The first call draws the object using exclusive-or mode. Because the screen was blank, exclusive-or has the same effect here as copy. The next pair of calls performs another exclusive-or at the same location, and then a second exclusive-or at a new location. Because the exclusive-or toggles the display bits, the first call of the pair has the effect of erasing the object; the second call then redraws it at a new location. With a little practice, this routine is quite easy to use, as we'll show in the Pong program later in this chapter.

After rect(0,0,640,200,grayPattern,1,0):

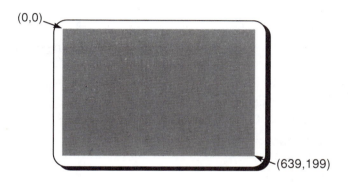

After rect(100,100,500,200,0,0,3):

Figure 14-5. Drawing Rectangles with rect

After rect(100,100,116,116,ballPattern,0,1):

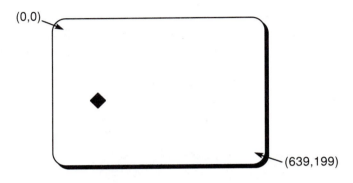

After rect(100,100,116,116,ballPattern,0,1)
and rect(500,100,516,116,ballPattern,0,1):

Figure 14-6. Moving a Ball with rect

Inside the rect Function

If we could deal with the display one dot at a time, the rect function wouldn't be very hard to write. It becomes complex because not only do we have to deal with the display in larger chunks, we actually want to. The reason we want to is to make the function as fast as possible. We will, in fact, access and manipulate the display memory in 16-bit units, called "words," which is the most efficient size for the IBM PC processor—some 16 times more efficient than dealing with the display a dot at a time. This operation is complicated because the rectangle we're going to display might start at any bit position within a 16-bit word; similarly, it may end at any bit position. Because of this, we will deal with the first and last words of each display line as a special case—not forgetting that they might even be the same word if the width of the rectangle is 16 dots or less.

The rect function's code is shown in Listing 14-1. This is a complex function that requires some study to understand. But it is worth the time, since it illustrates most aspects of manipulating a graphic display from assembly language. We will discuss it here from the point of view of functionality, rather than proceeding linearly through the listing.

The rect function uses several local variables, which are allocated on the stack at the beginning of the function. They are conveniently accessed using negative offsets from the BP register (just as the parameters can be accessed using positive offsets). To make it clear in the code which of these two types of variables is being referenced, both the parameter and the local variable offsets are declared as positive numbers and the code uses "[bp-offset]" for local variables and "[bp+offset]" for parameters. Figure 14-7 illustrates this arrangement, using word (int) variables.

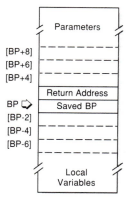

Figure 14-7. Parameters and Local Variables

This function also uses the ES register, which is an extra segment register specifically intended for references outside the normal data segment. In this case, it is used to manipulate the display memory. At the beginning of the function, it's set to B8000. All display memory references will be relative to this register, and will therefore use offsets starting at 0 for the first byte of the display memory.

It is possible that the application program may specify a rectangle that is partially or entirely off the screen. If rect handles these special cases properly, the calling program doesn't have to check explicitly for them. This process is called "clipping," since it clips the rectangle at the screen boundaries. In order to clip the rectangle, the rect function computes a new set of left, top, right, and bottom values. Taking the screen boundaries into account, it stores them in the local variables clipLeft, clipTop, clipRight, and clipBottom. An example is shown in Figure 14-8. If, in the process, the rect function discovers that the rectangle is entirely off the screen, it immediately jumps to the exit code. Note that the original values of left and top may be used later, since the pattern may still be repeated relative to these values.

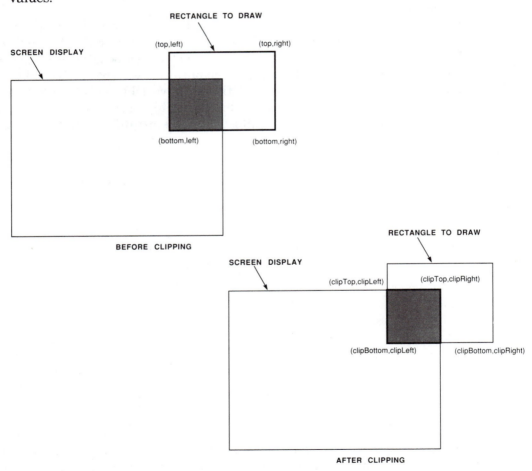

Figure 14-8. Clipping

The number of lines to be processed is computed by taking the difference between clipTop and clipBottom. It is stored in lCnt. This variable is then used to control the number of times the line processing code is executed. If this number is zero (clipTop equals clipBottom) or negative (clipTop greater than clipBottom), the function exits. Note that the negative case corresponds to the top and bottom parameters being reversed. It would not be a bad idea to detect this case—and the corresponding case for left and right—and correct it. We leave this exercise to the reader.

Four local variables specify the start and end of the line: lStart, lEnd, lSMask, and lEMask. The first two are the offsets to the first and last words in the line. They are generated by computing the byte address by shifting clipLeft and clipRight three bits to the right, then making it a word address by clearing the lowest bit. The second two are masks containing a 1 bit for each dot inside the rectangle. They are generated by setting a register to all 1s, and then rotating zeros into it according to the bottom four bits of clipLeft and clipRight. An example of these variables is shown in Figure 14-9. The masks stay the same for all the lines in the rectangle. The word offsets, however, are changed after processing each line, to point to the next line to be processed. Note that if lStart equals lEnd, the proper mask for that word is the logical AND of lSMask and lEMask.

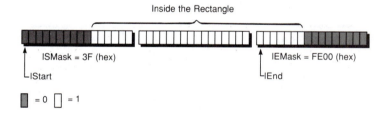

Figure 14-9: Line Start/End Offsets and Masks

The pattern may start repeating from (0,0) or from (left,top). In either case, we will start drawing it at (clipLeft, clipTop). The rect function first copies the original pattern into a local variable, pattRot (so named because it will be a rotation of the original pattern). While being copied, the pattern may be replaced with the default pattern of all 1s, if the pattern parameter is zero. And it is rotated (circularly bit-shifted) based on the globalPatt parameter and the difference between clipLeft and left. This takes care of adjusting the pattern horizontally. Vertically, the pattern words stored in pattRot must be taken sequentially as subsequent lines are processed. This is done by maintaining a variable pattCnt, and using it (modulo 32) to index into the pattRot array. This use of pattCnt in the main processing loop lets us adjust the pattern's starting point—as specified by globalPatt and the difference between clipTop and top—by selecting the appropriate initial value for pattCnt.

Finally we come to the main processing loop which is actually four main processing loops. There is one loop for each of the different transfer modes: copy, exclusive-or, bit-set, and bit-clear. We use four loops rather than one so that the routine runs as quickly as possible. Each loop follows basically the same model:

1. Get the mask for the first word of the line.

2. If the first word is the same word as the last one, go to 5.

3. Process the first word.

4. Process all inside words (neither first nor last).

5. Process the last word.

6. Increment lStart and lEnd to point to the next line.

7. Decrement lCnt; if non-zero, go to 1.

"Process" means one of the following four operations (in this table, "pattern" is the pattern for this word, "mask" is a mask of the bits that fall within the rectangle in this word, and "display" is the display memory word):

Mode	Function
Copy	display = (display & ˜mask)|(pattern & mask)
Exclusive-or	display = display ˆ(pattern & mask)
Bit-set	display = display|(pattern & mask)
Bit-clear	display = display & ˜(pattern & mask)

One special case worth noting occurs when the first and last words of the line are the same. In this case, the proper mask to use is formed by ANDing together the masks for the first and last words of the line. The code that processes the last word assumes that AX will contain a mask to be ANDed with the last word mask. Under normal circumstances, AX contains all 1s; but in this special case, it will contain the first word mask, lSMask.

Remember that every other display line is in a different part of the display memory. This complicates the process of incrementing lStart and lEnd to point at the next line. The rect function handles this by toggling bit 13 (the difference between the two areas of display memory) and then testing it. If it's on, then we have just gone from the first area to the second and are done with that increment.

If it's zero, we've gone in the other direction, and must also increment the pointers by one line's worth of bytes—decimal 80.

There is one last complication: the 8086/8088/80286 stores words byte-backwards from what we'd like. While the highest bit in a byte is the first dot to appear on the screen, the highest byte in a word is the second set of dots. To put that another way, if you take the first word at B8000, the bit corresponding to the first dot on the screen is bit 7, not 15. The second is 6, then 5,..., then 0, then 15, then 14,..., then 8. This could really mess up our rotation and masking procedure. But luckily there is an easy way out: We compute the masks and pattern rotations as if the words were not stored byte-reversed, and then reverse the bytes in the masks and pattern before doing the line processing. This corrects for the byte-backwards storage.

That's it. You should spend some time making sure you understand this routine. It will be useful virtually every time you manipulate a graphics display. Of course, you can use the routine even if you don't understand all of the internal details of how it works.

The Pong Program

Now we can get to the Pong program, as shown in Listing 14-2.

The main job of the Pong program is to keep track of the variables ballX, ballY, ballXV, ballYV, and padY, and to update the display to reflect their current values. The current position of the upper-left corner of the ball pattern is (ballX,ballY), with ballXV and ballYV being the current X and Y velocities of the ball. The padY variable is the Y coordinate of the upper end of the paddle—the paddle extending from (10,padY) to (20,padY + padHeight). When the ball runs into something, ballX, ballY, ballXV, and ballYV change. These variables also change under two other conditions. With every five successful rebounds, they both increase in magnitude by one, thus speeding up the ball; and if the ball hits the edge of the paddle, ballYV is adjusted by one to simulate the effect of that type of glancing hit. The padY variable changes only when the keyboard is used to change the paddle's position: keystrokes are discovered and processed using the keyboard routines first presented in Chapter Nine. In addition to these variables, goodHits keeps track of the number of times the user has successfully bounced the ball off the paddle.

The program starts by initializing the screen to 640x200 graphics mode ("setMode(6)") and the variables to their initial values. Then it draws the walls and the initial positions of the paddle and ball. The main loop checks first for keyboard input and then updates the ball position. Finally, the program resets the display mode to 80x25 text mode ("setMode(2)").

When blanking the screen initially, the program uses a bit-clear call to rect. Then it draws the walls using a copy mode call to rect. When drawing the paddle and the ball, the program uses the exclusive-or mode.

Summary

The graphics display memory of the CGA contains bits that correspond to the dots on the screen. In black and white mode, each bit represents one dot; in color mode, more than one bit is needed for each dot. A very general purpose graphics drawing routine has been presented, implemented as an assembly language routine. The routine directly accesses the color graphics adapter display memory in order to achieve the highest possible drawing speed. This routine, called "rect", draws rectangles of arbitrary size on the screen, filled with an arbitrary pattern. We have discussed the internal details and complexities of this routine in some detail. And we have then developed the program Pong, which makes extensive use of the rect function.

Exercises

1. Change Pong to shorten the paddle height instead of speeding up the balls every five successful bounces.

2. Change Pong to display the current value of goodHits, together with the highest value it's reached so far. This is the score.

3. Change Pong to use mode 4 rather than mode 6 — i.e., color rather than black and white. Note that now each dot is specified by two bits; patterns will therefore be 8x16 rather than 16x16. First, try just changing the setMode call. Then try changing ballXV to 2, always incrementing or decrementing it by 2. Note the difference in operation.

4. Write a program using the rand random number function and rect to draw random rectangles on the screen. Each new rectangle's corners should be selected using rand, and one of four different patterns should also be chosen using rand. This program will give you a good feeling for the drawing speed of the rect function.

5. Change rect to check for the cases of top greater than bottom or left greater than right. Swap the input parameters correctly before starting.

6. [advanced] Write a function, named outline, that draws an outline of the rectangle specified without filling it in (and does not have pattern and globalPatt parameters).

Listing 14-1. "rect.asm":

```
;                   Rectangle Drawing Routine

_TEXT     segment byte public 'CODE'
          assume CS:_TEXT

; rect(left,top,right,bottom,pattern,globalPatt,mode)
;
; Function: Draw a rectangle consisting of the bits (left,top) up to but
; not including (right,bottom), filling the rectangle with the pattern
; pointed to by pattern; if globalPatt is true, lock the pattern to a
; global reference otherwise start it at (left,top). mode specifies which
; type of operation to use to combine the new and old dots: 0 for copy,
; 1 for exclusive-or, 2 for bit-set (or), and 3 for bit-clear.
;
; Algorithm: First, clip the rectangle to the display. Second, figure out
; the start and end words and word masks. Third, rotate the pattern as
; needed. Fourth, branch to and perform the appropriate type of copying.
; Finally, restore the saved registers and exit.

          public _rect          ; Routine is available to other modules

; Parameters:

          left = 4              ; Offset from BP to parameter left
          top = 6               ; Offset to parameter top
          right = 8             ; Offset to right
          bottom = 10           ; Offset to bottom
          pattern = 12          ; Offset to pattern
          globPatt = 14         ; Offset to globPatt
          mode = 16             ; Offset to mode

; Local variables:

          lStrt = 2             ; Offset from BP to lStrt local variable
          lEnd = 4              ; Offset to lEnd local variable
          lSMask = 6            ; Offset to lSMask
          lEMask = 8            ; Offset to lEMask
          lCnt = 10             ; Offset to lCnt
          pattCnt = 12          ; Offset to pattCnt
          clipLeft = 14         ; Offset to clipLeft
          clipTop = 16          ; Offset to clipTop
          clipRight = 18        ; Offset to clipRight
          clipBottom = 20       ; Offset to clipBottom
          pattRot = 52          ; Offset to pattRot

_rect     proc near            ; NEAR type subroutine
          push    bp           ; Save BP register
          mov     bp,sp        ; Set BP to SP; to allow access to parameters
                               ;    and local variables
          sub     sp,52        ; Allocate space on the stack for loca vars
          push    di           ; Save the DI register
          push    si           ; Save SI register
          push    es           ; Save ES register
          mov     ax,0B800H    ; Set ES to the base of the graphics display
          mov     es,ax
;
; Clip left to produce clipLeft:
;
```

Listing 14-1. "rect.asm" *(cont.)*:

```
        mov     ax,[bp+left]     ; AX = left
        cmp     ax,640           ; Is AX >= 640 (i.e., off screen right)?
        jge     getOut1          ; If yes, there's nothing to do -- exit
        or      ax,ax            ; Is AX < 0 (i.e., off screen left)?
        jns     clip1            ; If no, leave it alone
        xor     ax,ax            ; If yes, set it to zero
clip1:  mov     [bp-clipLeft],ax ; Set clipLeft
;
; Clip top to produce clipTop:
;
        mov     ax,[bp+top]      ; AX = top
        cmp     ax,200           ; Is AX >= 200 (i.e., off screen bottom)?
        jge     getOut1          ; If yes, there's nothing to do, so exit
        or      ax,ax            ; Is AX < 0 (i.e., off screen top)?
        jns     clip2            ; If no, leave it alone
        xor     ax,ax            ; If yes, set it to zero
clip2:  mov     [bp-clipTop],ax  ; Set clipTop
;
; Clip right to produce clipRight:
;
        mov     ax,[bp+right]    ; AX = right
        or      ax,ax            ; Is AX < 0 (i.e., off screen left)?
        js      getOut1          ; If yes, there's nothing to do, so just exit
        cmp     ax,640           ; Is AX > 640 (i.e., off screen right)?
        jle     clip3            ; If no, leave it alone
        mov     ax,640           ; If yes, set it to 640
clip3:  mov     [bp-clipRight],ax ; Set clipRight
;
; Clip bottom to produce clipBottom:
;
        mov     ax,[bp+bottom]   ; AX = bottom
        or      ax,ax            ; Is AX < 0 (i.e., off screen top)?
        jns     clip4            ; If no, continue clipping
getOut1: jmp    getOut           ; If yes, there's nothing to do -- exit
clip4:  cmp     ax,200           ; Is AX > 200 (i.e., off screen bottom)?
        jle     clip5            ; If no, leave it alone
        mov     ax,200           ; If yes, set it to 200
clip5:  mov     [bp-clipBottom],ax ; Set clipBottom
;
; Compute lCnt:
;
        sub     ax,[bp-clipTop]  ; AX = clipBottom - clipTop
        jz      getOut1          ; If lCnt is zero, exit (nothing to do)
        js      getOut1          ; If lCnt is negative, also exit
        mov     [bp-lCnt],ax     ; Set lCnt
;
; Compute lSMask:
;
        mov     cl,[bp-clipLeft] ; CL = clipLeft & 15 (i.e., bottom 4 bits)
        and     cl,15
        xor     ax,ax            ; AX = FFFF
        not     ax
        shr     ax,cl            ; Shift AX right according to CL
        mov     bl,ah            ; BX = AX byte-reversed
        mov     bh,al
        mov     [bp-lSMask],bx   ; lSMask = BX
;
; Compute lEMask:
```

Listing 14-1. "rect.asm" *(cont.)*:

```
;
        mov     cl,[bp-clipRight] ; CL = clipRight & 15 (bottom 4 bits)
        and     cl,15
        xor     ax,ax             ; AX = FFFF
        not     ax
        shr     ax,cl             ; Shift AX right according to CL
        not     ax
        mov     bl,ah             ; BX = AX byte-reversed
        mov     bh,al
        mov     [bp-lEMask],bx    ; lEMask = BX
;
; Compute pattCnt (assuming globalPatt is FALSE):
;
        mov     ax,[bp-clipTop]   ; AX = clipTop - top
        sub     ax,[bp+top]
        shl     ax,1              ; AX = 2 * AX
        mov     [bp-pattCnt],ax   ; pattCnt = AX
;
; Transfer pattern to pattRot, rotated as specified by globalPatt (and, if
; globalPatt is TRUE, replace pattCnt with a recomputed value):
;
        mov     ch,16             ; CH = 16 (number of words to transfer)
        mov     bl,[bp+left]      ; BL = left & 15 (bottom four bits)
        and     bl,15
        mov     ax,[bp+globPatt]; Is globalPatt TRUE?
        or      ax,ax
        jz      locPat            ; If not, branch
        mov     ax,[bp-clipTop]   ; If yes, recompute pattCnt = 2 * clipTop
        shl     ax,1
        mov     [bp-pattCnt],ax
        xor     bl,bl             ; And set BL = 0
locPat: mov     si,[bp+pattern]   ; SI = pattern
        lea     di,[bp-pattRot]   ; DI = pattRot
        xor     ax,ax             ; AX = FFFF (used when pattern == 0)
        not     ax
nxtPat: or      si,si             ; Is SI (from pattern) == 0?
        jz      rotIt             ; If yes, use the FFFF already in AX
        lods    word ptr [si]     ; Otherwise, AX = *SI++
rotIt:  mov     cl,bl             ; Rotate the pattern according to BL
        ror     ax,cl
        mov     dl,ah             ; DX = AX byte-reversed
        mov     dh,al
        mov     [di],dx           ; *DI = DX
        inc     di                ; DI++
        inc     di
        dec     ch                ; CH--
        jnz     nxtPat            ; If more pattern left, go back and do it again
;
; Compute the initial lStrt:
;
        mov     ax,[bp-clipTop]   ; AX = clipTop
        xor     bx,bx             ; BX = 0
        shr     ax,1              ; AX = AX/2, with the bottom bit going to CF
        mov     cl,14             ; Shift CL into BX
        rcl     bx,cl
        mov     cl,80             ; AX = 80 * AX (multiple by # of columns)
        mul     cl
        add     ax,bx             ; Add in the bit in BX
```

Listing 14-1. "rect.asm" *(cont.)*:

```
        mov     bx,[bp-clipLeft]; BX = clipLeft
        mov     cl,3            ; BX = BX/8 (convert from bits to bytes)
        shr     bx,cl
        and     bx,0FFFEH       ; Convert to word address (clear bottom bit)
        add     bx,ax           ; BX += AX
        mov     [bp-lStrt],bx   ; lStrt = BX
;
; Compute the initial lEnd:
;
        mov     bx,[bp-clipRight]; BX = clipRight
        mov     cl,3            ; BX = BX/8 (convert to word)
        shr     bx,cl
        and     bx,0FFFEH       ; Convert to word address (clear bottom bit)
        add     ax,bx           ; AX += BX (AX had column offset from above)
        mov     [bp-lEnd],ax    ; lEnd = AX
;
; Set up for processing:
;
        mov     di,[bp-lStrt]   ; DI = lStrt
        mov     si,[bp-lEnd]    ; SI = lEnd
;
; Switch on mode:
;
        mov     ax,[bp+mode]    ; AX = mode
        dec     ax              ; AX == 0 (COPY)?
        jns     tryXor          ; If not, go try XOR
;
; Do COPY mode:
;
cpNxt:  push    di                      ; Save DI (line start)
        mov     di,[bp-pattCnt] ; DI = pattCnt
        and     di,31           ; DI &= 31 (get bottom five bits)
        mov     bx,[bp-pattRot+di] ; BX = pattRot[DI] (the pattern word)
        inc     di              ; DI++
        inc     di              ; DI++
        mov     [bp-pattCnt],di ; pattCnt = DI
        pop     di              ; Restore line start DI
        mov     ax,[bp-lSMask]  ; AX = lSMask
        cmp     di,si           ; Line start == line end?
        je      cpLast          ; If yes, go process it as one word
        mov     dx,ax           ; If not, copy line start mask to DX
        not     ax              ; Complement start mask in AX
        and     ax,es:[di]      ; AX &= *DI (old word with new bits cleared)
        and     dx,bx           ; DX &= BX (new word, with old bits cleared)
        or      ax,dx           ; AX |= DX (combine new and old)
        stos    word ptr es:[di]; *DI++ = AX (store processed word)
        mov     cx,si           ; CX = (SI-DI)/2 (converted from byte to word)
        sub     cx,di
        shr     cx,1
        jz      cpLast2         ; If CX == 0 (SI and DI in same word), branch
        mov     ax,bx           ; AX = BX (the pattern)
        rep stos word ptr es:[di] ; Block move the words between the 1st & last
cpLast2: xor    ax,ax           ; AX = FFFF
        not     ax
cpLast: and     ax,[bp-lEMask]  ; AX &= lEMask (AX is now mask of last word)
        mov     dx,ax           ; Copy mask to DX
        not     ax              ; Complement mask in AX
        and     ax,es:[di]      ; AX &= *DI (AX = old word with new bits clear)
```

Listing 14-1. "rect.asm" *(cont.)*:

```
        and     dx,bx           ; DX &= BX (DX = new word with old bits clear)
        or      ax,dx           ; AX |= DX (combine the two)
        mov     es:[di],ax      ; *DI = AX (put the processed word back)
;
; Increment line start and line end pointers to next line:
        mov     di,[bp-lStrt]   ; DI = lStrt
        xor     si,2000H        ; Toggle even/odd line bit in SI and DI
        xor     di,2000H
        mov     ax,di           ; DI & 0x2000?
        and     ax,2000H
        jnz     cpOdd           ; If yes (odd), don't add in 80
        add     si,80           ; If no (even), add 80 to the start and end
        add     di,80
cpOdd:  mov     [bp-lStrt],di   ; lStrt = DI
        dec     word ptr [bp-lCnt] ; lCnt--
        jnz     cpNxt           ; If we're not done, go back and do another line
        jmp     getOut          ; Otherwise, exit
;
; Try exclusive-or:
;
tryXor: dec     ax              ; Exclusive-or mode?
        jns     tryBst          ; If not, go try bit set
;
; Do EXCLUSIVE-OR mode:
;
xrNxt:  push    di              ; Save DI (line start)
        mov     di,[bp-pattCnt] ; DI = pattCnt
        and     di,31           ; DI &= 31 (get bottom five bits)
        mov     bx,[bp-pattRot+di] ; BX = pattRot[DI] (the pattern word)
        inc     di              ; DI++
        inc     di              ; DI++
        mov     [bp-pattCnt],di ; pattCnt = DI
        pop     di              ; Restore line start DI
        mov     ax,[bp-lSMask]  ; AX = lSMask
        cmp     di,si           ; Line start == line end?
        je      xrLast          ; If yes, go process it as one word
        and     ax,bx           ; AX &= BX (clip pattern to mask into AX)
        xor     ax,es:[di]      ; AX ^= *DI (exclusive-or in old word)
        stos    word ptr es:[di]; *DI++ = AX (store processed word)
        mov     cx,si           ; CX = (SI-DI)/2 (converted from byte to word)
        sub     cx,di
        shr     cx,1
        jz      xrLast2         ; If CX == 0 (SI and DI in same word), branch
xrLoop: mov     ax,es:[di]      ; AX = *DI (get next word to process)
        xor     ax,bx           ; AX ^= BX (exclusive-or word with pattern)
        stos    word ptr es:[di]; *DI++ = AX (store processed word)
        loopnz  xrLoop          ; Repeat until all word are processed
xrLast2: xor    ax,ax           ; AX = FFFF
        not     ax
xrLast: and     ax,[bp-lEMask]  ; AX &= lEMask (AX is now mask of last word)
        and     ax,bx           ; AX &= BX (clip pattern to mask into AX)
        xor     ax,es:[di]      ; AX ^= *DI (exclusive-or word into AX)
        mov     es:[di],ax      ; *DI = AX (put the processed word back)
;
; Increment line start and line end pointers to next line:
        mov     di,[bp-lStrt]   ; DI = lStrt
        xor     si,2000H        ; Toggle even/odd line bit in SI and DI
        xor     di,2000H
```

Listing 14-1. "rect.asm" *(cont.)*:

```
        mov     ax,di            ; DI & 0x2000?
        and     ax,2000H
        jnz     xrOdd            ; If yes (odd), don't add in 80
        add     si,80            ; If no (even), add 80 to the start and end
        add     di,80
xrOdd:  mov     [bp-lStrt],di    ; lStrt = DI
        dec     word ptr [bp-lCnt] ; lCnt--
        jnz     xrNxt            ; If we're not done, go back a do another line
        jmp     getOut           ; Otherwise, exit

;
; Try bit set:
;
tryBst: dec     ax               ; Bit set mode?
        jns     tryBcl           ; If not, go try bit clear
;
; Do BIT SET mode:
;
bsNxt:  push    di               ; Save DI (line start)
        mov     di,[bp-pattCnt]  ; DI = pattCnt
        and     di,31            ; DI &= 31 (get bottom five bits)
        mov     bx,[bp-pattRot+di] ; BX = pattRot[DI] (the pattern word)
        inc     di               ; DI++
        inc     di               ; DI++
        mov     [bp-pattCnt],di  ; pattCnt = DI
        pop     di               ; Restore line start DI
        mov     ax,[bp-lSMask]   ; AX = lSMask
        cmp     di,si            ; Line start == line end?
        je      bsLast           ; If yes, go process it as one word
        and     ax,bx            ; AX &= BX (clip pattern to mask into AX)
        or      ax,es:[di]       ; AX |= *DI (or in old word)
        stos    word ptr es:[di] ; *DI++ = AX (store processed word)
        mov     cx,si            ; CX = (SI-DI)/2 (converted from byte to word)
        sub     cx,di
        shr     cx,1
        jz      bsLast2          ; If CX == 0 (SI and DI in same word), branch
bsLoop: mov     ax,es:[di]       ; AX = *DI (get next word to process)
        or      ax,bx            ; AX |= BX (or word with pattern)
        stos    word ptr es:[di] ; *DI++ = AX (store processed word)
        loopnz  bsLoop           ; Repeat until all word are processed
bsLast2: xor    ax,ax            ; AX = FFFF
        not     ax
bsLast: and     ax,[bp-lEMask]   ; AX &= lEMask (AX is now mask of last word)
        and     ax,bx            ; AX &= BX (clip pattern to mask into AX)
        xor     ax,es:[di]       ; AX ^= *DI (exclusive-or word into AX)
        mov     es:[di],ax       ; *DI = AX (put the processed word back)
;
; Increment line start and line end pointers to next line:
        mov     di,[bp-lStrt]    ; DI = lStrt
        xor     si,2000H         ; Toggle even/odd line bit in SI and DI
        xor     di,2000H
        mov     ax,di            ; DI & 0x2000?
        and     ax,2000H
        jnz     bsOdd            ; If yes (odd), don't add in 80
        add     si,80            ; If no (even), add 80 to the start and end
        add     di,80
bsOdd:  mov     [bp-lStrt],di    ; lStrt = DI
        dec     word ptr [bp-lCnt] ; lCnt--
```

Listing 14-1. "rect.asm" *(cont.)*:

```
        jnz     bsNxt           ; If we're not done, go back a do another line
        jmp     getOut          ; Otherwise, exit
;
; Try bit clear:
;
tryBcl: dec     ax              ; Bit clear mode?
        jns     getOut          ; If not, exit (not a legal mode)
;
; Do BIT CLEAR mode:
;
bcNxt:  push    di              ; Save DI (line start)
        mov     di,[bp-pattCnt] ; DI = pattCnt
        and     di,31           ; DI &= 31 (get bottom five bits)
        mov     bx,[bp-pattRot+di] ; BX = pattRot[DI] (the pattern word)
        inc     di              ; DI++
        inc     di              ; DI++
        mov     [bp-pattCnt],di ; pattCnt = DI
        pop     di              ; Restore line start DI
        mov     ax,[bp-1SMask]  ; AX = 1SMask
        cmp     di,si           ; Line start == line end?
        je      bcLast          ; If yes, go process it as one word
        and     ax,bx           ; AX &= BX (clip pattern to mask into AX)
        not     ax              ; AX = ~AX (prepare to clear bits)
        and     ax,es:[di]      ; AX &= *DI (clear bits in old word)
        stos    word ptr es:[di]; *DI++ = AX (store processed word)
        mov     cx,si           ; CX = (SI-DI)/2 (converted from byte to word)
        sub     cx,di
        shr     cx,1
        jz      bcLast2         ; If CX == 0 (SI and DI in same word), branch
bcLoop: mov     ax,bx           ; AX = BX (make a copy of the pattern)
        not     ax              ; AX = ~AX (prepare to clear bits)
        and     ax,es:[di]      ; AX &= *DI (clear bits in next word)
        stos    word ptr es:[di]; *DI++ = AX (store processed word)
        loopnz  bcLoop          ; Repeat until all word are processed
bcLast2: xor    ax,ax           ; AX = FFFF
        not     ax
bcLast: and     ax,[bp-1EMask]  ; AX &= 1EMask (AX is now mask of last word)
        and     ax,bx           ; AX &= BX (clip pattern to mask into AX)
        xor     ax,es:[di]      ; AX ^= *DI (exclusive-or word into AX)
        mov     es:[di],ax      ; *DI = AX (put the processed word back)
;
; Increment line start and line end pointers to next line:
        mov     di,[bp-1Strt]   ; DI = 1Strt
        xor     si,2000H        ; Toggle even/odd line bit in SI and DI
        xor     di,2000H
        mov     ax,di           ; DI & 0x2000?
        and     ax,2000H
        jnz     bcOdd           ; If yes (odd), don't add in 80
        add     si,80           ; If no (even), add 80 to the start and end
        add     di,80
bcOdd:  mov     [bp-1Strt],di   ; 1Strt = DI
        dec     word ptr [bp-1Cnt] ; 1Cnt--
        jnz     bcNxt           ; If we're not done, go back a do another line
        jmp     getOut          ; Otherwise, exit
;
; Save registers and return:
;
getOut: pop     es              ; Restore the ES register
```

Listing 14-1. "rect.asm" (*cont.*):

```
        pop    si           ; Restore the SI register
        pop    di           ; Restore the DI register
        mov    sp,bp        ; Free the local variable stack space
        pop    bp           ; Restore the BP register
        ret                 ; Return to calling program
_rect   endp                ; End of subroutine

_TEXT   ends                ; End of code segment
        end                 ; End of assembly code
```

Listing 14-2. "pong.c":

```c
/*              Pong Game Main Program
 */

/* Copying modes for rect: */

#define COPY 0
#define XOR 1
#define BITSET 2
#define BITCLEAR 3

/* Gray pattern for the wall: */
wallPattern[] = {
    0xAAAA, 0x5555, 0xAAAA, 0x5555, 0xAAAA, 0x5555, 0xAAAA, 0x5555,
    0xAAAA, 0x5555, 0xAAAA, 0x5555, 0xAAAA, 0x5555, 0xAAAA, 0x5555
};

/* Diamond pattern for the ball: */
ballPattern[] = {
    0x0180, 0x03C0, 0x07E0, 0x0FF0, 0x1FF8, 0x3FFC, 0x7FFE, 0xFFFF,
    0xFFFF, 0x7FFE, 0x3FFC, 0x1FF8, 0x0FF0, 0x07E0, 0x03C0, 0x0180
};

#define FALSE 0
#define TRUE 1

/*      main()

        Function: Play pong. Simulate a ball moving around the display and
        bouncing off the walls and paddle. If the users hits the up or
        down arrow keys, move the paddle.

        Algorithm: Initialize the display and draw the walls, paddle, and
        ball. Then iterate checking the keyboard for up/down arrow hits,
        and simulating the moving ball.
 */

main()

{
        int ballX, ballY;        /* Current location of ball. */
        int newX, newY;          /* Next ball location. */
        int ballXV, ballYV;      /* Current velocity of ball. */
        int padHeight;           /* Paddle height. */
        int padY;                /* Current paddle location. */
        int ch;                  /* Input character from user. */
        int goodHits;            /* Number of successful rebounds. */
```

Listing 14-2. "pong.c" *(cont.)*:

```
/* Set the display to graphics mode. */
setMod(6);

/* Set the initial positions and velocities of everything. */
ballX = 431;
ballY = 97;
ballXV = ballYV = 1;
padHeight = 60;
padY = 10;
goodHits = 0;

/* Draw the wall, paddle, and ball. */
rect(0,0,640,200,blankPattern,1,COPY);              /* Clear screen. */
rect(0,0,640,10,wallPattern,1,COPY);                /* Top wall. */
rect(0,190,640,200,wallPattern,1,COPY);             /* Bottom wall. */
rect(630,10,640,190,wallPattern,1,COPY);            /* Right wall. */
rect(10,padY,20,padY+padHeight,0,1,XOR);            /* Paddle. */
rect(ballX,ballY,ballX+16,ballY+16,ballPattern,0,XOR); /* Ball. */

/* Loop, simulating movement and waiting for commands from the user. *
while (TRUE) {
        /* Check if there's a keypress waiting. */
        if (keyChk(&ch)) {
                /* If so, read it from the keystroke queue. */
                keyRd();
                /* If it was an ESC, exit the main loop. */
                if ((ch & 0xFF) == 0x1B) break;
                /* If it was an extended key, switch on that key. */
                if ((ch & 0xFF) == 0)
                        switch ((ch>>8) & 0xFF) {
                                /* Up arrow: move paddle up. */
                                case 72:
                                        /* Check for at top. */
                                        if (padY <= 20) break;
                                        /* Draw new paddle. */
                                        rect(10,padY-20,20,
                                            padY+padHeight-20,0,1,1);
                                        /* Erase old paddle. */
                                        rect(10,padY,20,
                                            padY+padHeight,0,1,1);
                                        /* Update position. */
                                        padY -= 20;
                                        break;
                                /* Down arrow: move paddle down. */
                                case 80:
                                        /* Check for at bottom. */
                                        if ((padY+padHeight) >= 180)
                                                break;
                                        /* Draw new paddle. */
                                        rect(10,padY+20,20,
                                            padY+padHeight+20,0,1,1);
                                        /* Erase old paddle. */
                                        rect(10,padY,20,
                                            padY+padHeight,0,1,1);
                                        /* Update position. */
                                        padY += 20;
                                        break;
                        };
```

Listing 14-2. "pong.c" *(cont.)*:

```
};
/* If the ball is still on the display... */
if (ballX > -16) {
        /* Compute where the ball will go next. */
        newX = ballX+ballXV;
        newY = ballY+ballYV;
        /* Check and adjust for running into top or bottom. */
        if ((newY < 10) || (newY > 174)) {
                ballYV = -ballYV;
                newY = ballY+ballYV;
        };
        /* Check and adjust for running into the right wall. */
        if (newX > 614) {
                ballXV = -ballXV;
                newX = ballX+ballXV;
        /* Check and adjust for running into the paddle. */
        } else if ((padY <= (ballY+15)) &&
                ((padY+padHeight) >= ballY) &&
                (ballX >= 20) &&
                (newX < 20)) {
                /* Reverse direction. */
                ballXV = -ballXV;
                newX = ballX+ballXV;
                /* Check for edge of paddle hit. */
                if (ballY < padY) {
                        if (--ballYV == 0) ballYV--;
                } else if ((ballY+15) > (padY+padHeight)) {
                        if (++ballYV == 0) ballYV++;
                };
                /* If he's gotten five, speed it up. */
                if (((++goodHits) % 5) == 0) {
                        if (ballXV > 0) ballXV++;
                        else ballXV--;
                                if (ballYV > 0) ballYV++;
                                else ballYV--;
                                };
                };
                /* Draw the new ball. */
                rect(newX,newY,newX+16,newY+16,ballPattern,0,XOR);
                /* Erase the old ball. */
                rect(ballX,ballY,ballX+16,ballY+16,ballPattern,0,XOR);
                /* Update the ball position. */
                ballX = newX; ballY = newY;
        /* Otherwise, the ball is off the screen -- he missed. */
        } else {
                /* Put the ball ack on the screen, and reset hits. */
                ballX = 431;
                ballY = 97;
                ballXV = ballYV = 1;
                goodHits = 0;
                /* Draw the ball. */
                rect(ballX,ballY,ballX+16,ballY+16,ballPattern,0,1);
        };
};

/* Reset the display mode to text. */
setMod(2);
}
```

Chapter 15

Interrupt Driven Serial I/O:
Term II

- Terminal Program Revisited: Getting Above 300 Baud

- Interrupts Signal Incoming Characters

- Serial Port I/O: 8250 Registers Exposed

- Serial Port Interrupts: IRQ3 and IRQ4

- Circular Buffers: Producers and Consumers

- Interrupt Driven Serial Interrupt

- The Term2 Program

I n this chapter, we will return to the terminal program developed in Chapter Eleven. That program used calls to the ROM BIOS to take data from the serial port of the PC and display it on the screen, and to take data from the keyboard and send it out the serial port. This direct polling approach works well in many circumstances, but it has a significant flaw: it can lose data at speeds higher than 300 bits per second. This happens because the hardware will only buffer one character of input. If the program does not get to the hardware to read that character before the next character arrives, the input will be overrun with the new character, and the first character will be lost forever. This happens when the processor is busy doing something else, perhaps something prompted by the previous character that arrived at the serial port. For example, when the Term program displays a character, the character may cause the display to be scrolled up—i.e., a line feed at the bottom of the screen. This scroll operation takes some time, long enough so that a character will be missed if the input is arriving at more than 300 bits per second. This is not a problem at very low speeds, but at higher than 300, it will cause the program to lose data.

To avoid this problem, we will replace the serial I/O routines with new ones, making the following changes: first, the receive character routine will be invoked by interrupts from the serial port hardware so that it's executed immediately, without having to wait for polling to occur. And second, the characters that are read in will be stored in a circular buffer. This buffer will allow a number of characters to accumulate before the non-interrupt portion of the program needs to read them.

Serial Port I/O

The serial port hardware consists of an Intel 8250 serial interface, plus a number of supporting chips. The software accesses the 8250 using IN and OUT instructions to I/O port addresses 3F8-3FF (hex) for COM1, and to 2F8-2FF (hex) for COM2.

There are a number of registers and configuration possibilities. We will let the ROM BIOS handle most of the configuration, and concentrate only on a few of the registers, which are described below. The details of the other registers, having to do with configuring the port for bit rate, number of data bits, parity, etc., can be found in the *Technical Reference* manual. The registers that we need to be concerned with are summarized below:

Receiver Buffer (3F8 or 2F8, read only) — This is the register where the hardware places a newly received character. The program reads the character by doing an IN instruction from this address.

Transmit Holding Register (3F8 or 2F8, write only) — This is where the program stores a character to be output. When the hardware is ready for it — i.e., when the transmitter has been enabled and the previous characters (if any) are completely out — it is moved from here to the Transmitter Shift Register.

Transmitter Shift Register (no address) — This is an internal register (i.e., not accessible from the processor), from which the character is shifted out of the serial port hardware onto the external transmit line. Characters are automatically transferred from the transmit holding register into this register when the current contents have been completely transmitted. Because characters are actually transmitted from this register, rather than from the transmit holding register, it is possible to load the next character into the holding register, where it will wait until this register is empty. Otherwise, as soon as the current character is finished, the processor must be ready to output the next character or the output line will sit idle waiting for a character to send.

Interrupt Enable (3F9 or 2F9) — This register, shown in Figure 15-1, is used to enable selected interrupts from the port; for each bit in this register that is 1, the associated interrupt is enabled:

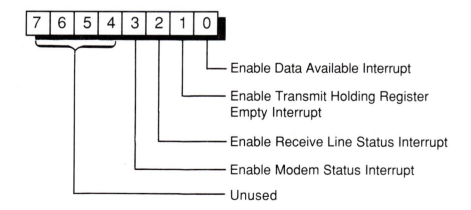

Figure 15-1. Interrupt Enable Register

The interrupts occur under the following conditions:

Interrupt	Cause
Data Available	A character has been received and is available in the receive register.
Transmit Holding Register Empty	The last character written to the transmit holding register has been transferred to the shift register.
Receive Line Status	One of several possible receive errors has occurred—overrun, parity error, framing error, or a break on the line.
Modem Status	A change has occurred in one of the modem control lines.

Interrupt Identification Register, or IIR (3FA or 2FA, read only)—After an interrupt has occurred, this register tells which specific interrupt it is. If the bottom bit is 1, there is no interrupt; if the bottom bit is 0, the contents of this register specify the type of interrupt. The register will continue to contain the same value until cleared by an action of the program. Once cleared, it's ready to show the next interrupt.

IIR Value	Meaning	Caused by	Cleared by
1	No interrupt	None	None
0	Modem status	Change in: clear to send, data set ready, ring indicator, receive line signal detect	Reading Modem Status Register
2	Transmit holding register empty	Transmit holding register becomes empty	Reading the IIR, or writing to the Transmit Holding Register
4	Received data available	Receive Buffer has data	Reading the Receive Buffer Register
6	Receive line status	Overrun error, parity error, framing error, break interrupt	Reading Line Status Register

Modem Control Register (3FC or 2FC)—This register, shown in Figure 15-2, manipulates the outgoing modem control lines, but it also includes the port's general interrupt enable output.

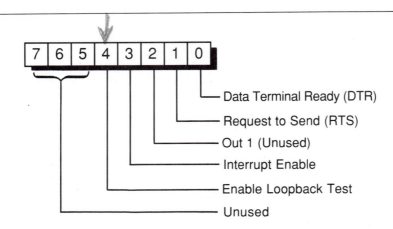

Figure 15-2. Modem Control Register Format

Line Status Register (3FD or 2FD)—This register reports the status of the line, including any errors that occurred. It has exactly the same format as the top byte of the Serial Port Status, which was described in Chapter Eleven.

Modem Status Register (3FE or 2FE)—This register reports the status of the modem control lines. It has the same format as the lower byte of the Serial Port Status which was described in Chapter Eleven.

In general, when dealing with registers that can be read as well as written, it's a good idea to minimize changes made to the register's value. If you want to set the third bit in the register, for instance, don't just write an 8. Instead, read the current contents, OR that with 8, and then write the result. That way, all the other bits will retain their previous values.

Serial Port Interrupts

There are two hardware interrupts reserved for the serial ports: IRQ3 and IRQ4, with vectors at memory locations 2C and 30 (hex). IRQ3 is generated by COM2, and IRQ4 is generated by COM1. Before they can be used, the interrupts must be enabled in the serial port hardware, both within the 8250 and in a separate interrupt line enable. Then, interrupts must also be enabled in the 8259 interrupt controller. Once enabled, interrupts originate in the serial port hardware, travel through the I/O channel onto the main PC-board, and into the 8259 interrupt controller. The 8259 then informs the processor that an interrupt is pending. When the processor finishes the current instruction, it calls the routine indicated by interrupt vector IRQ3 or IRQ4, depending on which of the two serial ports generated the interrupt. This system is shown in Figure 15-3:

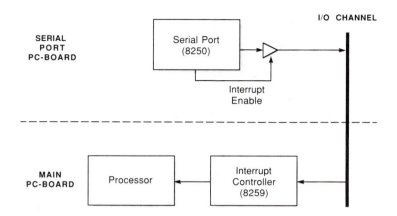

Figure 15-3. Serial Port Interrupt Requests

When the processor gets the interrupt, it executes the interrupt service routine specified by the interrupt vector. That routine knows that the interrupt must have come from the serial port, but it must determine from the hardware which specific type of interrupt occurred. This is accomplished by reading the Interrupt Identification Register, which was described above. The interrupt service routine must then clear the interrupt before returning; otherwise, the same interrupt will continue to interrupt the processor forever.

Circular Buffers

The purpose of a buffer is to allow two parts of a program to interact without having to be in lock step. One part of the program, the producer, generates data; and the other part, the consumer, uses the data. With a buffer between them, each part of the program can operate at a different and variable rate without unduly affecting the other part. This can be especially useful when working with interrupts, since they occur independent of the execution of the main program.

A circular buffer is a particular implementation of the general idea of a buffer. A block of contiguous memory is used to hold the data contained in the buffer. Two variables define the current state of the buffer: one points to the place where the producer is placing data into the buffer; the other points to the place where the consumer is removing it. When either the producer or consumer pointer reaches the end of the buffer area, it is reset to the beginning—hence the name "circular buffer". Another way to look at this is to consider the last byte of the buffer to be contiguous with the first byte; or to think of the pointer arithmetic as being performed modulo the length of the buffer. Figure 15-4 illustrates a circular buffer in two different states.

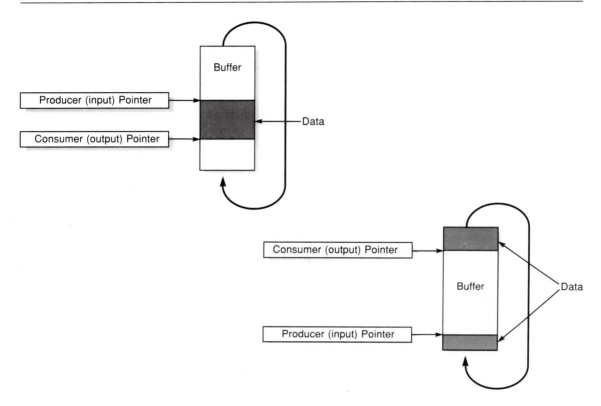

Figure 15-4. Circular Buffers

The producer pointer points to the next location in which to store data; the consumer pointer points to the next location from which to take data. When the producer and consumer pointers are equal, the buffer is empty. When the producer pointer is one less than the consumer pointer, the buffer is full: the producer has entered so much data that its pointer has looped around the buffer and is about to run into the consumer pointer.

The Interrupt Driven Serial Interface

Putting all of this together, we arrive at the new serial port interface library routines shown in Listing 15-1. A block diagram of the interface is shown in Figure 15-5. There are two main functional changes. The first is the addition of a serClose function, which must be called before the application program exits; and which restores the serial port to its original state, turning off interrupts and replacing the original interrupt vector. And the second is a change in the operation of the serRecv function, where serRecv returns immediately rather than waiting for a character. If no character is available, it returns -1; if a character is available, it returns that character.

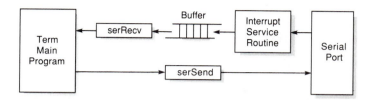

Figure 15-5. Serial Port Interface

Storage is set aside for two circular buffers, one for each port. We will use them only for incoming data. The best size for the buffers depends on the application. In this application, data taken from the buffer will be displayed on the screen, most likely in blocks no larger than one screenful. Therefore, a buffer roughly the same size as the screen should be enough for any eventuality.

The serInit routine still calls the ROM BIOS initialization function and lets it do most of the work, especially setting the data format and speed. But it then initializes the circular buffer for this port, sets up the appropriate vector, and enables receive interrupts in both the serial port hardware and in the interrupt controller. The existing interrupt vector is saved so it can be restored later. Interrupts are not used for transmitting data out the port, although they could be. For this application, where the outgoing data is generated by someone typing, it is not necessary to use an interrupt-driven approach. The serClose function disables the interrupts and returns the vector to its original value. Note that both serInit and serClose disable processor interrupts; this keeps an unexpected interrupt from using a partially completed interrupt vector.

The interrupt service routine carefully saves all the registers it will use, and then determines the type of interrupt. Even if the other interrupt types are not being used, it is a good idea to clear them. Otherwise, if an unexpected interrupt occurs, the program will be stuck permanently with an interrupt it refuses to clear. If the interrupt was a receive buffer full type interrupt, the service routine gets the new character from the hardware and adds it to the circular buffer. Regardless of its cause, the interrupt is acknowledged at the 8259 interrupt controller as well.

The new serRecv routine checks the circular buffer. If it's empty, it returns -1. If it has data available, it returns the first available character.

Although its function has not changed, the serSend function is now implemented differently. Rather than calling the ROM BIOS, it goes directly to the hardware to transmit the character, waiting for the hardware to finish with the previous character first. This is necessary because the ROM BIOS send character routine unconditionally turns interrupts off, which would keep our receive character code from being called properly.

The getb and putb functions at the end of the listing implement the circular buffer. The old version of serStat can still be used, so it is not shown here.

The Term2 Program

With this new serial port interface library, the C code for Term needs to change very little. Rather than checking for new incoming data with serStat, the new serRecv function simply returns -1 if there is no new data. Also, there must be a call added to the serClose function. Without this, the interrupt vectors changed during initialization would still point to the location where the interrupt service routine had been, and the interrupts would still be enabled. The next time an interrupt occurred from the serial port, the processor would vector off to what would then be jibberish, the memory area having been replaced with new code. This sort of bug can be very hard to find, since it may not occur until some completely different program is running. It is very important, therefore, to remember the serClose call. Listing 15-2 shows the complete new version of Term.

Summary

There is often more than one way to implement a given function. In this chapter, we have presented an alternative implementation for the program that was originally introduced in Chapter Eleven. This version has the advantage of eliminating the chance of losing data while the processor is busy elsewhere. It has the disadvantage of being much more complicated than the original. The complexity is found not only in the fact that the algorithm is more sophisticated, but also in the fact that more of the code is in assembly, and the implementation is much more hardware specific—in this case, specific even to the I/O addresses and the bit assignments of the data at those addresses.

More of this program could have been implemented in C. Instead of writing the entire interrupt service routine in assembly, it could have saved the registers and called a C function. Similarly, the circular buffer routines could have been implemented entirely in C. The decision of which way to implement the function is not clear-cut. C is generally more readable and maintainable, but indiscriminate jumping between C and assembly can make the program harder to understand. And, of course, interrupts are time-critical activities. In order to service the interrupt, the processor is pulled away from some other activity, and the sooner it's returned to its normal activities the better.

Exercises

1. Rewrite Term2, using as much C and as little assembly as possible.
2. Rewrite the send character portion of s2lib.asm (Chapter Eleven), so that it too uses a circular buffer.
3. If you have already implemented the additional features described in the exercises in Chapter Eleven, change your expanded program to use the serial port library developed here.

Listing 15-1. "slib2.asm":

```
;                  Serial Port Direct Interface Library

          BUFSIZE = 2000                    ; Size of buffer to use for receive

_BSS      segment word public 'BSS'         ; Global variables segment
_BSS      ends

_TEXT     segment byte public 'CODE'        ; Code segment
_TEXT     ends

DGROUP    group _BSS                        ; Global variables are in this group

_BSS      segment                  ; Declare variables

intSav    dw      4 dup(?)         ; Storage for saved interrupt vectors
bufIn     dw      2 dup(?)         ; Buffer input pointers
bufOut    dw      2 dup (?)        ; Buffer output pointers
buff0     db      BUFSIZE dup(?)   ; The COM1 circular buffer
buff1     db      BUFSIZE dup(?)   ; The COM2 buffer

_BSS      ends                     ; End of variables

_TEXT     segment                  ; Place the code in the code segment

          assume CS:_TEXT, DS:DGROUP ; Assume CS points to code segment, and
                                     ;    DS points to DGROUP segment (where
                                     ;    the variables are)

; _serInit(port,config)
;
; Function: Initialize and configure serial port port (0 for COM1, 1 for
; COM2). See the main text of the chapter for details on the format of the
; config parameter. Also set up incoming interrupts and buffering.
;
; Algorithm: Call the ROM BIOS to configure and initialize the port. Then
; save the existing interrupt vector and replace it with our own. Enable
; interrupts at the port, and return.

          public  _serInit        ; Routine is available to other modules

          port = 4                ; Offset from BP to parameter port
          config = 6              ; Offset to parameter config

; These two tables are used to get the buffer pointers based on the
; port number. The first table contains pointers to the beginning of
; the buffers; the second contains pointers to the first byte immediately
; after the buffers.
bufAddr dw      offset DGROUP:buff0, offset DGROUP:buff1
bufLim  dw      offset DGROUP:buff0+BUFSIZE, offset DGROUP:buff1+BUFSIZE

_serInit proc near                ; NEAR type subroutine
         push    bp               ; Save the BP register
         mov     bp,sp            ; Set BP to SP; easier to get parameters
         push    di               ; Save the DI register
         push    si               ; Save the SI register
         mov     dx,[bp+port]     ; DX = port number
```

Listing 15-1. "slib2.asm" *(cont.)*:

```
        mov     al,[bp+config]     ; AL = port configuration
        mov     ah,0               ; Call ROM BIOS port init function
        int     14H
        cli                        ; Disable interrupts
        push    es                 ; Save the ES register
        xor     ax,ax              ; ES = 0 (to access low memory)
        mov     es,ax
        mov     si,[bp+port]       ; SI = port # * 2
        shl     si,1
        mov     ax,cs:[si+bufAddr] ; Set the buffer to empty:
        mov     [si+bufIn],ax      ;    bufIn = bufOut = start of buffer
        mov     [si+bufOut],ax
        mov     bx,es:[si+400H]    ; BX = base port address of serial port
        mov     si,1               ; SI = (1 - port #) * 4 (offset to vector)
        sub     si,[bp+port]
        shl     si,1
        shl     si,1
        mov     ax,es:[si+2CH]     ; Save the old vector in intSav
        mov     [si+intSav],ax
        mov     ax,es:[si+2CH+2]
        mov     [si+intSav+2],ax
        mov     ax,OFFSET intServ  ; Replace the vector with intServ
        mov     es:[si+2CH],ax
        mov     ax,_TEXT
        mov     es:[si+2CH+2],ax
        mov     dx,bx              ; Read the serial port to clear it
        in      al,dx
        add     dx,4               ; Get modem control register address
        in      al,dx              ; Get contents of modem control registers
        or      al,8               ; Set the OUT2 bit (enables interrupt line)
        out     dx,al              ; Output it
        sub     dx,3               ; Get interrupt enable register address
        mov     al,1               ; Enable receive interrupts only
        out     dx,al              ; Set it
        in      al,21H             ; Get enable register from the 8259
        mov     ah,0EFH            ; Get mask
        mov     cl,[bp+port]       ; Rotate it according to the port number
        ror     ah,cl
        and     al,ah              ; Clear the appropriate bit (enable it)
        out     21H,al             ; Output it to enable interrupts
        sti                        ; Enable interrupts
        pop     es                 ; Restore ES
        pop     si                 ; Restore the SI register
        pop     di                 ; Restore the DI register
        pop     bp                 ; Restore the BP register
        ret                        ; Return to calling program
_serInit endp                      ; End of subroutine

; intServ
;
; Function: Serial receive interrupt service routine. Handle an interrupt
; from a serial port and return.
;
; Algorithm: Save registers. Figure out which port the interrupt is from.
; Figure out what kind of interrupt it is, and process it accordingly.
; Acknowledge the interrupt at the 8259. Then restore registers and return
```

Listing 15-1. "slib2.asm" *(cont.)*:

```
; from interrupt.

intServ proc near                   ; NEAR type subroutine (doesn't matter which
                                     ;   type actually, since we do a IRET rather
                                     ;   than a RET)
        push    ax                  ; Save the AX register
        push    bx                  ; Save BX
        push    cx                  ; Save CX
        push    dx                  ; Save DX
        push    si                  ; Save SI
        push    ds                  ; Save DS
        push    es                  ; Save ES
        mov     ax,DGROUP           ; Set DS to DGROUP for access to variables
        mov     ds,ax
        xor     ax,ax               ; Set ES to 0 for access to low memory
        mov     es,ax
;
; Find which port the interrupt is from:
;
        xor     si,si               ; SI = 0 (assume COM1)
        mov     dx,es:400H          ; DX = base port address for COM1
        add     dx,2                ; Get IIR address
        in      al,dx               ; Get IIR contents
        mov     ah,al               ; Make a copy of the input
        and     ah,1                ; Any interrupts here?
        jz      intC1               ; If there is an interrupt, go process it
        mov     dx,es:402H          ; Otherwise, DX = base port address for COM2
        add     dx,2                ; Get IIR address for COM2
        in      al,dx               ; Get IIR contents
        mov     ah,al               ; Make a copy of it
        and     ah,1                ; Are there interrupts?
        jnz     notC2               ; If not, forget this interrupt
        add     si,2                ; If yes, increment SI for use with COM2
;
; Find out which type of interrupt it is, and handle it:
;
intC1:  cmp     al,0                ; Is it a modem status change?
        jne     notMSt              ; If not, try the next interrupt type
        add     dx,4                ; If it is, read the modem status to clear it
        in      al,dx
        jmp     endInt              ; And exit
notMSt: cmp     al,2                ; Is it a transmit register empty interrupt?
        jne     notTRE              ; If not, try other types
        jmp     endInt              ; If it is, exit (we shouldn't get these)
notTRE: cmp     al,4                ; Is it a receiver register full interrupt?
        jne     notRRF              ; If not, try other types
        sub     dx,2                ; If yes, read in the received character
        in      al,dx
        call    putb                ; Put it in the buffer
        jmp     endInt              ; And exit
notRRF: cmp     al,6                ; Is it a receive line status interrupt?
        jne     endInt              ; If not, it's no known type -- ignore it
        add     dx,3                ; If yes, read the status to clear it
        in      al,dx
;
; Send end-of-interrupt to the 8259:
```

Listing 15-1. "slib2.asm" *(cont.)*:

```
;
endInt: mov     al,20H          ; Send EOI
        out     20H,al
;
; Restore registers and exit:
;
notC2:  pop     es              ; Restore the ES register
        pop     ds              ; Restore DS
        pop     si              ; Restore SI
        pop     dx              ; Restore DX
        pop     cx              ; Restore CX
        pop     bx              ; Restore BX
        pop     ax              ; Restore AX
        iret                    ; Return from interrupt
intServ endp                    ; End of routine

; serClose(port)
;
; Function: Close the port; restore it to the state it was in before serInit
; was called.
;
; Algorithm: Turn off interrupts and restore the interrupt vector to its
; original state.

        public  _serClose       ; Routine is available to other modules

        port = 4                ; Offset from BP to parameter port

_serClose proc near             ; NEAR type subroutine
        push    bp              ; Save the BP register
        mov     bp,sp           ; Set BP to SP; easier to access parameters
        push    di              ; Save the DI register
        push    si              ; Save the SI register
        push    es              ; Save the ES register
        xor     ax,ax           ; Set ES to 0, for access to low memory
        mov     es,ax
        cli                     ; Disbale interrupts
        mov     si,[bp+port]    ; SI = 2*port #
        shl     si,1
        mov     bx,es:[si+400H] ; BX = I/O port base address
        mov     si,1            ; SI = 4*(1 - port #)
        sub     si,[bp+port]
        shl     si,1
        shl     si,1
        mov     ax,[si+intSav]  ; Restore the interrupt from intSav
        mov     es:[si+2CH],ax
        mov     ax,[si+intSav+2]
        mov     es:[si+2CH+2],ax
        mov     dx,bx           ; Get modem control register address
        add     dx,4
        in      al,dx           ; Get current value
        and     al,0F7H         ; Turn off OUT2 bit (interrupt enable)
        out     dx,al           ; Set it
        sub     dx,3            ; Get interrupt enable register address
        xor     al,al           ; Clear all interrupt enable bits
        out     dx,al           ; Set them
```

Listing 15-1. "slib2.asm" *(cont.)*:

```
        in      al,21H          ; Get 8259 enable byte
        mov     ah,10H          ; Get a mask for the enable for this port
        mov     cl,[bp+port]
        ror     ah,cl
        or      al,ah           ; Turn off the enable bit for this port
        out     21H,al          ; Set it
        mov     al,20H          ; Write an EOI just in case
        out     20H,al
        sti                     ; Re-enble interrupts at the processor
        pop     es              ; Restore the ES register
        pop     si              ; Restore SI
        pop     di              ; Restore DI
        pop     bp              ; Restore BP
        ret                     ; Return to calling program
_serClose endp                  ; End of subroutine
;   _serSend(port,char)
;
; Function: Send the character char out over serial port port.
;
; Algorithm: Wait for the transmit holding register to be empty, and then
; output the character to be sent to that register.

        public  _serSend        ; Routine is available to other modules

        port = 4                ; Offset from BP to parameter port
        char = 6                ; Offset to parameter char

_serSend proc near              ; NEAR type subroutine
        push    bp              ; Save the BP register
        mov     bp,sp           ; Set BP to SP; easier to access parameters
        push    di              ; Save the DI register
        push    si              ; Save the SI register
        push    es              ; Save ES
        mov     dx,[bp+port]    ; DX = port #
        xor     ax,ax           ; ES = 0 (for access to low memory)
        mov     es,ax
        mov     si,[bp+port]    ; SI = 2*port #
        shl     si,1
        mov     dx,es:[si+400H] ; DX = I/O port base address
        add     dx,5            ; DX = address of line status register
sendWt: in      al,dx           ; Get line status
        and     al,20H          ; Transmit holding register empty?
        jz      sendWt          ; If not, keep asking...
        sub     dx,5            ; If yes, DX = address of trasmit holding reg.
        mov     al,[bp+char]    ; Send character
        out     dx,al
        pop     es              ; Restore the ES register
        pop     si              ; Restore SI
        pop     di              ; Restore DI
        pop     bp              ; Restore BP
        ret                     ; Return to caller
_serSend endp                   ; End of subroutine
;   _serRecv(port)
;
; Function: If a character is available from serial port port, return it.
```

Listing 15-1. "slib2.asm" *(cont.)*:

```
; Otherwise, return -1.
;
; Algorithm: Get the port number, turn off interrupts (so one doesn't sneak
; in and mess us up), and call getb to get a character out of the input
; buffer (if there's a character available).

        public  _serRecv         ; Routine is available to other modules

        port = 4                 ; Offset from BP to parameter port

_serRecv proc near               ; NEAR type subroutine
        push    bp               ; Save the BP register
        mov     bp,sp            ; Set BP to SP; easier to access parameters
        push    di               ; Save the DI register
        push    si               ; Save the SI register
        mov     si,[bp+port]     ; SI = 2 * port #
        shl     si,1
        cli                      ; Disable interrupts
        call    getb             ; Get a character from the buffer
        sti                      ; Enable interrupts
        pop     si               ; Restore SI register
        pop     di               ; Restore DI
        pop     bp               ; Restore BP
        ret                      ; Return to caller
_serRecv endp                    ; End of subroutine

; _serStat(port)
;
; Function: Return the status of the serial port specified.
;
; Algorithm: Call the ROM BIOS serial status function.

        public  _serStat         ; Routine is available to other modules

        port = 4                 ; Offset from BP to the parameter port

_serStat proc near               ; NEAR type subroutine
        push    bp               ; Save the BP register
        mov     bp,sp            ; Set BP to SP; easier to access parameters
        push    di               ; Save the DI register
        push    si               ; Save the SI register
        mov     dx,[bp+port]     ; DX = port #
        mov     ah,3             ; AH = 3 (serial status function)
        int     14H              ; Call ROM BIOS serial port interrupt
        pop     si               ; Restore the SI register
        pop     di               ; Restore DI
        pop     bp               ; Restore BP
        ret                      ; Return to caller
_serStat endp                    ; End of subroutine

; putb(AL = byte, SI = offset)
;
; Function: Put a byte into a circular buffer; AL contains the byte,
; SI contains a word offset within the buffer pointers (0 for the COM1
; buffer, 2 for the COM2 buffer). If the character didn't fit in the
; buffer, putb returns with AH == -1; otherwise AH == 0.
```

Listing 15-1. "slib2.asm" *(cont.)*:

```
;
; Algorithm: Get the bufIn pointer. Compute what the new bufIn will be.
; If it equals bufOut, the buffer is full. Otherwise, the character can
; be stored and bufIn updated.

putb    proc near               ; NEAR type subroutine
        mov     ah,-1           ; Assume the buffer'll be full
        mov     bx,[si+bufIn]   ; BX = bufIn
        mov     cx,bx           ; CX = (BX+1) modulo buffer
        inc     cx              ; CX++
        cmp     cx,cs:[si+bufLim] ; Is it past the end of the buffer?
        jne     putb2           ; If not, continue
        mov     cx,cs:[si+bufAddr] ; If yes, reset it to the beginning
putb2:  cmp     cx,[si+bufOut]  ; Is the buffer full?
        je      putb3           ; If it is, don't store this byte
        mov     [bx],al         ; Otherwise, store the byte
        xor     ah,ah           ; Set AH to indicate success
        mov     [si+bufIn],cx   ; Update bufIn
putb3:  ret                     ; Return
putb    endp                    ; End of subroutine

; getb(SI = offset); returns AL = char
;
; Function: Get a byte into a circular buffer; SI contains a word
; offset within the buffer pointers (0 for the COM1 buffer, 2 for
; the COM2 buffer). On return, AX will contain a character from the
; buffer, or -1 if there were no bytes left in the buffer.
;
; Algorithm: Get the bufOut pointer. If it equals bufIn, the buffer
; is full. Otherwise, get a byte and increment bufOut.

getb    proc near               ; NEAR type subroutine
        mov     ax,-1           ; Assume we'll fail
        mov     bx,[si+bufOut]  ; BX = bufOut
        cmp     bx,[si+bufIn]   ; bufOut == bufIn?
        je      getb2           ; If yes, go exit
        mov     al,[bx]         ; Otherwise, get byte from buffer
        xor     ah,ah           ; Clear top byte of AX
        inc     bx              ; Increment bufOut
        cmp     bx,cs:[si+bufLim] ; Past end of buffer?
        jne     getb3           ; If not, continue
        mov     bx,cs:[si+bufAddr] ; If yes, reset to the beginning
getb3:  mov     [si+bufOut],bx  ; Update bufOut
getb2:  ret                     ; Return
getb    endp                    ; End of subroutine

_TEXT   ends                    ; End of code segment
        end                     ; End of assembly code
```

Listing 15-2. "term2.c":

```
/*                  Terminal Emulator Program (Version 2)
*/

#define SERCONFIG 0x83  /* 1200 baud, 8 bits, 1 stop bit, no parity. */
```

Listing 15-2. "term2.c" *(cont.)*:

```
#define SERDRDY 0x100    /* Serial receiver data ready bit mask. */

#define TRUE 1
#define FALSE 0

/*      main()

        Function: Display data coming from COM1 on the screen, and send
        keystrokes from the keyboard out to COM1.

        Algorithm: Loop, waiting for data from either side to appear.
        Use keyChk to see if there's anything from the keyboard; if
        there is, send it using serSend. Use serRecv to check if
        there's anything from the serial port; if there is, display
        it using putTty.
*/

main()

{
        int ch; /* Character to transfer. */

        /* Initialize the port. */
        serInit(0,SERCONFIG);

        /* Main loop. */
        while (TRUE) {
                /* Check for keyboard input. */
                if (keyChk(&ch)) {
                        /* If yes, clear the character from the queue. */
                        keyRd();
                        /* Check for non-ASCII. */
                        if ((ch & 0xFF) == 0) {
                                break;
                        };
                        /* Send the character out the serial port. */
                        serSend(0,ch);
                };
                /* Anything available from the serial port? */
                if ((ch = serRecv(0)) != -1)
                        /* If so, display it. */
                        putTty(0,ch,3);
        };

        /* Close the serial port. */
        serClose(0);
}
```

Chapter 16

Direct Access Sound I/O: *NoiseMaker*

- The Sound Hardware: Accessing the 8253 (PC) or 8254 (AT) Timer Chip

- The Three Timers, Sound Control Bits

- The NoiseMaker Program: snd(cnt) and sndOff( )

- Siren, Overload, Whoop and Blaster

- Processor Speed Independent Sound: Percent of a Standard PC Approach

- Direct Speaker Control

I n this chapter, we will develop a sound effects program and present an assembly language interface to the sound hardware. The sound generation capabilities of the PC are somewhat limited, but, if properly programmed, it can still produce a wide range of interesting noises. In order to make noise on the PC, we will need to access the sound hardware directly. This hardware consists of one-third of the 8253 timer chip (8254 on the PC/AT), which is used to generate a continuous square wave. The square wave is filtered by external hardware to turn it into a sine wave, which then goes to the speaker, which actually generates the sound. We will use an assembly language interface to the sound hardware in our sound effects program.

The Sound Hardware

The sound hardware on the IBM PC consists of one-third of an 8253 timer chip (8254 on the PC/AT), two output bits of a general output register, and some external analog filtering, as shown in Figure 16-1. The timer chip contains three timers which can be configured to count a specific time interval or to generate a repeating square wave on an output pin (a square wave is a signal that is on for half of the time and off for half of the time). It is this latter mode that is used for sound generation. By programming the timer count value, the application sets the frequency of the output square wave: the longer the time, the lower the frequency. The filtering hardware then turns the square wave into a more pleasant sine wave (square waves sound coarse and jarring). The two output bits from the 8255 allow the program to turn the sound off entirely, and also to control the speaker directly without using the timer.

The 8253 is a general purpose timer chip that contains three independent timers. The 8254, used in the PC/AT, is a superset of the 8253. For our purposes, they are functionally identical. The chip has a clock input with a frequency of 1.193MHz. Each of the timers on the chip can use the clock input for one of two purposes: as a basis to measure out intervals that are an integer multiple of one cycle of this clock (838 nanoseconds), or to generate another signal that has a frequency an integral fraction of the original 1.193MHz frequency. The first of the three timers is used by the ROM BIOS to record the passage of time. It causes a clock-tick interrupt (interrupt 8) to occur 18.2 times per second (every 54.9 milliseconds). This interrupt can be used by the program to keep track of time. The ROM BIOS interrupt service routine for this interrupt increments a four-byte count in low memory location 46C (hex), which can be accessed either directly or by using ROM BIOS interrupt 1A (hex). It contains the number of ticks since midnight. The second of the three timers is used by the hardware in connection with dynamic memory refresh—this one should never be touched, unless you really know what you're doing, and maybe not even then.

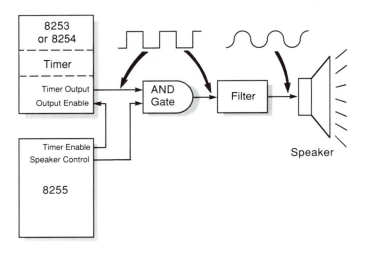

Figure 16-1. Sound Generation Hardware

The third timer is used to generate sounds. The value programmed into the timer determines the frequency of the sound that will be heard. A value of 1 will generate a frequency of 1.193MHz, a value of 2 will generate 0.596MHz, 3 will generate 0.397MHz, etc. The frequency is exactly 1,193,180/c, where c is the count programmed into the timer. All the frequencies just mentioned are well above the range of human hearing, which covers approximately 20Hz to 20,000Hz. If we want to pick a count based on a frequency, the formula is 1,193,180/f, where f is the frequency. So, if we want to sound a tone at 10KHz, we would program the timer with a value of 119. If we want 100Hz, we'd use 11,932.

The timer chip registers are at I/O port addresses 40-43 (hex). Setting the value into the timer involves three steps. First, we write the constant B6 (hex) to the control register at I/O address 43 (hex). This constant informs the chip that we want to write to the third timer, that we want to write the low byte of the count first, followed by the high byte; and that once it's programmed, we want the timer to act as a signal generator, using the count as a frequency divisor. We could have placed the timer in a number of other modes of operation, but this is the most convenient mode for sound generation. Second, we write the low byte of the count to I/O address 42 (hex). And third, we write the high byte, also to address 42 (hex). Once these three values are output to the timer, it will generate a square wave of the specified frequency forever; or at least until we write a different value to the register, or turn off the power.

At this point, the timer chip is generating the signal, but the signal is blocked from the speaker. The two other output bits act as enables to the signal, one enabling the output from the timer chip and the other enabling the signal at the AND gate. These must both be turned on before the signal can get to the speaker. These bits are controlled from an 8255 chip, which is a general purpose output chip: it has three output ports, each eight bits in size. The two bits we need share one of the three ports with several other outputs. They can be read and changed by reading and writing I/O port 61 (hex). (Note: The AT does not use an 8255 for this interface, but it uses one that is functionally identical in this area.) It is important that we don't change any of the other bits that share this output port, since they are used for other purposes. We must first read the current value of the byte, change only the bits we want to change, then write it back. Figure 16-2 shows the bits we're interested in.

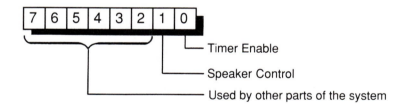

Figure 16-2: Sound Control Bits at I/O Port 61 (hex)

Listing 16-1 presents two assembly language routines that allow a C program to control the sound generation hardware just discussed. They perform the following functions:

Function

---

sound(cnt) — Set the timer to the count specified, and turn on the timer output and speaker.

sndOff() — Turn off the sound generation hardware.

The NoiseMaker Program

We can now write a C main program that uses the sound interface routines described above. Using these routines, it is easy to produce a single tone of a given frequency, and not much harder to produce a series of tones. It can be more interesting, however, to vary the frequency rapidly in order to produce sound effects. This is what the NoiseMaker program does. Figure 16-3 shows the four ways that NoiseMaker changes the frequency of the sound over time:

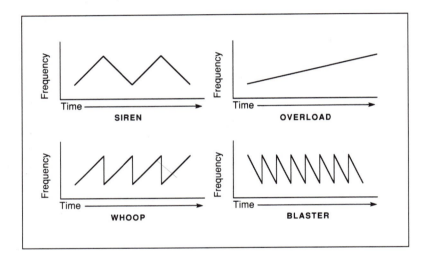

Figure 16-3. NoiseMaker Sound Patterns

Listing 16-2 presents the NoiseMaker program. The main loop asks the user which type of sound to play, and how many times to make that sound. A while statement is used to repeat the sound the specified number of times. The program then uses a switch statement to branch into one of four cases, corresponding to the four patterns presented above. The main loop repeats until the user selects exit.

When the frequency is changed, it momentarily disrupts the normal, balanced square wave output. This isn't noticeable if it happens infrequently, but if the delay between changing frequencies is too short, the listener starts to hear clicking noises. If the delay is too long, the listener can distinguish the individual frequency changes—it no longer sounds smooth and continuous. In designing sound effects like these, you have to decide which trade-off is best for you. We recommend that you try other frequency changing patterns. There are literally thousands of possibilities, and by experimenting with them you will get a feeling for the trade-offs involved.

Processor Speed

The program presented above will work fine on an IBM PC or an IBM PC/XT. But it won't work well at all on an IBM PC/AT, or on any IBM PC compatible machine that runs at a higher processor clock rate. The individual tones are still generated properly, since their frequencies are controlled by the timer chip; but the rate at which the processor changes those frequencies is different, because the processor is running at a different speed. The result is a program that works on some of the PC family machines, but fails on others.

The problem comes down to the delay function and how it does the delaying. In essence, the delay function is using the execution speed of the processor—how long the processor takes to complete a given number of iterations of a for loop—to accomplish its task, pausing for a set interval. There are two ways to fix this problem. The first involves rewriting the function so it uses some other means of measuring time. The second involves adjusting the count value we pass to the delay function according to the speed of the processor executing the program.

The first solution, keeping delay's function the same, but making it independent of the processor speed, is the best solution. We don't need to change any other parts of the program, and the resulting function will be useful in future work. Unfortunately, this is also the more complicated solution. The only readily available time source is the system timer, which ticks at a rate of only 18.2 times per second. This is much too slow for our needs. We can change the tick rate, but that is a complex operation. We will be showing how to modify the timer tick rate in Chapter Seventeen, so we encourage you to return to this problem after reading that chapter and rewrite the delay function yourself. For our purposes here, we will take a simpler approach.

The second solution involves discovering how much faster (or slower) the current processor is than a "standard" IBM PC processor. Using that information, we can adjust the count values passed to the delay function. This involves writing a function that returns the speed of the processor as a percent of a standard PC—i.e., it will return 100 for a normal PC, 200 for a PC that is running twice as fast, etc. We use percent because the speed of the processor may not be an integral multiple of a standard PC, but we don't want to incur the overhead of using floating point. Percentages give us two digits resolution while still using integers.

We can discover the speed of the processor by counting how many times a loop is executed between two system timer ticks. Listing 16-3 shows calib, a function that does this by using a far pointer to access the system time-of-day stored in low memory. We used far pointers in C rather than an assembly language routine for two reasons. First, it will tend to make the code portable to new C compilers, since it takes into account the way the compiler performs for loops, as well as the processor speed. This technique is not guaranteed to work, but it is more likely to work than using assembly language. Second, we wanted to illustrate the use of far pointers. Although most of the examples in this book have used assembly language to access data outside the normal data space of the C program, it is sometimes simpler to use far pointers within C—assuming, of course, that your C compiler provides them, as does the Microsoft compiler.

The function's result is calculated by multiplying the iteration count by 100 (to turn it into a percentage) and dividing by the number of iterations required on a standard IBM PC. Note that the arithmetic which calculates the final result uses long integers to avoid overflow before the final division. The number of iterations that a standard PC takes is found by inserting a statement to print the iteration value before the return statement. The number printed is then inserted into the formula in the last statement.

Using this function, we can easily write a program to display the power of the current processor as compared with a standard PC. This program is given in Listing 16-4. This is not a complete or fair test of the processor's power, however, since it really tests only the processor's ability to execute empty for loops. But, it does give a ball-park idea of the processor speed. This program shows the processor speed of the IBM PC/AT, for example, as being 289% greater than that of a standard IBM PC—in other words, it runs almost three times as fast. (Note that the value displayed by this program is accurate to plus or minus 1, so don't be alarmed if it says your machine is only 99% of an IBM PC.)

Armed with the calib function, we can rewrite NoiseMaker to be independent of processor speed. This version of the program is shown in Listing 16-5. At the beginning of the program, the calib function calculates the equivalent of the delay counts used in the program; these are stored in local variables adj100, adj200, and adj700. In the body of the program, the parameters to the delay function are replaced with these precomputed counts.

Direct Speaker Control

There is another, more direct way to control the speaker. If the timer enable output is zero, the timer outputs a constant high (1) signal. The program can then use the speaker control output to control the state of the speaker directly and immediately. The program is not limited to the square waves that the timer can generate; it can generate an arbitrary signal to the speaker. This technique allows the program to generate a much richer set of sounds, but it has two disadvantages. First, the program must be actively controlling the output: if it isn't, no sound is generated (unlike the timer, which continues to run even without the program). And second, because of the first disadvantage, nothing can be allowed to interfere with the program while it's generating the sound signal. This includes the ROM BIOS timer interrupt, which will occur 18.2 times every second, and, of course, any other interrupts that the program uses, such as the serial port interrupts described earlier. But if the program disables the ROM BIOS timer interrupt, the PC will lose track of the current time. It may be necessary to control the speaker directly for some special applications requiring the added flexibility, but we do not recommend it for everyday use.

Summary

The sound generation facility of the IBM PC consists of one-third of the system timer chip, together with two output enables. The output is passed through a filter to produce a more pleasant tone, and then delivered to a speaker. Using the timer, the PC can generate a continuous tone. We have presented an assembly language library that allows a C program to turn on the tone, and to turn off the speaker entirely. The frequency can be changed continuously to make more interesting noises. The NoiseMaker program uses this technique to generate a variety of sounds.

Because the sounds are changed in proportion to the speed of the processor, NoiseMaker will not work properly on machines with different processor speeds. One such machine is the IBM PC/AT. It is possible, however, to determine the speed of the processor and correct for it.

We presented a routine that discovers the current processor speed, as well as a program that prints out the results, showing the speed of the processor as a percentage of a "standard" IBM PC. We then used this same function to produce a new version of NoiseMaker that is independent of the speed of the processor.

Exercises

1. Try as many variations as possible on the sound effects presented in the NoiseMaker program.
2. Write a program that directly controls the speaker. Generate a constant tone. Notice the interference from the 18.2Hz timer interrupts.
3. Using the routines developed in this chapter, write a C program that uses the keyboard as a musical keyboard. Each key should cause a specific note to be sounded. Use the shift, control, and alt keys to modify the duration of the note.
4. [advanced] Discover how to disable the ROM BIOS timer interrupt. Rerun the program in the first exercise with the interrupt disabled.

Listing 16-1. "sndlib.asm":

```
;                     Noise Library

_TEXT    segment byte public 'CODE'        ; Place the code in the code segment
         assume  CS:_TEXT                   ; Assume the CS register points to it

; _sound(count)
;
; Function: Turn on the speaker and have it play the note specified by
; count.
;
; Algorithm: Write the count to the portion of the timer that drives the
; speaker, and then enable the speaker output.

         public _sound                      ; Routine is available to other modules

         count = 4                          ; Offset from BP to the parameter count

_sound   proc near                          ; NEAR type subroutine
         push    bp                         ; Save the BP register
         mov     bp,sp                      ; Set BP to SP; easier to access parameters
         mov     al,0B6H                    ; Tell timer to prepare for a new count
         out     43H,al
         mov     ax,[bp+count]              ; Write new count to the timer, low byte 1st
         out     42H,al
         mov     al,ah                      ; Then high byte
         out     42H,al
         in      al,61H                     ; Enable speaker output from timer
         or      al,3
         out     61H,al
         pop     bp                         ; Restore the BP register
         ret                                ; Return to caller
_sound   endp                               ; End of subroutine

; _sndoff()
;
; Function: Turn off speaker.
;
; Algorithm: Disable speaker output from timer.

         public _sndOff                     ; Routine is available to other modules

_sndOff  proc near                          ; NEAR type subroutine
         in      al,61H                     ; Disable speaker output from timer
         and     al,0FCH
         out     61H,al
         ret                                ; Return to caller
_sndOff  endp                               ; End of subroutine

_TEXT    ends                               ; End of code segment
         end                                ; End of assembly code
```

Listing 16-2. "noise.c":

```
/*                    Noise Maker Main Program
 */

#define FALSE 0
#define TRUE 1

/*       main()

         Function: Produce sound-effect. Repeatedly ask the user what
         sound to make, and then make it.
```

Listing 16-2. "noise.c" *(cont.)*:

```
Algorithm: Loop, asking the user for which sound and how many
times to make it. Then repeat the sound generation code the
number of times requested. To generate the sound, switch on the
type of sound to generate. Each sound is generated by sweeping
through a set of frequencies in a particular order at a particular
rate.
*/

main()

{
        int snd;        /* Which sound to produce. */
        int cnt;        /* Number of times to repeat sound. */
        int note;       /* Current note, when sweeping frequencies. */

        while (TRUE) {
                /* Make sure any previous sounds are turned off. */
                sndOff();
                /* Ask the user for which type of sound. */
                printf("1-siren; 2-overload; 3-whoop; 4-phaser; 0-exit: ");
                /* Read the answer. */
                scanf("%d",&snd);
                /* If the answer is to exit, do so. */
                if (snd == 0) break;
                /* Ask how many times to repeat the sound. */
                printf("Number of times: ");
                /* Get the answer. */
                scanf("%d",&cnt);
                /* Repeat the sound the number of time specified. */
                while (cnt--) {
                        /* Switch on type of sound to produce. */
                        switch (snd) {
                                case 1:
                                        /* Do a siren: sweep up. */
                                        for (note = 1000; note > 150;
                                            note -= 10) {
                                                sound(note); delay(200);
                                        };
                                        /* Sweep down. */
                                        for (; note < 1000; note += 10) {
                                                sound(note); delay(200);
                                        };
                                        break;
                                case 2:
                                        /* Do an overload: sweep up. */
                                        for (note = 4000; note > 10;
                                            note -= 10) {
                                                sound(note); delay(700);
                                        };
                                        break;
                                case 3:
                                        /* Do a whoop: sweep up. */
                                        for (note = 1000; note > 10;
                                            note -= 10) {
                                                sound(note); delay(200);
                                        };
                                        break;
                                case 4:
                                        /* Do a phaser: sweep down. */
                                        for (note = 60; note < 2000;
                                            note += 10) {
                                                sound(note); delay(100);
                                        };
                                        break;
```

Listing 16-2. "noise.c" *(cont.)*:

```
                            default:
                                    /* Unknown, ask again. */
                                    printf("Invalid entry; try again.\n");
                                    break;
                    };
            };
    };
}

/*      delay(cnt)

        Function: Delay for an amount of time proportional to cnt.

        Algorithm: Just waste time in a for loop.
*/

delay(cnt)

{
        int i;

        /* Loop to burn time... */
        for (i = 0; i < cnt; i++);
}
```

Listing 16-3. "calib.c":

```
/*                      Processor Speed Calibration Function
 */

/*      calib()

        Function: Return the speed of this processor, as a percent of
        the speed of a standard IBM-PC.

        Algorithm: Iterate for one system timer tic (as found in low
        memory location 46C). Multiply the result by 100 (conver to %)
        add in 50 (so the next divide will round rather than truncate),
        and divide by the number of iterations on a normal PC. Do all
        the calculations in long format to avoid overflow.
*/

calib()

{
        /* Pointer to system timer in low memory: */
        unsigned far *timerLow = {(unsigned far *) 0x46C};
        unsigned lastTime;      /* Last value read from *timerLow. */
        unsigned iter;          /* Iteration count. */

        /* Wait until timer has just ticked. */
        for (lastTime = *timerLow; lastTime == *timerLow;);
        /* Count iterations until the next tick. */
        for (iter = 0, lastTime = *timerLow; lastTime == *timerLow; iter++);
        /* Calculate and return the percent of a standard IBM-PC. */
        return ((100L*((long) iter) + 50L)/1878L);
}
```

Listing 16-4. "speed.c":

```
/*                      Display Processor Speed
 */

/*      main()

        Function: Display the speed of the current processor, as a
        percentage of a standard IBM-PC.

        Algorithm: Just call calib and print out the result.
*/

main()

{
        printf("This processor is %u%% of a standard IBM-PC.\n",calib());
}
```

Listing 16-5. "noise2.c":

```
/*                      Noise Maker Main Program
 */

#define FALSE 0
#define TRUE 1

/*      main()

        Function: Produce sound-effect. Repeatedly ask the user what
        sound to make, and then make it.

        Algorithm: Loop, asking the user for which sound and how many
        times to make it. Then repeat the sound generation code the
        number of times requested. To generate the sound, switch on the
        type of sound to generate. Each sound is generated by sweeping
        through a set of frequencies in a particular order at a particular
        rate.
*/

main()

{
        int snd;        /* Which sound to produce. */
        int cnt;        /* Number of times to repeat sound. */
        int note;       /* Current note, when sweeping frequencies. */
        int adj100;     /* A delay of 100, adjusted for processor speed. */
        int adj200;     /* Delay of 200, adjusted for processor speed. */
        int adj700;     /* Delay of 700, adjusted for processor speed. */

        /* Calculate the delays needed for this processor. */
        adj100 = calib();
        adj200 = 2*adj100;
        adj700 = 7*adj100;

        while (TRUE) {
                /* Make sure any previous sounds are turned off. */
                sndOff();
                /* Ask the user for which type of sound. */
                printf("1-siren; 2-overload; 3-whoop; 4-phaser; 0-exit: ");
                /* Read the answer. */
                scanf("%d",&snd);
                /* If the answer is to exit, do so. */
                if (snd == 0) break;
```

Listing 16-5. "noise2.c" (cont.):

```
                /* Ask how many times to repeat the sound. */
                printf("Number of times: ");
                /* Get the answer. */
                scanf("%d",&cnt);
                /* Repeat the sound the number of time specified. */
                while (cnt--) {
                        /* Switch on type of sound to produce. */
                        switch (snd) {
                                case 1:
                                        /* Do a siren: sweep up. */
                                        for (note = 1000; note > 150;
                                            note -= 10) {
                                                sound(note); delay(adj200);
                                        };
                                        /* Sweep down. */
                                        for (; note < 1000; note += 10) {
                                                sound(note); delay(adj200);
                                        };
                                        break;
                                case 2:
                                        /* Do an overload: sweep up. */
                                        for (note = 4000; note > 10;
                                            note -= 10) {
                                                sound(note); delay(adj700);
                                        };
                                        break;
                                case 3:
                                        /* Do a whoop: sweep up. */
                                        for (note = 1000; note > 10;
                                            note -= 10) {
                                                sound(note); delay(adj200);
                                        };
                                        break;
                                case 4:
                                        /* Do a phaser: sweep down. */
                                        for (note = 60; note < 2000;
                                            note += 10) {
                                                sound(note); delay(adj100);
                                        };
                                        break;
                                default:
                                        /* Unknown, ask again. */
                                        printf("Invalid entry; try again.\n");
                                        break;
                        };
                };
        };
}

/*      delay(cnt)

        Function: Delay for an amount of time proportional to cnt.

        Algorithm: Just waste time in a for loop.
*/

delay(cnt)

{
        int i;

        /* Loop to burn time... */
        for (i = 0; i < cnt; i++);
}
```

Chapter 17

Supercharging
Tool: *IP Histogram*

- Introduction to Instruction Pointer Histograms

- 64 Byte Address Resolution and 1,025 Counters

- Increasing the Timer Interrupts on the 8253 and 8254 to 1,165/Second

- The IP Histogram Module

- Link Maps

- Analyzing RamSort

W e're now ready to develop a very useful tool for supercharging programs: the IP histogram module. This module records statistically where a program spends its time, allowing the programmer to see into the program as it executes. With this tool, the programmer can find the 10% of the code where 90% of the execution time is spent, and therefore can optimize the processor execution time much more effectively.

The IP histogram module collects information by using the timer interrupt to stop program execution periodically and record where the program is executing at that moment. This builds a histogram in the PC's memory of the locations to which the processor instruction pointer (IP) pointed. When execution is finished, the histogram can be displayed and the programmer can interpret it. This module can be incorporated into any program as part of the testing and calibration conditional compilation.

IP Histograms

In general, it is difficult for a programmer to get a real feeling for how a program executes, where it spends its time, what are the bottlenecks, and so on. Most programs are composed of thousands of instructions—without even counting the underlying operating system—and the PC executes hundreds of thousands of instructions per second. Programs are large, complex systems. It is possible to understand them at the micro level, perhaps using a debugger to single-step the program execution one instruction at a time. But the program is qualitatively different when executed at one instruction per second rather than the normal hundred thousand instructions per second. And at a rate of one instruction per second, it would take over a day to step through what the program does in the first second of execution.

When dealing with large quantities, we find it easier to work with statistics than with distinct events. Instead of considering the entire chain of execution, a record of which would quickly fill up all the disk space available and take a life-time (literally) to weed through, we can take another approach. For each address in the program, we can keep a record of how many times that instruction was executed. By doing this, we discard all the information about the order of execution—which instruction followed which—and retain only the number of times each instruction was executed. This reduces the amount of information by an order of magnitude, and simplifies the problems of both collection and interpretation.

An IP histogram is a record of where the program spent its time. A histogram counter is associated with each instruction, or block of instructions. The value in the counter, relative to the sum of the values in all the counters, tells what percentage of its total execution time the program spent executing this particular instruction. IP histograms can be used to help the programmer better understand the program. They are particularly useful in optimizing processor execution time, since they show where in the program improvements will do the most good.

To build an IP histogram, we must construct an array of counters, increment them according to where the program is executing, and then display them for the programmer after the program has finished execution. The final display should look something like Figure 17-1. The histogram module could be constructed as a separate program, which loads and runs the program much like debug loads and runs the program to be debugged. But the loading process can be complicated. A much simpler technique, from the point of view of writing the histogram module, is to have the programmer writing the program to be measured take into account the fact that the program is going to be measured, probably as a part of the test and calibration conditional compilation. The programmer can then add calls to the histogram module to initialize the counters and to display the final results after the program has finished. Actually incrementing the counters, however, will be done using timer interrupts, so the programmer will not need to worry about that part.

ADDRESS	COUNT	PERCENT	GRAPH
0000-0040	0	0%	
0040-007F	0	0%	
0080-00BF	0	0%	
00C0-00FF	0	0%	
0100-013F	5	10%	
0140-017F	27	54%	
0180-01BF	18	36%	
01C0-01FF	0	0%	

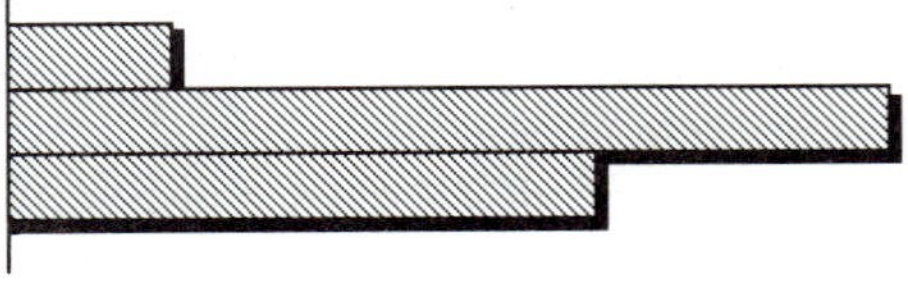

Figure 17-1. Execution Histogram

We will keep track of execution by using counters that count the number of times the program was "caught" executing at a particular location. On the IBM PC, we're primarily interested in the program's code segment. Even though the program will sometimes be executing outside that segment in MS-DOS and the ROM BIOS, we have little control over that part of the execution: we cannot rewrite the operating system, much less the ROM BIOS. We therefore clump all the addresses outside the program code segment into one counter, which we'll call "other."

Even within the program code segment, we don't need a counter for every instruction. We will use 64 byte chunks, making 1,024 counters in the 64K code segment. So all together, the IP histogram module will need to keep 1,025 counters, one for every 64 bytes in the program's code segment, plus one for all the addresses outside the code segment, as shown in Figure 17-2. To make sure that the counters don't overflow, we'll use long integers, which are four bytes long. The total histogram table size is then 4,100 bytes, which will fit easily within the normal data segment of the program. For most programs, 64 byte resolution on where the program spends its time is sufficient; if more detail is needed, another version of the histogram module can be easily produced with smaller blocks.

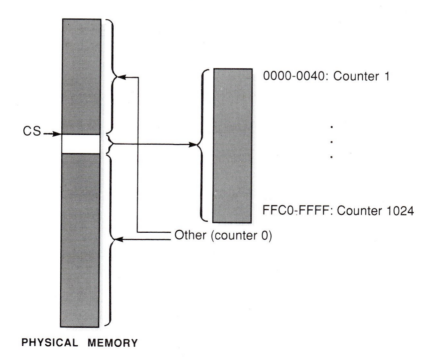

Figure 17-2. Histogram Counters

There are two ways to interrupt the program and collect the information about the current value of the IP. The first is to use the trap bit of the processor. When this bit is set, a processor interrupt is generated after every instruction executed; i.e., an interrupt service routine is invoked after every single instruction. This facility is used by the debugger to implement single-stepping of a program. The disadvantage of this approach is that it dramatically slows down the execution of the program. Since some 20 or 30 instructions must be executed to save and restore registers and find and record the histogram information in the histogram interrupt service routine, the program would run 20 or 30 times slower than normal.

A second technique slows the program down much less by periodically sampling the IP, not after every instruction, but at set intervals of time. In the IBM PC, the timer interrupt, normally used to increment the time of day, can provide this periodic interrupt. Once a millisecond is about the right sampling rate. Again, we are using statistical techniques to simplify the data collection problem. Also, note that because not every instruction is sampled, the histogram cannot be interpreted as a complete record of which parts of the code were executed, only which parts were executed most frequently.

The Timer Interrupt

We used one-third of the 8253 timer chip (8254 in the PC/AT) in Chapter Sixteen to produce a continuous signal for the speaker. Another third of the timer is normally used by the ROM BIOS to interrupt the processor 18.2 times every second. We could simply use this existing interrupt to record the IP status, but at only 18.2 samples per second, it would take some time to build up a reasonable histogram. Instead, we will increase the interrupt rate by a factor of 64, yielding a sampling rate of approximately 1,165 times every second, or a little more than once a millisecond. In order not to interfere with the normal timer interrupt operation—which is used to keep track of the time of day and also to shut off the floppy disk drive after a certain period of inactivity—we will call the original timer interrupt service routine once every 64 times through our IP sampling routine, as illustrated in Figure 17-3.

In order to change the timer interrupt rate, we must change the count value in the timer. This value is exactly like the one we wrote to change the sound frequency in Chapter Sixteen, except with timer zero it changes the interrupt frequency rather than the sound frequency. To do this, we first write a 36 (hex) to address 43 (hex)—this tells the timer that we're going to write a new count value. It is the equivalent, for timer zero, of the B6 (hex) we wrote to set up timer two back in Chapter Sixteen. Then we write the low and high bytes of the count to port address 40 (hex). In normal operation, the ROM BIOS sets the timer count to zero. This is really equivalent to 65,536, since the counter is decremented first and then checked to see if it reached zero, not the other way around. In order to interrupt 64 times more often, the counter must be set to 65,536/64, or 1,024, which is 400 in hexadecimal.

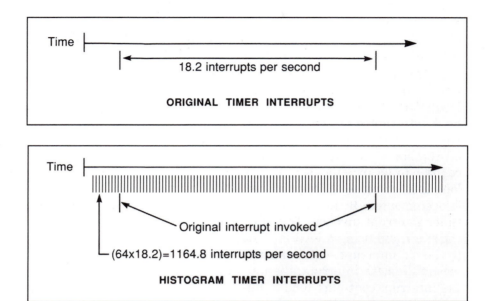

Figure 17-3. Timer Interrupt Rates

Besides setting the timer value, the old interrupt vector must be saved and a new one put in its place. And after the interrupt service routine finishes, the interrupt must be acknowledged in the 8259 interrupt controller, just as we did in Chapter Fifteen for the serial port interrupt, by outputting 20 (hex) to port 20 (hex). This tells the 8259 that we're done servicing this interrupt and that it can proceed with the next pending interrupt (if any).

The IP Histogram Module

Listings 17-1 and 17-2 contain the IP histogram module. The second part of the module is in C because it is much easier to manipulate floating point numbers and perform formatted output—in this case, computing and writing the histogram information—in C than in assembly.

The startH function sets up the histogram storage area and changes the timer interrupt rate and vector. It begins by zeroing the histogram data area using a "rep stos" instruction; this clears all the histogram counters. Note that the first histogram counter is used for "other," the second for the first 64 bytes of the code segment, the third counter for the second 64 bytes, and so on. Next, the program saves the old vector and replaces it with a vector to the intServ interrupt service routine that we'll be using. And after setting the interrupt count to 64, which will be used in the service routine to determine when the interrupt has occurred 64 times, it changes the timer zero interrupt rate. Finally, it restores the registers it changed and returns to the function that called it.

The interrupt service routine, intServ, saves the registers it will change, and sets up the BP register to point to the stack and the DS register to point to the DGROUP group. Remember that we don't know what code the interrupt might have interrupted, and therefore we cannot count on the DS register to have the value we want. The values of the interrupted CS and IP registers, which are found on the stack, are then used to compute the offset within the histogram of the counter to be incremented. This address is stored in the BX register. The 32-bit long integer value at this address is then incremented. Next, the interrupt count is decremented. If this was the 64th interrupt, the count is reset and the normal timer interrupt invoked. This involves pushing the original timer IP and CS onto the stack and using a FAR RET instruction—note that the routine could not JMP to the old interrupt routine since all of the registers must be restored first. If this wasn't the 64th interrupt, the interrupt is acknowledged by sending a 20 (hex) to the interrupt controller (end-of-interrupt), the registers are restored, and an IRET instruction returns the processor to whatever it was doing before the interrupt.

The endH routine restores the timer to normal operation and prints the results of the histogram. First it saves the registers that will be changed. It sets the timer zero counter back to its normal, zero value and restores the old timer interrupt vector. Then it calls the prHist function to print out the histogram results. This operation is much easier to do in C than in assembly, since it involves manipulating long and floating point type numbers, and it is not at all time-critical. Finally, endH restores the registers and returns to the caller.

The prHist C function first prints a message that it is starting to compile the information from the histogram table. This is done, not because the operation takes a long time, but in case the program is being timed: when a stopwatch is used to time the program, we need a clear indication to the programmer when to hit the stop button on the watch. The routine then sums up all the counters; a floating point number is used for the sum to prevent any possibility of overflow, and also to speed up later percentage calculations. This number is printed. Then, for each histogram counter which is not zero, the address with which it is associated, the value of the counter, and the percentage of the total of all counters and the percentage of all counters except the "other" counter, are printed. Two percentages are presented because most of the time the programmer is interested in the percentage of the total time, but sometimes the "other" counter is so large that it drowns out the code segment counters, making it hard to interpret them. This is particularly true in disk-bound programs, where the bulk of the time is spent in the disk I/O routines.

Using the IP Histogram Module

The IP histogram module must be linked with the program to be measured. Calls must also be added to invoke the startH and endH functions. This is best done by adding a HIST constant which conditionally compiles those calls. The HIST constant can be considered a sub-mode of the CALIBRATE mode discussed earlier. As an example, we'll use the RamSort program developed in Chapter Four. Listing 17-3 contains a modified version of that application's main function.

Note that the startH call is placed after the code that outputs "Starting sort..." and the endH is placed before the code that outputs "done." Otherwise, the execution of those two puts calls would also be measured in the histogram. Compiling this modified RamSort, linking it with the original C version of the sort routine, sortl.c, and with the histogram module, and then running it, produces the following histogram:

```
Starting sort...
Program done. Compiling histogram data.

Total recorded hits:          116645.

Address      Count      % with Other   % without Other
---------    ---------  -------------  ---------------
  Other          0         0.000%
 240- 27f      32385       27.764%         27.764%
 280- 2bf       3610        3.095%          3.095%
1200-123f      73904       63.358%         63.358%
1240-127f       6746        5.783%          5.783%
done.
```

We now know that the program is spending about 69% of its time at the addresses between 1200 and 127F (hex). But what routines are found at those addresses? The answer is found in link maps produced by the linker.

Link Maps

Knowing where in the code segment the program is spending most of its time is not useful unless you can translate the code segment address into the module and function in the source code to which that address corresponds. Luckily, the linker produces a map of where it placed the various modules in the final, linked code segment. However, it tells only where the globally defined symbols (function names, global variables, etc.) are located, and does not provide information about the internal layout of the function. In other words, if you have two functions, a and b, defined in a source module, the link map will show where in the code segment a starts and where b starts, but it will not tell you the location of a particular statement inside a. This is yet another argument for keeping functions small and modular.

Listing 17-4 shows the link map for the modified RamSort program presented above (with the histogram module also linked in). The map has four parts. The first lists all the segments in the program. The second lists all the groups. The third lists all the global symbols—those available to other modules—ordered alphabetically. And the fourth also lists all the global symbols, but ordered by address. The global symbols ordered by address is the most useful part of the load map for interpreting histograms.

You will have noticed that there are a lot more symbols, and segments too, for that matter, than you ever consciously included in your program. These are included because a C run-time routine was called, either explicitly or implicitly, causing the linker to include that routine and its associated functions and data in the final linked file. An example of an explicit call is the printf function. Implicit calls happen in two ways. One way is that a call to one library function causes several other functions to be loaded, since the function explicitly called, calls those functions in turn. The second way is that the compiler needs a library function to perform some function, such as adding floating point numbers together. Exactly which functions show up in the link map will vary from application to application, and also, of course, from compiler to compiler. A lot can go on when you innocently invoke some routine from the run-time library. The use of printf and floating point numbers in the prHist function brings in a number of extra functions over what RamSort would need if the histogram module was not being used. For the purpose of interpreting histograms, you can ignore most of the extraneous entries in the link map. Only when you find your program spends a large part of its time in one of those functions do you need to figure out what the function is and what it does.

Analyzing RamSort

Now that we have the link map for RamSort, we can interpret its histogram: the program is spending 69% of its time in strcmp, and another 31% in sortLines. Recall that in Chapter Four we came to roughly the same conclusions, although through a much longer and more painful route. The obvious thing to do is recode strcmp in assembly, and incorporate it into sortLines, just as we did in Chapter Four. If we rerun the histogram on RamSort, using the final, assembly language version of sortLines from sortl.asm, we get the following histogram:

```
Starting sort...
Program done. Compiling histogram data.

Total recorded hits:            76555.

  Address      Count      % with Other    % without Other
  ---------    ---------  -------------    ---------------
    Other          0         0.000%
   240- 27f     76488        99.912%           99.912%
   280- 2bf        66         0.086%            0.086%
   2c0- 2ff         1         0.001%            0.001%
done.
```

Of course the link map changes somewhat in this version, but sortLines still starts at the same location. So, with this version of RamSort, virtually all of the time is spent in sortLines. This doesn't mean that the program is as efficient as possible. It means that any improvements in speed must come from changes to the sortLines routine, since that's where the processor is spending all of its time. Changes elsewhere will have negligible effect.

Note that because of our timer-based sampling, the fact that the other histogram counters are zero does not mean that the program never executed those instructions. It means only that the program didn't spend much time there, not enough for the timer interrupt to catch it in the act. For much the same reason, the percentages given are not as accurate as the three digits of precision would seem to indicate. The extra digits are there so that even very low counter values show some non-zero percentage.

Summary

It is difficult to tell what a program is doing when it's executing. The IP histogram module provides one tool for looking into the operation of the program and getting a little better idea what's actually happening. Using this tool, we can isolate those parts of a program that will have the most impact if rewritten; and we can better understand and measure the effects of the rewrite.

The IP histogram module increases the frequency of the system timer interrupt by a factor of 64. This allows it to sample the instruction pointer of the processor approximately once a millisecond and to record the value in the histogram table. Every 64 times through the interrupt, the original, time-of-day interrupt is invoked, giving the regular system timer routine a chance to perform its normal function. Changing the timer rate involves the same sort of timer manipulation as that presented in Chapter Sixteen. Changing the interrupt vector involves the same sort of procedure as that presented in Chapter Fifteen. Once the histogram has been collected in memory, it can be presented to the user. The most useful presentation displays it as a list of percentages of where the processor spent its time. This tells the programmer where further code optimization will be most effective.

Exercises

1. Incorporate the histogram module into the other time-sensitive examples in the book (TicTac, Encrypt, TextDisplay, Fractals).

2. Modify the histogram module to accept a starting offset within the code segment, and a chunk size (rather than the fixed 64 bytes) as parameters to the startH function. This will let you measure programs more closely than before; i.e., with a greater resolution.

3. Change the module in the second exercise to ask the user for the values to be used when it runs. This will allow the programmer to zero in interactively on the most active parts of the program, without having to recompile.

4. Write a separate program that reads in histograms (generated by running the histogram module with the output redirected to a file), and produces a graphic bar chart of the data in the histogram.

5. [very advanced] Write a program that loads another program and produces a histogram of that program's execution i.e., no changes should be required to the program to be measured.

Listing 17-1. "histalib.asm":

```
;                       Histogram Assembly Library

        HISTSIZE = 4100             ; The size of the histogram table

_BSS    segment word public 'BSS' ; Define data segment
_BSS    ends

_TEXT   segment byte public 'CODE' ; Define code segment
_TEXT   ends

DGROUP  group _BSS                 ; Define the DGROUP group

_BSS    segment                    ; Place variables in data segment

histtab db      HISTSIZE dup(?) ; The histogram table
oldVIP  dw      ?               ; Storage for old timer vector IP
oldVCS  dw      ?               ; Storage for old timer vector CS
intCnt  db      ?               ; Count of times thru interrupt

_BSS    ends                       ; End of variable storage

_TEXT   segment                    ; Place code in the code segment

        assume CS:_TEXT, DS:DGROUP, ES: DGROUP ; Assume CS points to code
                                   ;       segment, and DS and ES
                                   ;       to data segment

        extrn   _prHist:near    ; We'll use prHist from the C module

; _startH()
;
; Function: Initialize and start IP histogram collection.
;
; Algorithm: Zero the histogram table. Save the old timer interrupt
; vector and replace it with the new one. And reset the timer interrupt
; rate.

        public  _startH            ; Routine is available to other modules

_startH proc near                  ; NEAR type subroutine
        push    bp                 ; Save the BP register
        mov     bp,sp              ; Set BP to SP; easier access to parameters
        push    di                 ; Save the DI register
        push    es                 ; Save the ES register
        mov     ax,ds              ; Make sure ES = DS
        mov     es,ax
        mov     di,offset DGROUP:histtab ; DI = histtab
        xor     ax,ax              ; AX = 0
        mov     cx,HISTSIZE/2      ; CX = size of histtab in words
        rep stos word ptr [di]     ; Zero histtab
        cli                        ; Disable interrupts
        xor     ax,ax              ; ES = 0
        mov     es,ax
        mov     ax,es:20H          ; Save the old timer vector
        mov     oldVIP,ax
        mov     ax,es:22H
```

Listing 17-1. "histalib.asm" *(cont.)*:

```
        mov     oldVCS,ax
        mov     ax,OFFSET intServ  ; Set the timer vector to intServ
        mov     es:20H,ax
        mov     ax,_TEXT
        mov     es:22H,ax
        mov     al,64              ; Set interrupt count
        mov     intCnt,al
        mov     al,36H             ; Tell timer to prepare for a new count
        out     43H,al
        mov     ax,400H            ; Write count; first low byte
        out     40H,al
        mov     al,ah              ; Then high byte
        out     40H,al
        sti                        ; Enable interrupts
        pop     es                 ; Restore ES register
        pop     di                 ; Restore DI register
        pop     bp                 ; Restore BP register
        ret                        ; Return to caller
_startH endp                       ; End of subroutine

; intServ
;
; Function: Service a timer interrupt, updating histogram counters and
; calling the normal timer interrupt routine if appropriate.
;
; Algorithm: Save registers. Increment the appropriate counter. Check
; if we should call the old timer interrupt vector; if so, do it. Otherwise,
; just ack the interrupt at the 8259, restore registers, and return.

intServ proc far                   ; FAR type subroutine (this is used to let
                                   ;    us do a RET to the old vector, even if
                                   ;    it's in a different segment)
        push    ax                 ; Push room for a second return address
        push    ax                 ;    (this may be used below)
        push    ax                 ; Save the AX register
        push    bx                 ; Save BX
        push    cx                 ; Save CX
        push    bp                 ; Save BP
        push    ds                 ; Save DS
        mov     bp,sp              ; Set BP to SP, to access interrupts CS:IP
        mov     ax,DGROUP          ; DS = DGROUP, to access variables
        mov     ds,ax
        xor     bx,bx              ; BX = 0; offset to "other" counter
        mov     ax,[bp+16]         ; AX = interrupted CS
        cmp     ax,_text           ; Is it in the code segment?
        jne     intS2              ; If not, then "other" was correct
        mov     bx,[bp+14]         ; BX = IP
        mov     cl,6               ; BX /= 64 (i.e., make BX counter number)
        shr     bx,cl
        shl     bx,1               ; BX = 4*BX + 4 (i.e., make histogram offset)
        shl     bx,1
        add     bx,4
intS2:  inc     word ptr [histtab+bx] ; Increment low word of counter
        jnz     intS3              ; If no overflow from low word, skip
        inc     word ptr [histtab+2+bx] ; Increment high word of counter
intS3:  dec     intCnt             ; Decrement count of interrupts
```

Listing 17-1. "histalib.asm" (cont.):

```
        jnz     intS4           ; If 64 haven't gone by yet, go exit
        mov     al,64           ; Otherwise, reload count of interrupts
        mov     intCnt,al
        mov     ax,oldVCS       ; Set up stack for RET to old timer vector
        mov     [bp+12],ax
        mov     ax,oldVIP
        mov     [bp+10],ax
        pop     ds              ; Restore DS register
        pop     bp              ; Restore BP
        pop     cx              ; Restore CX
        pop     bx              ; Restore BX
        pop     ax              ; Restore AX
        ret                     ; Return to old vector address

intS4:  mov     al,20H          ; Send end-of-interrupt to 8259
        out     20H,al
        pop     ds              ; Restore DS register
        pop     bp              ; Restore BP
        pop     cx              ; Restore CX
        pop     bx              ; Restore BX
        pop     ax              ; Restore AX
        pop     ax              ; Pop space for vector return
        pop     ax
        iret                    ; Return to interrupted code
intServ endp                    ; End of subroutine

; _endH()
;
; Function: Turn off histogram collection, and print out the results.
;
; Algorithm: Reset the timer interrupt rate to the old one. Restore the
; timer interrupt vector. And call _prHist to print out the histogram
; results.

        public  _endH           ; Routine is available to other modules

_endH   proc near               ; NEAR type subroutine
        push    bp              ; Save the BP register
        mov     bp,sp           ; Set BP to SP; easier to access parameters
        push    es              ; Save the ES register
        xor     ax,ax           ; ES = 0, to access low memory vectors
        mov     es,ax
        cli                     ; Turn off interrupts
        mov     al,36H          ; Tell timer to accept a new count value
        out     43H,al
        xor     al,al           ; Write zero to the timer counter
        out     40H,al          ; First the low byte
        out     40H,al          ; Then the high byte
        mov     ax,oldVIP       ; Restore the old interrupt vector
        mov     es:20H,ax
        mov     ax,oldVCS
        mov     es:22H,ax
        sti                     ; Turn on interrupts
        pop     es              ; Restore the ES register
        mov     ax,offset DGROUP:histtab ; _prHist(histtab): push histtab
        push    ax
```

Listing 17-1. "histalib.asm" *(cont.)*:

```
        call    _prHist         ; Call _prHist
        pop     ax              ; Pop histtab
        pop     bp              ; Restore BP
        ret                     ; Return to caller
_endH   endp                    ; End of subroutine

_TEXT   ends                    ; End of code segment
        end                     ; End of assembly code
```

Listing 17-2. "histclib.c":

```c
/*              Histogram Library; C portion.
 */

/*      prHist(hist)

        Function: Given a pointer to a table of 1025 histogram counters,
        print out the address that each counter covers, the count for that
        counter, and the percentage of the total both with and without
        the "other" counter included. Don't print counters that are zero.

        Algorithm: Add up all the counters. Print out the heading. Then
        cycle through all the counters, printing out the information.
*/

prHist(hist)

long *hist;

{
        float total, totalWo;
        long *hptr;
        unsigned addr;

        /* Alert the user that we're done running, and are now computing
           the histogram. */
        printf("Program done. Compiling histogram data.\n\n");
        /* Add up all the counters. */
        for (total = 0, hptr = hist+1; hptr < hist+1025; total += *hptr++);
        /* Compute the total without the "other" category. */
        totalWo = total + ((float) *hist);
        /* Print the total count without "other." */
        printf("Total recorded hits: %15.0f.\n\n",totalWo);
        /* Print the header for the main list. */
        printf(" Address     Count     %% with Other  %% without Other\n");
        printf("---------  ---------   -----------   ---------------\n");
        /* Print the "other" counter. */
        printf("  Other    %9ld      %7.3f%%\n",*hist,
                100.0*(((float) *hist)/total));
        /* Loop through all of the counters... */
        for (hptr = hist+1, addr = 0; hptr < hist+1025; hptr++, addr += 64)
                /* If it isn't zero, print it. */
                if (*hptr != 0L)
                        printf("%4x-%4x  %9ld      %7.3f%%          %7.3f%%\n",
                                addr,addr+63,*hptr,
```

Listing 17-2. "histclib.c" *(cont.)*:

```
                100.0*(((float) *hptr)/totalWo),
                100.0*(((float) *hptr)/total));
}
```

Listing 17-3. "RamSort main":

```
/*      main(argc,argv)

        Function: Read the standard input into memory, sort it, and
        write it to the standard output. If there's a switch "/+<n>",
        then sort starting at column <n>.

        Algorithm: Call readLines to read it in, offLines to adjust
        the sort column if the appropriate switch is present, sortLines
        to sort it, and writeLines to write it out. If CALIBRATE is
        defined, skip the reading and writing and fill the buffer up
        with hard-to-sort stuff; this is used to check the timing.
*/

main(argc,argv)

int argc;
char *argv[];

{
        int i;

        /* Read in the lines, or fill up the buffer with test data. */
#ifdef CALIBRATE
        fillLines();
        puts("Starting sort...");
#ifdef HIST
        startH();
#endif HIST
#else CALIBRATE
        readLines();
#endif CALIBRATE

        /* Check for a starting column parameter. */
        for (i = 1; i < argc; i++)
                if ((argv[i][0] == '/') && (argv[i][1] == '+'))
                        /* Column sort switch found, so set the
                           columns to sort from. */
                        offLines(atoi(&argv[i][2])-1);

        /* Sort the lines. */
        sortLines();

        /* Write the lines back out again. */
#ifdef CALIBRATE
#ifdef HIST
        endH();
#endif HIST
        puts("done.\n");
```

Listing 17-3. "RamSort main" *(cont.)*:

```
#else CALIBRATE
        writeLines();
#endif CALIBRATE
}
```

Listing 17-4. "rsort.map":

Start	Stop	Length	Name	Class
00000H	028BEH	028BFH	_TEXT	CODE
028C0H	04B11H	02252H	EMULATOR_TEXT	CODE
04B12H	04B12H	00000H	C_ETEXT	ENDCODE
04B20H	04C6FH	00150H	EMULATOR_DATA	FAR_DATA
04C70H	04CBEH	0004FH	NULL	BEGDATA
04CC0H	05189H	004CAH	_DATA	DATA
0518AH	05197H	0000EH	CDATA	DATA
05198H	05198H	00000H	XCB	DATA
05198H	05198H	00000H	XC	DATA
05198H	05198H	00000H	XCE	DATA
05198H	05198H	00000H	XIB	DATA
05198H	05198H	00000H	XI	DATA
05198H	05198H	00000H	XIE	DATA
05198H	051ABH	00014H	CONST	CONST
051ACH	061DFH	01034H	_BSS	BSS
061E0H	0B7E9H	0560AH	c_common	BSS
0B7F0H	0BFEFH	00800H	STACK	STACK

Origin	Group
04C7:0	DGROUP
0000:0	IGROUP

Address		Publics by Name	Address *(cont.)*	Publics by Name
0000:253D		$i8_input	04C7:044E	_errno
0000:0A5A		$i8_output	0000:1175	_exit
0000:0D1B		$i8_tpwr10	0000:0203	_fatal
0000:FE32	Abs	FIARQQ	0000:2076	_fflush
0000:0E32	Abs	FICRQQ	0000:0077	_fillLines
0000:5C32	Abs	FIDRQQ	0000:20E1	_flushall
0000:1632	Abs	FIERQQ	0000:0E99	_fputs
0000:0632	Abs	FISRQQ	0000:21E8	_free
0000:A23D	Abs	FIWRQQ	0000:16AF	_fwrite
0000:4000	Abs	FJARQQ	0000:0D58	_gets
0000:C000	Abs	FJCRQQ	0000:2015	_isatty
0000:8000	Abs	FJSRQQ	04C7:1970	_lPtr
04C7:021C		STKHQQ	0000:0002	_main
0000:0EEC		_atof	0000:21F6	_malloc
0000:0F5C		_atoi	0000:1124	_memcpy
0000:243A		_brkctl	0000:0F2D	_memset
04C7:4850		_buffer	04C7:6B78	_nextLPtr
0000:23E6		_clearerr	0000:01B0	_offLines
04C7:053C		_edata	0000:038E	_PRHIST
04C7:6B80		_end	0000:10EE	_printf
0000:0361		_endH	0000:11A6	_puts
04C7:045A		_environ	0000:1F4F	_read

(listing continued in the next column)

Listing 17-4. "rsort.map" *(cont.)*:

Address	Publics by Name	Address *(cont.)*	Publics by Name
0000:0107	_readLines	0000:04CE	__fadd
0000:023F	_sortLines	0000:0500	__faddd
0000:02BD	_startH	0000:0536	__fadds
0000:1212	_strcmp	0000:05F9	__fassign
0000:0DC4	_strcpy	0000:04EA	__fchs
0000:118D	_strlen	0000:08C7	__fcmp
0000:2035	_strncmp	0000:04DE	__fdiv
0000:1F47	_ultoa	0000:0510	__fdivd
0000:2115	_write	0000:0514	__fdivdr
0000:0185	_writeLines	0000:04E2	__fdivr
04C7:0340	__abrkp	0000:0546	__fdivs
04C7:02F0	__abrktb	0000:054A	__fdivsr
04C7:0340	__abrktbe	0000:04E6	__fdup
0000:0001 Abs	__acrtused	0000:1246	__filbuf
04C7:02E8	__aintdiv	0000:04EE	__fldd
0000:223F	__amalloc	0000:051E	__fldl
0000:236A	__amallocbrk	0000:0524	__flds
04C7:04C2	__amblksiz	0000:0518	__fldw
0000:230E	__amexpand	0000:1301	__flsbuf
0000:2348	__amlink	0000:24FE	__fltin
04C7:04BC	__aseg1	0000:09D2	__fltout
04C7:04B2	__asegds	0000:0001 Abs	__fltused
04C7:04BE	__asegn	0000:04D2	__fmul
04C7:04C0	__asegr	0000:0504	__fmuld
04C7:02EC	__asizds	0000:053A	__fmuls
0000:0F5F	__astart	0000:054E	__forcdecpt
0000:10C7	__astkovr	028C:06BB	__fpemulator
04C7:02EE	__atopsp	028C:01F9	__FPEXCEPTION87
04C7:1770	__bufin	04C7:051C	__fpinit
04C7:1570	__bufout	028C:2143	__FPINSTALL87
0000:1EF2	__catox	028C:0020	__fpmath
0000:0858	__cfltcvt	0000:0999	__fpsignal
0000:063C	__cftoe	04B2:0142	__fptaskdata
0000:072C	__cftof	028C:21BF	__FPTERMINATE87
0000:07F8	__cftog	0000:0DE7	__fptostr
04C7:0486	__child	0000:10E7	__fptrap
0000:0DB0	__chkstk	0000:04FA	__fstd
0000:1401	__cinherit	0000:04F4	__fstdp
0000:2389	__cltoasub	0000:0530	__fsts
0000:0587	__cropzeros	0000:052A	__fstsp
04C7:0488	__csigtab	0000:04D6	__fsub
04C7:0342	__ctype	0000:0508	__fsubd
04C7:0342	__ctype_	0000:050C	__fsubdr
0000:2397	__cxtoa	0000:04DA	__fsubr
04C7:0452	__cyfunc	0000:053E	__fsubs
04C7:045C	__doserrno	0000:0542	__fsubsr
0000:23F2	__dosret0	0000:1651	__ftbuf
0000:23FA	__dosretax	04C7:021E	__iob
04C7:0454	__dosvermajor	04C7:02BE	__iob2
04C7:0455	__dosverminor	04C7:02E6	__lastiob
04C7:045E	__eofflag	0000:2406	__maperror
0000:0E55	__exit	0000:21E8	__nfree
04C7:0444	__fac	0000:21F6	__nmalloc

(listing continued in the next column)

Listing 17-4. "rsort.map" *(cont.)*:

Address	Publics by Name
0000:17ED	__nullcheck
04C7:045C	__oserr
04C7:0472	__osfile
04C7:0454	__osmajor
04C7:0455	__osminor
0000:1828	__output
0000:05DB	__positive
04C7:044C	__psp
0000:14CB	__setargv
0000:146F	__setenvp
0000:15CF	__stbuf
04C7:0450	__umaskval
04C7:0456	___argc
04C7:0458	___argv

Address		Publics by Value		Address *(cont.)*		Publics by Value
0000:0001	Abs	__acrtused		0000:053E		__fsubs
0000:0001	Abs	__fltused		0000:0542		__fsubsr
0000:0002		_main		0000:0546		__fdivs
0000:0077		_fillLines		0000:054A		__fdivsr
0000:0107		_readLines		0000:054E		__forcdecpt
0000:0185		_writeLines		0000:0587		__cropzeros
0000:01B0		_offLines		0000:05DB		__positive
0000:0203		_fatal		0000:05F9		__fassign
0000:023F		_sortLines		0000:0632	Abs	FISRQQ
0000:02BD		_startH		0000:063C		__cftoe
0000:0361		_endH		0000:072C		__cftof
0000:038E		_PRHIST		0000:07F8		__cftog
0000:04CE		__fadd		0000:0858		__cfltcvt
0000:04D2		__fmul		0000:08C7		__fcmp
0000:04D6		__fsub		0000:0999		__fpsignal
0000:04DA		__fsubr		0000:09D2		__fltout
0000:04DE		__fdiv		0000:0A5A		$i8_output
0000:04E2		__fdivr		0000:0D1B		$i8_tpwr10
0000:04E6		__fdup		0000:0D58		_gets
0000:04EA		__fchs		0000:0DB0		__chkstk
0000:04EE		__fldd		0000:0DC4		_strcpy
0000:04F4		__fstdp		0000:0DE7		__fptostr
0000:04FA		__fstd		0000:0E32	Abs	FICRQQ
0000:0500		__faddd		0000:0E55		__exit
0000:0504		__fmuld		0000:0E99		_fputs
0000:0508		__fsubd		0000:0EEC		_atof
0000:050C		__fsubdr		0000:0F2D		_memset
0000:0510		__fdivd		0000:0F5C		_atoi
0000:0514		__fdivdr		0000:0F5F		__astart
0000:0518		__fldw		0000:10C7		__astkovr
0000:051E		__fldl		0000:10E7		__fptrap
0000:0524		__flds		0000:10EE		_printf
0000:052A		__fstsp		0000:1124		_memcpy
0000:0530		__fsts		0000:1175		__exit
0000:0536		__fadds		0000:118D		_strlen
0000:053A		__fmuls		0000:11A6		_puts

(listing continued in the next column)

Listing 17-4. "rsort.map" *(cont.)*:

Address		Publics by Value	Address *(cont.)*		Publics by Value
0000:1212		_strcmp	04C7:0340		__abrktbe
0000:1246		__filbuf	04C7:0340		__abrkp
0000:1301		__flsbuf	04C7:0342		__ctype_
0000:1401		__cinherit	04C7:0342		__ctype
0000:146F		__setenvp	04C7:0444		__fac
0000:14CB		__setargv	04C7:044C		__psp
0000:15CF		__stbuf	04C7:044E		_errno
0000:1632	Abs	FIERQQ	04C7:0450		__umaskval
0000:1651		__ftbuf	04C7:0452		__cyfunc
0000:16AF		_fwrite	04C7:0454		__dosvermajor
0000:17ED		__nullcheck	04C7:0454		__osmajor
0000:1828		__output	04C7:0455		__osminor
0000:1EF2		__catox	04C7:0455		__dosverminor
0000:1F47		_ultoa	04C7:0456		___argc
0000:1F4F		_read	04C7:0458		___argv
0000:2015		_isatty	04C7:045A		_environ
0000:2035		_strncmp	04C7:045C		__oserr
0000:2076		_fflush	04C7:045C		__doserrno
0000:20E1		_flushall	04C7:045E		__eofflag
0000:2115		_write	04C7:0472		__osfile
0000:21E8		_free	04C7:0486		__child
0000:21E8		__nfree	04C7:0488		__csigtab
0000:21F6		_malloc	04C7:04B2		__asegds
0000:21F6		__nmalloc	04C7:04BC		__asegl
0000:223F		__amalloc	04C7:04BE		__asegn
0000:230E		__amexpand	04C7:04C0		__asegr
0000:2348		__amlink	04C7:04C2		__amblksiz
0000:236A		__amallocbrk	04C7:051C		__fpinit
0000:2389		__cltoasub	04C7:053C		_edata
0000:2397		__cxtoa	0000:5C32	Abs	FIDRQQ
0000:23E6		_clearerr	04C7:1570		__bufout
0000:23F2		__dosret0	04C7:1770		__bufin
0000:23FA		__dosretax	04C7:1970		_lPtr
0000:2406		__maperror	0000:8000	Abs	FJSRQQ
0000:243A		_brkctl	04C7:4850		__buffer
0000:24FE		__fltin	0000:A23D	Abs	FIWRQQ
0000:253D		$i8_input	04C7:6B78		_nextLPtr
028C:0020		__fpmath	04C7:6B80		_end
028C:01F9		__FPEXCEPTION87	0000:C000	Abs	FJCRQQ
028C:06BB		__fpemulator	0000:FE32	Abs	FIARQQ
0000:4000	Abs	FJARQQ			
028C:2143		__FPINSTALL87	Program entry point at 0000:0F5F		
028C:21BF		__FPTERMINATE87			
04B2:0142		__fptaskdata			
04C7:021C		STKHQQ			
04C7:021E		_iob			
04C7:02BE		__iob2			
04C7:02E6		__lastiob			
04C7:02E8		__aintdiv			
04C7:02EC		__asizds			
04C7:02EE		__atopsp			
04C7:02F0		__abrktb			

(listing continued in the next column)

Part IV

Appendices

Appendix A

C Programmers' Assembly Language Introduction

Y
ou've spent a lot of time and energy learning how to program in C. You've learned a lot of concepts and how those concepts combine to produce working programs. There's no reason for you to start all over again to learn assembly language programming. C and assembly language are very different in style, but most of the underlying concepts are the same. This chapter teaches assembly language assuming that you already know C. By assuming C, we can take a number of shortcuts that greatly reduce the amount of time it takes to understand and be comfortable with writing a program or function in assembly language.

Clearly it isn't possible, in the space available, to present a complete guide to assembly language programming. We will go quickly through some concepts and eliminate the less frequently used parts of the 8086/8088/80286 entirely. With a little care, however, you should be able to write assembly language routines to be called by C, after reading this book and the manual for the assembler.

A Simple Example

Listing A-1 shows a simple C program that prints "Hello, world!" and exits. Listing A-2 shows an assembly language program that does the same thing. Comparing the two listings, you'll notice that they're dramatically different in appearance. In fact, at first glance, it's hard to believe that they're functionally the same. But underlying the surface differences, the two programs have a lot in common.

The most obvious and immediate difference is that the assembly program is several times longer than the C program. There are three reasons for this. First, assembly language works in smaller chunks than C does. One statement in C may translate into a dozen assembly language statements. Second, the C compiler automatically takes care of a number of things that must be done explicitly in assembly language. And third, the C programmer has access to a large library of run-time routines, such as the printf function used in the example; while the assembly programmer must often invent his own.

The syntax of assembly language is simpler than C. Each statement is on a line by itself. Each element of the statement—label, operation, operand, and comment—is in a fixed position. Writing in assembly language is like writing in a very restricted subset of C. Most operations can only be performed on a limited number of predefined variables, known as registers, and the operations available are more limited.

Segments are one of the elements of a complete IBM PC program that the C compiler handles for the programmer. Segments are needed because the processor addresses the memory in 64-K byte chunks. Even though the total amount of available memory can be much larger, the processor can deal only with chunks, or segments, of this size. Every piece of code or data that an IBM PC program uses must reside in a segment. In the example program, the segments are enclosed in SEGMENT and ENDS statements. This is how the programmer tells the assembler which segment to place code or data in. Two segments are used here, the stack segment and the code segment; very often, more segments are needed.

The stack is another element of an IBM PC program that is handled by the C compiler. The compiler uses the stack to store the return address whenever a function call is made, and to hold local variables and intermediate results of calculations. Before the stack can be used, space must be allocated for it. In the assembly example, this is done by defining a stack segment.

One of the other differences between the C version of the example and the assembly version is that the C version uses the printf function, while the assembly version does not. The assembly version uses, instead, a call to the ROM BIOS, a set of built-in routines that are always available on the PC. The C version can pass the string to be printed all at once, while the assembly version must iterate through the string, displaying each character individually.

In the remainder of this appendix, we will discuss in more detail the nature and structure of assembly language. In the main body of the book, you can learn how to combine C and assembly language, which will allow you to achieve the best of both worlds.

Assembler Syntax

The most noticeable difference between C and assembly language is the syntax. As we've noted, assembly language programs have a much more restricted form than C programs do. While C statements can arbitrarily span multiple lines, assembly statements occur one per line. While C statements can be large and complex, assembly statements are always simple, with each line corresponding to a single 8086/8088/80286 instruction. While C statements can use complex expressions to compute addresses and values, assembly statements are limited to a few pre-set types of addressing. In general, 8086/8088/80286 instructions are much simpler than C statements. When your C program is compiled, the compiler usually produces several machine instructions for every statement in the original C code. Assembly language, on the other hand, is translated directly, one-for-one, into machine instructions: each instruction in the assembly language program is transformed by the assembler into one machine instruction. And since machine instructions are the ones actually executed by the 8086/8088/80286, the assembly language programmer is much closer to what's actually going on when a program executes.

Each line of assembly language code is composed of several parts: label, operation, operands, comment. Each part of an assembly language statement is called a "field." The label is optional and is used to allow other statements to reference this one. The label may correspond to C labels, which allow other statements to "go to" this one, in which case it is followed by a colon ("labelJ:"); it may correspond to a C function name, which can be called from other functions; or it may correspond to a C variable name. The operation specifies the action to be taken. There are two types of operation: the first is called an op-code, which corresponds to a machine instruction; the second is called a pseudo-op, which is actually a directive to the assembler and does not directly correspond to an 8086/8088/80286 instruction. The operands are the parameters to the operation, and there may be different numbers of them depending on the type of operation. If there is more than one operand, they are separated by commas. Finally, the comment field contains any descriptive comments the programmer wishes to include.

As an example, the following two pairs of statements show the C code and the corresponding assembly language code:

```
              C code:  int a;
                          .
                          .
                          .
                       a += 5;

Assembly language code:  a    dw       0         ; Define a word of storage
                                       .
                                       .
                                       .
                              add      a,5       ; Add 5 to a
```

Data Structures and Addressing Modes

Before we continue to discuss assembly language itself, we need to examine some background data structures. The organization of the 8086/8088 processor and the way it deals with memory impose certain structures on the data used by the processor. The most fundamental and obvious of these structures is the byte: data is clumped into eight bit units known as bytes; in C, this same size unit is declared as type char. The next natural unit is two bytes, also known as a word; in C, this is type int. C ints can be signed or unsigned, but this distinction doesn't really change the data itself; rather it changes the way the data is manipulated and tested. In assembly, this difference in manipulation is specified explicitly in every operation on the data; in C it is specified implicitly.

In this appendix, we will show many assembly concepts using C code. Note, however, that the C code presented here should not be taken literally. If you were to put this code all together, you would not get a program that simulates the IBM PC processor; in fact, you wouldn't even get a program that runs. This C code is intended to be illustrative; it is used as a shortcut to explain concepts that would otherwise take pages of text to cover.

To start, we'll define types "byte" and "word" using typedef:

```c
typedef unsigned char byte;
typedef unsigned int word;
```

Registers

Assembly language uses a number of special "variables" known as registers. The registers are built into the processor chip itself and can therefore be accessed very quickly. There are fourteen of these registers in all. Four of them can be viewed as either words or as pairs of bytes:

```c
union wordOrByteUnion {
        word x;
        struct {
                byte l;
                byte h;
        } b;
};

typedef union wordOrByteUnion wordOrByte;
```

The processor registers can then be defined as follows:

```c
wordOrByte A;    /* Accumulator. */
wordOrByte B;    /* Base. */
wordOrByte C;    /* Count. */
wordOrByte D;    /* Data. */
```

(listing continued)

```
word SP;          /* Stack Pointer. */
word BP;          /* Base Pointer. */
word SI;          /* Source Index. */
word DI;          /* Destination Index. */

word CS;          /* Code Segment. */
word DS;          /* Data Segment. */
word SS;          /* Stack Segment. */
word ES;          /* Extra Segment. */

word IP;          /* Instruction Pointer. */

word FLAGS;       /* Flag Register. */
```

When discussing assembly language, these registers are commonly presented as shown in Figure A-1. Note that the FLAGS register is actually a collection of individual flag bits. These will be discussed in detail later.

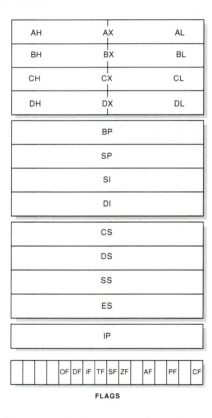

Figure A-1. Processor Registers

The registers cannot be used interchangeably for any purpose, as C variables can be. These registers each have their own special uses and capabilities, as their names suggest.

Memory & Segments

The 8086/8088 processor can address up to 1,048,576 bytes of memory outside the processor, as can the 80286 in "real" mode. This is also known as the physical memory address space. It doesn't mean that that much memory is or ever will be available to the processor; it simply means that the processor cannot address more than that directly. We can define the physical memory of the IBM PC as follows:

```
byte mem[1048576];
```

This memory is used to store programs and program variables, and also to allow the processor to access input/output hardware such as the display memory. It can be accessed as bytes or as words, a word being composed of two adjacent bytes:

```
wordData = mem[address+1]<<8 + mem[address];
```

In order to simplify the explanations in this appendix, we will not explicitly show the expression above when word references are made. It will be clear from the context when a word reference is intended. This means that the C code presented as equivalent to an assembly language construct will not be precisely correct. Those code fragments simply explain the operation of the processor; they are not meant to be actually executed.

Notice that the highest address of physical memory is a larger number than will fit in a word. This makes it impossible to address an arbitrary location in that memory using a word variable to specify the address. We could use larger registers; or, we could use segments, which is the approach used in the 8086/8088/80286. A segment is a block of physical memory 64K bytes in size — exactly the number of locations that can be addressed by a word. Segment registers are used to provide a "base" address, to which an offset is added to produce a physical memory address. The offsets can range from 0 to 65,535, the range of possible values of a word. The segment registers (CS, DS, SS, and ES) that provide the base address are also words, but are multiplied by 16 in order to form the base address:

```
    physical_address = 16*segment_register + offset;
or  physical_address = segment_register<<4 + offset;
```

This approach lets a program address all of the available physical memory address space without ever using a number larger than will fit in a word. The segment register approach can also be diagrammed as shown in Figure A-2:

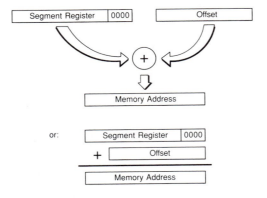

Figure A-2. Segment Register Usage

In order to let a program use more than a single segment at a time, four segment registers are available. One of these four segment registers is used whenever a memory reference is made, but the one to be used is chosen based on the type of reference: when code is being fetched, the CS (code segment) register is used; when data is being fetched, the DS (data segment) register is used; when the stack is referenced (more, later, on the stack and how it works), the SS (stack segment) register is used; and the ES (extra segment) register is used to easily access data that is not in any of the other three segments.

Instruction Execution

As we mentioned above, the main memory of the machine is used to store the program as well as the data manipulated by that program. Whenever the processor is ready to execute another instruction, it fetches the instruction from memory. The IP (instruction pointer) register and the CS (code segment) register together indicate where the next instruction should come from, as follows:

```
new_instruction = mem[CS<<4 + IP++];
```

Sometimes instructions are more than one byte long, in which case this same expression is used again to fetch subsequent bytes. The additional bytes may select one of several possible instructions, or they may supply data used to produce the operands of the instruction.

Addressing Modes

Machine instructions can be thought of as C functions, with each one taking zero, one, or two parameters. The forms of the parameters are restricted, however, to what are called the "addressing modes" of the processor. Each addressing mode tells the processor how to find a byte or word of data — as most instructions operate on either bytes or words. The following paragraphs detail each of the addressing modes of the 8086/8088/80286; they are followed by examples of the assembly language syntax used to specify the modes.

Immediate: The immediate addressing mode takes the data from the memory area following the instruction itself, which may be either a byte or a word:

```
data = mem[CS<<4 + IP++];
```

Register: The register addressing mode takes the data from one of the registers. Depending upon the instruction, only some of the registers may be used.

Direct: The direct addressing mode takes its data from a fixed offset into the data segment. The offset is taken from the memory location immediately following the instruction, just like immediate data. It can be either a byte or a word:

```
data = mem[DS<<4 + mem[CS<<4 + IP++]];
```

Register Indirect: The register indirect addressing mode takes its data from a register-specified offset into the data or stack segment. The register must be one of BX, BP, SI, or DI. Registers BX and BP are called base registers, and SI and DI are called index registers. If the BP register is used, the data is taken from the stack segment; otherwise it's taken from the data segment. For example, using the BX register, this is what the equivalent C code would be:

```
data = mem[DS<<4 + BX];
```

Register Indirect with Displacement: This addressing mode combines the previous two modes by allowing both a register and a fixed offset to be added to the segment register to produce the data to be used:

```
                data = mem[SS<<4 + BP + mem[CS<<4 + IP++]];
```

Register Indirect with Base and Index Register: This addressing mode allows one base register and one index register to be added to the segment register, to compute the address of the data. Only BX or BP may be used for the base register, and only DI or SI may be used for the index register. Here is an example, using BX and SI:

```
                data = mem[DS<<4 + BX + SI];
```

Register Indirect with Base and Index and Displacement: This is the most complicated addressing mode. It adds a base register, an index register, and an offset to the data segment register:

```
                data = mem[DS<<4 + BX + SI + mem[CS<<4 + IP++]];
```

In order to show the assembly language syntax of these addressing modes, we'll use the ADD instruction, which adds two bytes or words together. This works just like the C statement "dest + = data". We'll always use the accumulator as the destination, and show the addressing modes for the data to be added to the accumulator. Note that the size of the specified data determines whether the instruction performs a byte or word operation. In this case, it is specified by the choice of the register: AL or AH specify bytes while AX specifies words.

```
aByte    db      0                   ; A byte of storage
aWord    dw      0                   ; A word of storage

         add     al,5                ; Immediate byte
         add     ax,10000            ; Immediate word

         add     ah,bh               ; Register byte
         add     ax,di               ; Register word
         add     ax,dx               ; Register word

         add     al,aByte            ; Direct byte
         add     ax,aWord            ; Direct word

         add     al,[si]             ; Register indirect byte
         add     ah,[bx]             ; Register indirect byte
         add     ax,[bx]             ; Register indirect word
         add     ax,[di]             ; Register indirect word

         add     al,7[bp]            ; Reg. ind. w/disp. byte
         add     ah,[bx+5]           ; Reg. ind. w/disp. byte
         add     al,aByte[bx]        ; Reg. ind. w/disp. byte
         add     ax,[bp+20]          ; Reg. ind. w/disp. word
         add     ax,1000[di]         ; Reg. ind. w/disp. word
         add     ax,[aWord+si]       ; Reg. ind. w/disp. word

         add     al,[bx][di]         ; Reg. ind. base+indx byte
         add     ah,[bp+si]          ; Reg. ind. base+indx byte
         add     ax,[bp][di]         ; Reg. ind. base+indx word
         add     ax,[bp+si]          ; Reg. ind. base+indx word

         add     al,7[bp][di]        ; Reg. ind. base+indx+disp. byte
         add     al,[bp+si+20]       ; Reg. ind. base+indx+disp. byte
         add     al,[si+1+bp]        ; Reg. ind. base+indx+disp. byte
         add     ax,aWord[si][bp]    ;Reg ind base+indx+disp word
         add     ax,[bp+aWord+di]    ;Reg ind base+indx+disp word
         add     ax,[7+bp+di]        ; Reg. ind. base+indx+disp. word
```

In addition, a segment other than the default segment can be specified with any addressing mode that accesses memory. This adds to the instruction another byte, called the segment override prefix; but it gives the programmer considerable freedom to access different segments.

To use a different segment, the segment register name, followed by a colon, is placed before the address expression. For example:

```
add     ax,es:7         ; AX += mem[ES<<4 + 7]
add     al,ss:[bp]      ; AL += mem[SS<<4 + BP]
```

The Stack

The SS (stack segment) and SP (stack pointer) registers of the processor are used to implement a special and very useful data structure called a stack. Data is added to and taken away from the stack in a first-come-last-go fashion. You can think of it as a stack of dishes: the ones you put on the stack first are at the bottom of the stack. When you take dishes off the stack you first take the ones you put on most recently, and only at the end do you take the dishes you put on first.

The SS and SP registers specify a particular location in memory (mem[SS<<4 + SP]), which is the "top" of the stack. This is the address of the last thing to be placed on the stack. In order to put data on the stack, the SP register is first decremented, then the data is stored:

```
mem[SS<<4 + --SP] = data;
```

In order to take data off the stack, the data is retrieved and then the SP register is incremented:

```
data = mem[SS<<4 + SP++];
```

The stack has two main purposes: to hold local variables and the intermediate results of computations, and to keep the return address when a subroutine is called. There are several processor instructions that allow the programmer to make use of the stack. These will be discussed in a later section.

Flags

The FLAG register is the aspect of assembly language programming that is the least like C programming. Because an understanding of the operation of the processor requires a thorough understanding of flags and how they work, the FLAG register deserves special attention and a section all to itself.

There are two types of flags: mode flags, which determine how the processor operates; and condition flags, which remember the results of a previous operation performed on the machine. The condition flags are set as a side-effect of most arithmetic instructions, and they retain information about the result produced by the execution of the instruction. For example, if an add instruction produces a zero result, the ZF (zero flag) is set; if it produces a non-zero result, the ZF flag is cleared. The condition flags can then be tested, and the order of instruction execution changed, based on their value. The following condition flags are included in the FLAGS register:

Flag	Name	Definition
OF	Overflow	Set if an arithmetic overflow occurred
SF	Sign	Set to the high order (sign) bit of the result
ZF	Zero	Set if the result is zero
AF	Auxiliary carry	Set if there has been a carry low order four bits to the high order four bits (seldom used by programmers)

Flag *(cont.)*	**Name**	**Definition**
PF	Parity	Set if the result has even parity (i.e., if there are an even number of "1" bits)
CF	Carry	Set if there's been a carry or borrow to the high order bit of the result

There are a large number of instructions which can test these flags and branch to a different location in the program depending upon the results. It's as if the only conditional tests allowed in the language were tests of the form:

```
if (flag_expression) goto label;
```

This is considerably different than the "if...else...", "while...", and "do...while..." statements allowed in C, and takes some getting used to. Rather than writing

```
if (a == b) a = 0;
```

we have to write:

```
        mov     ax,a        ; Set AX to a
        cmp     ax,b        ; Set flags according to (AX-b)
        jne     label       ; Jump if not equal, to label
        mov     a,0         ; Set a to zero
label:
```

To make this situation even more complicated, not all instructions set all of the flags. For example, the addition instruction sets the carry flag but the increment instruction does not; both, on the other hand, do set the zero flag. A list of which instructions set which flags is included in the complete listing of 8086/8088 or 80286 instructions that should have come with your assembler documentation.

Processor Instructions

The instructions of the processor fall into the following broad categories:

- Arithmetic
- Data movement
- Flow of execution
- Input/output
- Strings

Note that the following explanations do not include all the 8086/8088/80286 instructions, especially not all of the 80286 instructions. They do include the commonly used instructions and all of the instructions used in assembly language routines presented in this book.

Not all addressing modes are allowed in all operands of all instructions. Generally speaking, the first operand (the destination) is limited to a register, while the second operand (the source) can use a broader range of addressing modes. For example, the ADD instruction used above has three forms. The first form is any of the addressing modes listed added to any register. The second form is immediate mode added to any of the modes listed. The third form is immediate mode added to the accumulator. This is a special ADD instruction that is one byte shorter than the equivalent version of the second form. A list of which instructions allow which addressing modes should be included with your assembler.

Arithmetic

The arithmetic operations allow the programmer to combine operands in a wide variety of ways. The following are the two operand instructions:

```
adc     ax,2        ; AX += 5 + CF (carry flag)(add with carry)
add     al,b        ; AL += b (add)
and     al,3        ; AL &= 3 (logical AND)
cmp     al,bl       ; AL - BL (sets condition flags) (compare)
or      ax,c        ; AX |= c (logical OR)
sbb     al,dh       ; AL -= DH + CF (carry flag) (subtract with
                    ;    borrow)
sub     ax,5        ; AX -= 5 (subtract)
test    al,bl       ; AL & BL (sets condition flags) (test)
xor     ax,8        ; AX ^= 8 (logical exclusive-or)
```

The shift and rotate instructions are a special case of the two operand arithmetic instructions. Although they take two operands, the second operand, which specifies the number of bits to shift or rotate by, must be either 1 or CL: 1 specifies a one-bit shift, while CL specifies a shift by the count contained in the CL register. Figure A-3 shows the various shift and rotate instructions:

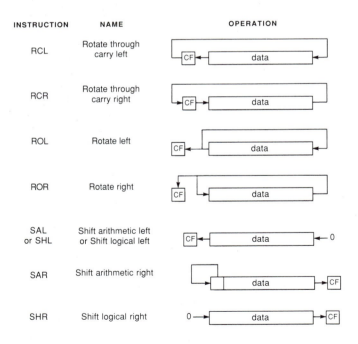

Figure A-3. Shift and Rotate Instructions

```
rcl     ax,1        ; Rotate AX 1 left, through carry
rcr     al,cl       ; Rotate AL CL bits left, through carry
rol     ax,cl       ; Rotate AX CL bits left
ror     al,1        ; Rotate AL 1 left
sal     ax,1        ; Shift AX 1 left, arithmetic
shl     ax,cl       ; Shift AX CL bits left, logical
sar     al,cl       ; Shift AL CL bits right, arithmetic
shr     al,1        ; Shift AL 1 left, logical
```

Single operand arithmetic instructions include:

```
dec     ax      ; AX-- (decrement)
inc     bp      ; BP++ (increment)
div     bl      ; AL = AX / BL, AH = AX % BL (unsigned divide)
div     bx      ; AX = AX,DX / BX, DX = AX,DX % BX (unsigned divide)
idiv    cl      ; AL = AX / CL, AH = AX % CL (signed divide)
idiv    cx      ; AX = AX,DX / CX, DX = AX,DX % CX (signed divide)
mul     cl      ; AX = AL*CL (unsigned multiply)
mul     cx      ; AX,DX = AX*CX (unsigned multiply)
imul    bl      ; AX = AL*BL (signed multiply)
imul    bx      ; AX,DX = AX*BX (signed multiply)
neg     ax      ; AX = -AX (arithmetic negative)
not     al      ; AL = ~AL (logical negative)
```

Finally, the following arithmetic instructions do not explicitly specify an operand; it is implicit in the instruction itself:

```
clc     ; CF = 0 (clear carry)
cmc     ; CF = ~CF (complement carry)
stc     ; CF = 1 (set carry)
```

Data Movement

The most important single instruction on the 8086/8088 is the MOV instruction, which moves data between registers and memory. This instruction has the widest range of possible addressing modes for use in either of its operands of any of the instructions:

To	From	Example	
Register	Any mode	mov	al,fred[bx]
Any mode	Register	mov	[bp + si],ax
Any mode	Immediate	mov	aWord,10000
Register	Immediate (short form)	mov	bx,26000
Accumulator	Direct memory (short form)	mov	al,aByte
Direct memory	Accumulator (short form)	mov	aWord,ax
Segment register	Any mode	mov	es,ax
Any mode	Segment register	mov	aWord,cs

In addition to the MOV instruction, there are several instructions just for manipulating data on the stack:

```
pop     cx      ; CX = mem[SS<<4 + SP++] (pop data)
popf            ; FLAGS = mem[SS<<4 + SP++] (pop flags)
```

(listing continued)

```
push      bx        ; mem[SS<<4 + --SP] = BX (push data)
pushf               ; mem[SS<<4 + --SP] = FLAGS (push flags)
```

Flow of Execution

There are four basic types of instructions for manipulating the flow of execution of the processor (that is, the order in which instructions are executed):

1. The JMP (jump) instruction.

2. The conditional jump instructions.

3. The loop instructions.

4. Subroutine and interrupt call and return instructions.

The JMP instruction allows the program to change the memory location from which it's taking instructions. In other words, it allows the program to change the IP register and, optionally, the CS register as well. It has the following format:

```
JMP       label
```

The conditional jump instructions differ from the JMP instruction in two ways: First, they test one or more of the condition flags, and only if those flags have particular values does the jump actually occur. If the jump doesn't occur, execution continues with the next instruction, as if the jump instruction were never executed. Second, the conditional jump instructions can only jump to other instructions within a limited range: -128 to +127 bytes of the jump instruction. Because of this restriction, it is sometimes necessary to combine the two types of instructions and have a conditional instruction branch to or over a JMP instruction. The conditional instruction performs the test, and the JMP instruction makes the long jump. The following conditional instructions are available (assume that a "CMP a,b" instruction has been executed immediately before the jump instruction):

Op-code	Operation	Condition for jump	Exact test
JA or JNBE	Jump if above / Jump if not below or equal	a > b (unsigned) / !(a <= b) (unsigned)	(CF = = 0) && (ZF = = 1)
JAE or JNB	Jump if above or equal / Jump if not below	a >= b (unsigned) / !(a < b) (unsigned)	CF = = 0
JB or JNAE	Jump if below / Jump if not above or equal	a < b (unsigned) / !(a >= b) (unsigned)	CF = = 1
JBE or JNA	Jump if below or equal / Jump if not above	a <= b (unsigned) / !(a > b) (unsigned)	(CF = = 1) (ZF = = 1)
JC	Jump if carry	CF set	CF = = 1
JCXZ	Jump if CX zero	CX = = 0	CX = = 0
JE or JZ	Jump if equal / Jump if zero	a = = b / result = = 0	ZF = = 1
JG or JNLE	Jump if greater / Jump if not less or equal	a > b (signed) / !(a <= b) (signed)	(SF = = OF)&& (ZF = = 0)
JGE or JNL	Jump if greater or equal / Jump if not less	a >= b (signed) / !(a < b) (signed)	SF = = OF

Op-code *(cont.)*	Operation	Condition for jump	Exact test
JL or JNGE	Jump if less Jump if not greater or equal	a ‹ b (signed) ! (a › = b) (signed)	SF! = OF
JLE or JNG	Jump if less or equal Jump if not greater	a ‹ = b (signed) ! (a › b) (signed)	(SF! = OF) (ZF = = 1)
JNC	Jump if no carry	Carry clear	CF = = 0
JNE or JNZ	Jump if not equal Jump if not zero	a! = b result! = 0	ZF = = 0
JNO	Jump if no overflow	Overflow clear	OF = = 0
JNS	Jump if no sign	Sign clear	SF = = 0
JNP or JPO	Jump if no parity Jump if parity odd	Parity clear	PF = = 0
JO	Jump if overflow	Overflow set	OF = = 1
JP or JPE	Jump if parity Jump if parity even	Parity set	PF = = 1
JS	Jump if sign	Sign set	SF = = 1

The loop instructions make it easy to repeat a block of instructions while using the CX register as a counter to determine how many times the block should be executed. There are three forms of the instruction, each of which takes one operand, the label to jump to:

Op-code	Operation	C Code
LOOP	Loop until CX zero	if (--CX != 0) goto label
LOOPE LOOPZ	Loop until CX zero or a != b Loop until X zero or result != 0	if ((--CX != 0) && (ZF = = 1)) goto label
LOOPNE or LOOPNZ	Loop until CX zero or a = = b Loop until CX zero or result = = 0	if ((--CX != 0) && (ZF = = 0)) goto label

The subroutine call facility allows the processor to save the current IP (and optionally the CS) on the stack, to go and execute a block of code at another location, and then to return to the point where the original execution left off. This is exactly like a function call in C and, in fact, C uses this facility to implement function calls. The CALL instruction initiates a subroutine call, and has the same operand variations as the JMP instruction. If the call is to a subroutine in the same code segment, only the IP is pushed onto the stack. If the call is to another segment, both the IP and CS are pushed. Subroutines are enclosed in PROC...ENDP pseudo-ops, which will be discussed later in the section on pseudo-ops. The RET instruction returns from a subroutine and takes no operands. For example:

```
        call    aFunc
          .
          .
          .
aFunc   proc near
        mov         ax,10
```

(listing continued)

```
            ret
aFunc       endp
```

An interrupt is exactly like a call with two exceptions. First, the FLAGS register is saved as well as the IP and CS registers. If the interrupt routine is careful to preserve all the other registers, this makes it possible for the interrupted routine to continue execution without ever being aware of the interrupt. Second, the means of invoking interrupts is different. Some interrupts are invoked from the processor, for instance when a divide by zero is attempted. Some interrupts are initiated by external hardware, as we've discussed in detail in this book. And some interrupts, called software interrupts, are invoked by executing the INT instruction. These are used to call MS-DOS and the ROM BIOS. The format of the INT instruction is as follows:

```
int     interrupt#      ; # is 0-255
```

The IRET instruction is used to return from an interrupt. Most of the hardware generated interrupts can also be turned off by clearing the interrupt flag (IF) in the FLAGS register, by using the CLI instruction. And the interrupts can be turned back on using the STI instruction.

Input/Output

In order to communicate with input/output devices, a separate address space is available to the processor. Locations in this space are called "I/O ports." There are up to 65,536 separate ports, and data can be written in byte or word size units. Data is read from and written to I/O devices using the IN and OUT instructions, which have one of the following forms:

```
in      al,constant     ; AL = port[constant]
in      ax,constant     ; AX = port[constant]
in      al,dx           ; AL = port[DX]
in      ax,dx           ; AX = port[DX]

out     constant,al     ; port[constant] = AL
out     constant,ax     ; port[constant] = AX
out     dx,al           ; port[DX] = AL
out     dx,ax           ; port[DX = AX]
```

However, when using the constant address form, the constant must be a byte. So this form of the IN and OUT instructions can only address the first 256 I/O ports. To address the rest of the ports, the other form, using the DX register to specify the port address, must be used.

String Operations

One powerful facility of the IBM PC processor is its set of string manipulation instructions. These instructions use the SI and DI index registers to efficiently load, store, move, or compare a block of bytes or words. The string operations consist of two types of instruction. The first type manipulates the data stored at the memory areas pointed to by the data segment and SI register, and the extra segment and DI register. (The SI register is also known as the source register, and the DI register is also known as the destination register.) Note that the DI uses the extra segment rather than the data segment, but only when it is used in string operations. The second type of instruction causes the first type to be repeated according to the contents of the CX register and also according to the condition flag values resulting from the manipulation instruction. The following string manipulation instructions are available:

Op-code	Operation	C Code

CMPS	Compare string	If byte: mem[ES··4 + DI]—mem[DS··4 + SI]; (for flags)
		    if (DF = = 0) DI + +; SI + +
		    else DI--; SI--;
		If word: mem[ES··4 + DI]—mem[DS··4 + SI]; (for flags)
		    if (DF = = 0) DI + = 2; SI + = 2
		    else DI - = 2; SI - = 2;

LODS	Load string	If byte: AL = mem[DS··4 + SI];
		    if (DF = = 0) SI + +
		    else SI--;
		If word: AX = mem[DS··4 + SI];
		    if (DF = = 0) SI + = 2
		    else SI - = 2;

MOVS	Move string	If byte: mem[ES··4 + DI] = mem[DS··4 + SI];
		    if (DF = = 0) DI + +; SI + +
		    else DI--; SI--;
		If word: mem[ES··4 + DI] = mem[DS··4 + SI];
		    if (DF = = 0) DI + = 2; SI + = 2
		    else DI - = 2; SI - = 2;

SCAS	Scan string	If byte: AL—mem[DS··4 + SI]; (for flags)
		    if (DF = = 0) SI + +
		    else SI--;
		If word: AX—mem[DS··4 + SI]; (for flags)
		    if (DF = = 0) SI + = 2
		    else SI - = 2;

STOS	Store string	If byte: mem[DS··4 + SI] = AL;
		    if (DF = = 0) SI + +
		    else SI--;
		If word: mem[DS··4 + SI] = AX;
		    if (DF = = 0) SI + = 2
		    else SI - = 2;

The DF flag, used to determine whether the SI and DI registers are incremented or decremented, is set using the STD instruction and cleared using the CLD instruction. You can specify whether a string operation is byte or word in two ways: by supplying a byte or word operand, which is ignored except to determine whether the operation should be byte or word; or, by using special versions of the op-codes given above—CMPSB, LODSB, MOVSB, SCASB, and STOSB for bytes, and CMPSW, LODSW, MOVSW, SCASW, and STOSW for words.

These string manipulation instructions are quite powerful and can be very useful by themselves. But combined with the repeat instructions that cause them to be executed repeatedly, they become the most powerful instructions of the processor. The repeat instructions are not specified as separate assembly statements, but go on the same line as the string instruction they modify. For example, "MOVSB" can be repeated CX times with the "REP MOVSB" instruction. The following repeat prefixes are available:

Op-code	Operation	C Code
REP	Repeat until CX = = 0	do string_op while (--CX != 0);
REPE or REPZ	Repeat until CX = = 0 or ZF set	do string_op while ((--CX != 0) && (ZF = = 1));
REPNE or REPNZ	Repeat until CX = = 0 or ZF clear	do string_op while ((--CX != 0) && (ZF = = 0));

The following code will clear 200 bytes starting at a (assuming the segment registers are set properly):

```
a:      db      200
        .
        .
        .
        mov     di,offset a    ; DI = &a
        xor     al,al          ; AL = 0 (value to write)
        mov     cx,200         ; CX = 200 (# of bytes)
        rep stos byte ptr [di] ; Zero the block
```

Pseudo-ops

Pseudo-ops are directives to the assembler rather than instructions to be included in the program, although they do sometimes cause data to be included in the program. There are many pseudo-ops available, but we will discuss only three types: data storage; segment & group; and procedure.

Data Storage

Data storage pseudo-ops are used to reserve memory for variables and to fill that memory in with initial values. There are a number of these types of pseudo-ops available, but the most commonly used ones are define byte (db) and define word (dw). Each takes a list of values, one for each byte or word to be defined. If a large number of locations are to be reserved with the same value, the expression "*n* dup (*value*)" can be used to make *n* copies of *value*. If the data is not to be initialized—thus saving space in the loadable program, since the initial values do not need to be included—the values in the definition list can be replaced with "?". And in the case of the define byte pseudo-op, an ASCII string can also be used to specify a series of character values.

Here are some examples:

```
aByte    db     ?             ; One uninitialized byte
aWordList dw    1,2,3,4        ; A list of words
aString  db     "A string"    ; An ASCII string
aBlock   db     2000 dup (?)  ; 2000 uninitialized bytes
```

SEGMENT, GROUP, and ASSUME

A segment is a block of data which will be pointed to by a segment register. A group is a collection of segments. Both of these are explained more thoroughly in the main part of the book. The segment and group pseudo-ops allow the programmer to specify which segment a given piece of code or data belongs in, which group the segment belongs in (if any), and which segment registers point to which segments or groups.

Segments are defined by enclosing the data within them in SEGMENT and ENDS pseudo-ops:

```
dataSeg segment para public 'DATA'

aByte   db      ?
aWord   db      ?,?,?

dataSeg ends
```

All of the data defined between the SEGMENT and ENDS pseudo-ops will be included in the dataSeg segment. The parameters to the SEGMENT pseudo-op—and note that they are separated by spaces, not commas—are:

Name	Value in example	Meaning
Align Type	para	Defines what sort of boundary the segment should start on—byte, word, para(graph—16 bytes, used for segments), or page (256 byte boundary).
Combine Type	public	How multiple segments of the same name should be combined—public, stack, common, memory, or "at addr" (see the assembler manual for more details).
Class Type	'DATA'	Segments having the same class type are loaded contiguously.

The GROUP pseudo-op allows the programmer to specify that several segments should be loaded contiguously so that they can then be referenced using a single segment register that points to the base of the group of segments, rather than pointing to one of the individual segments. Of course, the entire group must not be larger than 64K bytes. The GROUP pseudo-op has the following format:

```
aGroup          group   segment1, segment2, segment3
```

Finally, there is a pseudo-op to tell the assembler which segment registers point to which segments or groups:

```
assume  CS:codeSegment,DS:dataSegment
assume  ES:aGroup
```

Since data is defined within a segment, and the assembler is told which segment registers contain pointers to which segments or groups, the assembler can automatically generate segment override prefixes if an instruction references data in a segment other than the data segment—but only so long as another segment register contains the proper segment base address.

Procedures

A "procedure" is simply another name for a function. The assembler provides the PROC and ENDP pseudo-ops to clearly delineate procedures in the code. In addition, the PROC pseudo-op takes one parameter that specifies whether this procedure will be called using a "near" call (within a single code segment) or a "far" call (between segments). This also tells the assembler whether to generate code for a near or far return when it encounters a RET instruction within the procedure.

```
aProc    proc near

         mov     ax,10
         ret

aProc    endp
```

There is one final pseudo-op that does very little but is very important: each assembly language source code file ends with an END pseudo-op:

```
end
```

Summary

Assembly language is in some ways fundamentally different than C. It uses much smaller chunks of functionality to create a program; it uses a different style of syntax to specify the program; and, it is much closer to the actual processor that will execute the program. This combination makes it harder to write and maintain programs in assembly than in C, which is why higher level languages like C were invented in the first place. But assembly also gives better control and can often produce more efficient code than C, which is why assembly language is still in use now that we have compilers.

In other ways, however, assembly language is very similar to C. It uses bits and bytes, it performs arithmetic operations, and it controls the flow of execution using tests and jumps. This similarity has allowed us to explain assembly language in a much more concise fashion than is normally possible, by drawing on what you already know about programming from your experience with C.

At this point, you should have a basic understanding of assembly language. Since we have not presented a complete and comprehensive guide to assembly language, you may still want to read other material on the subject. We have, however, presented enough depth to allow you to read and understand the material in this book. You should now read over the assembler manual, and look at some of the assembly language examples in *Supercharging C*.

Listing A-1. "example.c":

```
/*              Example C Program

        This program simply prints "Hello, world!"
 */

main()

{
        printf("Hello, world!\n");
}
```

Listing A-2. "example.asm":

```
;               Example Assembly Program
;
; This program simply prints "Hello, world!" It demonstrates all the
; elements of an assembly language program.

;
; Stack segment:
;
stakseg segment stack           ; Define the stack segment

        db      20 dup ('stack   ') ; Fill it with "stack"

stakseg ends                    ; End of stack segment

;
; Code segment:
;
codeseg segment                 ; Define code segment

        assume  cs:codeseg, ds:codeseg ; Assume CS points to code segment

msg:    db      'Hello, world!',0DH,0AH,0

main    proc far                ; Main routine

        push    ds              ; Set up for return to DS:0, which will, in
        xor     ax,ax           ;   turn, return us to DOS
        push    ax

        mov     ax,codeseg      ; DS = codeseg
        mov     ds,ax
        mov     bx,offset msg   ; BX = &msg

loop:   mov     al,[bx]         ; AL = *BX
        inc     bx              ; BX++
        or      al,al           ; AL == 0?
        jz      done            ; If yes, exit the loop
        push    bx              ; Save BX
        mov     ah,14           ; Tell ROM BIOS we want function 14, TTY write
        mov     bl,3            ; Using an attribute of 3 (white on black)
        int     10H             ; Call ROM BIOS video function TTY write
        pop     bx              ; Restore BX
        jmp     loop            ; Go do the next character in the string

done:   ret                     ; Return to DOS
```

Listing A-2. "example.asm" *(cont.)*:

```
main    endp                ; End of main routine

codeseg ends                ; End of code segment

        end     main        ; End of assembly code; start at main
```

Appendix B

Mechanics of Running the Compiler, Assembler, and Linker

- Compiling and Assembling

- Linking

- Running the Compiler, Assembler, and Linker

I n this appendix, we'll discuss the process of actually creating a program in C and assembly language that will run on the IBM PC. This includes the concepts behind separate assembly and compilation, the operation of the compiler and assembler, and the process of combining the results of those programs into a final application using the linker.

Compiling and Assembling

Computers only understand a very rudimentary language called "machine language." This language consists of numbers stored in the memory of the machine. People, on the other hand, are much better at dealing with characters, words, sentences, and text in general. Two programs are available to the programmer which translate the world of text and characters into the world of machine language: the assembler and the compiler. Programs using assembly language and compiler languages such as C are entered into the machine using a program known as a text editor. Then they are translated by the compiler or assembler into machine language.

Assembly language, which is translated by an assembler, is very close to the final machine language that the IBM PC actually executes. The machine language consists of a series of instructions to the processor; assembly language also consists of a series of instructions, one per line in the source text file, which are translated one-for-one into the machine language instructions. A compiler language such as C, on the other hand, is much farther removed from machine language. One line of source text in a compiler language generally translates into several machine language instructions. Some compilers produce assembly language rather than machine language, and an assembler must then be used to complete the translation process. Most compilers, in fact, allow this at least as an option, so that the programmer can see the compiler's translation of his original program.

Linking

For a wide variety of reasons, it is desirable for parts of a program to be compiled or assembled separately and then to be combined together. First, this approach facilitates the creation of libraries of routines that can be reused in a number of programs. Second, it reduces the development time since the programmer doesn't have to recompile or reassemble all parts of the program every time. Third, it lets the program be structured into independently designed and developed modules. And finally, it allows the source text of the routines to be kept proprietary while still letting other developers incorporate the object code into their applications.

The process of combining separately compiled or assembled modules is called "linking." Linking is accomplished using a program called a "linker." The entire process of creating a set of modules and linking them together into a finished application is illustrated in Figure B-1.

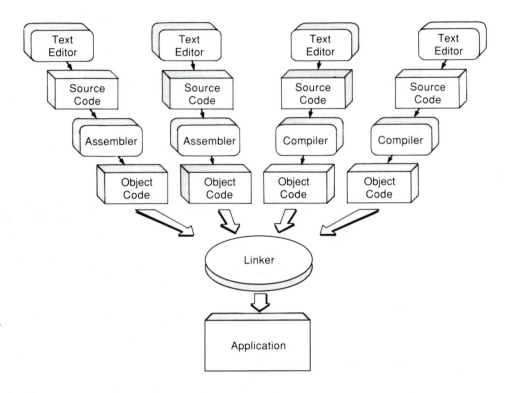

Figure B-1. Compiling, Assembling, and Linking

To summarize:

1. The source code files—the texts of the programs—are created using a text editor.

2. The source code files are translated into object code files using either an assembler or a compiler.

3. The object code files are combined and linked using a linker.

4. The user can then run the application just like any other program on the IBM PC.

Running the Compiler, Assembler, and Linker

For a detailed explanation of how to operate these programs and of the wide range of options available with them, the reader should study the manuals that come with the individual programs. We will only be discussing those aspects of operating the programs that are needed to assemble, compile, and link the programs in this book. Note also that we are talking here about Microsoft C (versions 3.0 and 4.0); Microsoft's macro assembler, MASM; and the standard MS-DOS linker, LINK. If you are using a different compiler, assembler, or linker, you should refer to the manuals for those programs.

All of these programming tools are programs just like any other. You invoke them from MS-DOS by typing their names, and you can supply parameters after the name on the same line. All three programs need you to enter file names indicating where the input should come from and what the output files should be named; and they allow options specifying variations on the operation of the program. All three also let you enter this information in one of two ways: you can enter it on the same line as the program name; or you can simply enter the program name and the program, itself, will prompt you for the rest of the information. Entering it on the command line is shorter and quicker, but for the beginner, the prompts are much easier to use. Each prompt asks for a file or list of files. It may also supply a default file name in brackets— the file name used if you simply type carriage return (i.e., leave the line blank).

Each of these programs also knows something about the file name extensions that are used. The convention to use is ".c" for C programs, ".asm" for assembly programs, ".obj" for object files, and, of course, ".exe" for applications. Because the programs know about these conventions, you only need to type in the base file name, not the extension.

The simplest of these programs is MASM. In this book we are not using any of the options available to change MASM's operation. All we need to do, therefore, is to let MASM know the name of the text file to be assembled. It will then provide a default object file name with the same base name and an ".obj" extension. In the example that follows, we type "masm" and "myfile" and then just enter carriage returns for the remaining three lines. There are other possibilities, of course, many of which are covered in the MASM user's guide.

```
A>masm
Microsoft (R) Macro Assembler  Version 4.00
Copyright (C) Microsoft Corp 1981, 1983, 1984, 1985.  All rights reserved.

Source filename [.ASM]: myfile
Object filename [myfile.OBJ]:
Source listing [NUL.LST]:
Cross-reference [NUL.CRF]:
```

A base file name of "NUL", like the default names for the source listing and cross-reference, indicates that no output file should be produced. The example above, for instance, will produce neither a source listing nor a cross-reference. If you want either of these files, simply type in the file name to be used, thus overriding the default "NUL" file name.

Compiling is a little more complicated for two reasons. One reason is that some programs require "#included" files such as "stdio.h", and the other reason is that compiler options are sometimes used to modify the behavior of the compiler. It is generally best to place system include files—that is, those that are included using angle-brackers to surround the name ("#include ‹file.h›")—in a sub-directory, and then use the MS-DOS command "set INCLUDE directory-name". The set command sets the MS-DOS variable INCLUDE to the directory name. This variable is used by the compiler to find the directory that contains the files to be included.

Options to the compiler can be specified on the command line. Options begin with a "/". In this book, we use only two of the options, "/Fa" and "/Ze". "/Fa" tells the compiler to produce a listing file that includes the assembly language equivalent of the machine language code that the compiler is generating. In other words, it tells the compiler to translate from C into assembly language. "/Ze" tells the compiler to allow the keyword "far", which is used to generate pointers that can point outside the normal C data segment. With both of these options selected, the compile process looks like this:

```
A>msc /Fa/Ze
Microsoft C Compiler   Version 3.00
(C)Copyright Microsoft Corp 1984 1985
Source filename [.C]: myprog
Object filename [myprog.OBJ]:
Object listing [NUL.ASM]:
```

Note that even with the "/Fa" option enabled, the object listing is shown as NUL.ASM. Despite that fact, a file named "myprog.asm" will be produced, containing the assembly language equivalent of the C source code. Without the options, it looks like this:

```
A>msc
Microsoft C Compiler   Version 3.00
(C)Copyright Microsoft Corp 1984 1985
Source filename [.C]: myprog
Object filename [myprog.OBJ]:
Object listing [NUL.COD]:
```

Operating the linker is very similar to operating the other programs. In this case, though, there are often multiple input files. These input files are all typed on the same line, with spaces between the file names; for example:

```
A>link
IBM Personal Computer Linker
Version 2.10 (C)Copyright IBM Corp. 1981, 1982, 1983

Object Modules [.OBJ]: file1 file2 file3
Run File [file1.EXE]:
List File [NUL.MAP]:
Libraries [.LIB]:
```

Note that the first name in the object module list is the one taken as the default name for the runnable application file. Note too that, by default, no list file, or "link map," is produced. You can produce one, however, simply by typing an output file name at that prompt. When used with Microsoft C, the linker will automatically look for a library file containing the C run-time support modules. This file, which is included with the compiler, should be placed in a subdirectory. The linker can then be told where to find it by issuing the MS-DOS command "set LIB sub_directory".

Compiling or assembling and linking a program is simply a matter of invoking the compiler or assembler for each module in the program, and then invoking the linker to put them all together. Each step should look just like the examples given above, but with different file names.

Appendix C

ROM BIOS
Interrupts
and Register Usage

This appendix includes a listing of most of the ROM BIOS interrupts. Three areas are not listed here. These are the diskette and fixed disk calls (as explained earlier, these are considered to be dangerous calls to use, and are not covered in this book), the cassette calls (which are virtually never used), and IBM PC/AT specific calls (these should be avoided so that programs will run on all members of the IBM PC and compatible family). The rest of the ROM BIOS interrupts are listed in concise form. More details can be found in the main text of the book and in the IBM *Technical Reference* manual.

Int	AH	Inputs	Outputs	Function
Display:				
10H	0	AL = mode		Set mode
10H	1	CH = starting line CL = ending line		Set cursor type
10H	2	BH = page DH = row DL = column		Set cursor position
10H	3	BH = page	DH = row DL = column CH = starting line CL = ending line	Read cursor type & position
10H	4		AH = 1 if pos. valid DH = row DL = column CH = raster line BX = pixel column	Read light pen position
10H	5	AL = page		Set active display page
10H	6	CH = top row CL = left column DH = bottom row DL = right column AL = # of lines to scroll BH = attr. for blank lines		Scroll active page up

Int	AH	Inputs	Outputs	Function
Display *(cont.)*:				
10H	7	Same as AH == 6		Scroll active page down
10H	8	BH = page	AL = character AH = attribute	Read character at current cursor position
10H	9	BH = page CX = # of chars to write AL = character to write AH = attribute to write	cursor position	Write character at current
10H	10	BH = page CX = # of chars to write AL = character		Write character only at current cursor position
10H	11	BH = palette to set BL = value to set		Set color palette
10H	12	BH = page DX = row CX = column AL = color		Write dot
10H	13	BH = page DX = row CX = column	AL = color	Read dot
10H	14	AL = character BL = foreground color		TTY-style character write
10H	15		AL = mode AH = # of columns BH = active page	Get current video state
Equipment Determination:				
11H			AX = equipment	Get equipment list

```
 15 14 13 12 11 10 9 8 7 6 5 4 3 2 1 0
                                     └── 1 if any diskette drives
                                   └──── Math co-processor
                             └────────── System board RAM in 16K blocks
                         └────────────── Initial video mode:
                                             00 - unused
                                             01 - 40x25 CGA
                                             10 - 80x25 CGA
                                             11 - 80x25 MA
                       └──────────────── # of diskette drives - 1
                     └────────────────── Unused
                └─────────────────────── # of serial ports
              └───────────────────────── Game I/O attached
            └─────────────────────────── Unused
      └───────────────────────────────── # of printer ports
```

Int	AH	Inputs	Outputs	Function
Memory Size Determination:				
12H			AX = # of blocks	Get # of contiguous 1K blocks of memory
Asynchronous Communications:				
14H	0	AL = configuration	AH = line status AL = modem status	Initialize line; see below for register values
14H	1	AL = character	AH = line status	Send character
14H	2		AH = line status AL = character	Receive character
14H	3		AH = line status AL = modem status	Get status

CONFIGURATION

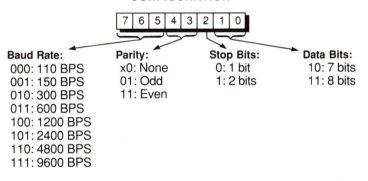

Baud Rate:
000: 110 BPS
001: 150 BPS
010: 300 BPS
011: 600 BPS
100: 1200 BPS
101: 2400 BPS
110: 4800 BPS
111: 9600 BPS

Parity:
x0: None
01: Odd
11: Even

Stop Bits:
0: 1 bit
1: 2 bits

Data Bits:
10: 7 bits
11: 8 bits

SERIAL PORT STATUS

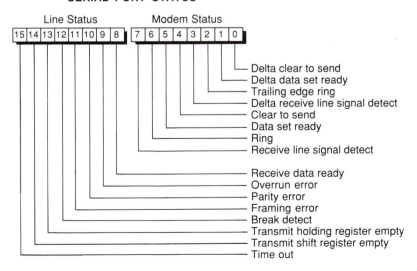

Line Status — 15 14 13 12 11 10 9 8
Modem Status — 7 6 5 4 3 2 1 0

- Delta clear to send
- Delta data set ready
- Trailing edge ring
- Delta receive line signal detect
- Clear to send
- Data set ready
- Ring
- Receive line signal detect
- Receive data ready
- Overrun error
- Parity error
- Framing error
- Break detect
- Transmit holding register empty
- Transmit shift register empty
- Time out

Int	AH	Inputs	Outputs	Function
Keyboard:				
16H	0		AH = scan code AL = ASCII character	Read character
16H	1		AH = scan code AL = ASCII character ZF = 0 if char available	Check for char available
16H	2		AL = shift status	Get shift status

SHIFT STATUS

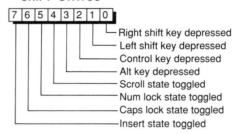

Right shift key depressed
Left shift key depressed
Control key depressed
Alt key depressed
Scroll state toggled
Num lock state toggled
Caps lock state toggled
Insert state toggled

Int	AH	Inputs	Outputs	Function
Printer:				
17H	0	DX = printer (0-2) AL = character	AH = status	Print character
17H	1	DX = printer (0-2)	AH = status	Initialize printer port
17H	2	DX = printer (0-2)	AH = status	Read status

PRINTER STATUS

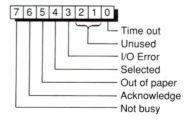

Time out
Unused
I/O Error
Selected
Out of paper
Acknowledge
Not busy

Int	AH	Inputs	Outputs	Function
Time-of-day:				
1AH	0		CX = hi count word DX = low count word	Read clock setting
1AH	1	CX = hi count word DX = low count word		Set clock

Appendix D

Keyboard Codes

Figures D-1–D-4 show the codes that are returned when a key is pressed. The returned code is enclosed in brackets and is shown in hexadecimal: pressing "a", for example, would return 61 (0x61 in C notation). If it's an extended key, the code is shown as "[0,n]" where n is the extended code. Figure D-1 shows the normal, unshifted keyboard; D-2 shows the codes returned when the shift key is held down; D-3 shows the codes when the control key is held down; and D-4 shows them when the alt key is held.

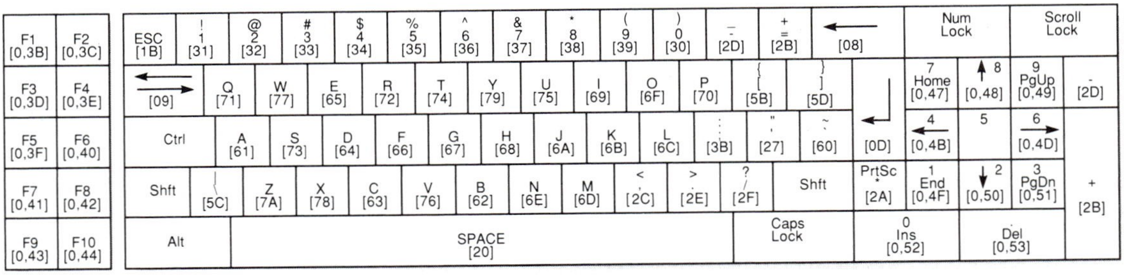

F1 [0,3B]	F2 [0,3C]	ESC [1B]	! 1 [31]	@ 2 [32]	# 3 [33]	$ 4 [34]	% 5 [35]	^ 6 [36]	& 7 [37]	* 8 [38]	(9 [39]	) 0 [30]	_ − [2D]	+ = [2B]	← [08]			Num Lock		Scroll Lock	
F3 [0,3D]	F4 [0,3E]	→ [09]	Q [71]	W [77]	E [65]	R [72]	T [74]	Y [79]	U [75]	I [69]	O [6F]	P [70]	{ [[5B]	}] [5D]			7 Home [0,47]	↑ 8 [0,48]	9 PgUp [0,49]	[2D]
F5 [0,3F]	F6 [0,40]	Ctrl	A [61]	S [73]	D [64]	F [66]	G [67]	H [68]	J [6A]	K [6B]	L [6C]	: ; [3B]	" ' [27]	~ ` [60]	↵ [0D]		4 ← [0,4B]	5	6 → [0,4D]	
F7 [0,41]	F8 [0,42]	Shft	| \ [5C]	Z [7A]	X [78]	C [63]	V [76]	B [62]	N [6E]	M [6D]	< , [2C]	> . [2E]	? / [2F]	Shft	PrtSc * [2A]	1 End [0,4F]	2 ↓ [0,50]	3 PgDn [0,51]	+ [2B]
F9 [0,43]	F10 [0,44]	Alt	SPACE [20]										Caps Lock		0 Ins [0,52]		Del [0,53]	

Figure D-1. Key Codes for Normal Keys

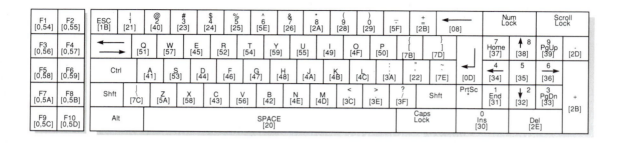

Figure D-2. Key Codes for Shifted Keys

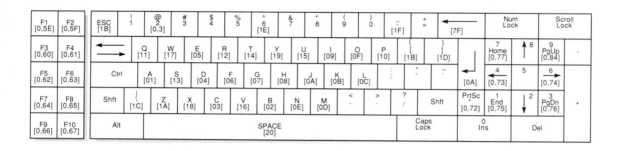

Figure D-3. Key Codes for Control Keys

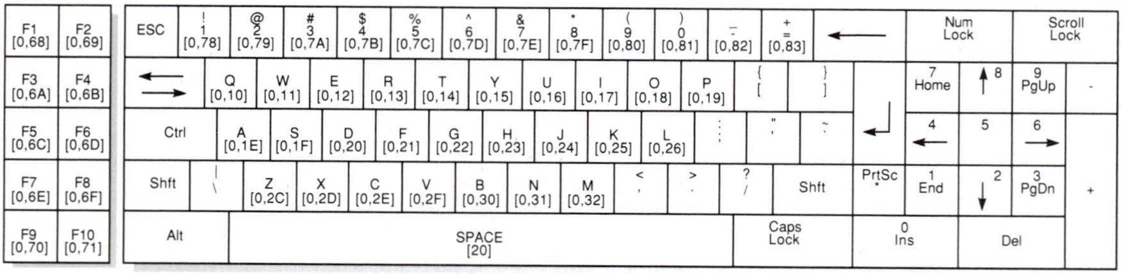

Figure D-4. Key Codes for Alt Keys

Glossary

Acknowledge—notify that a condition has occurred or that data has been accepted.

Address—a number specifying a particular memory location.

Addressing mode—in assembly language, one of a fixed number of ways to specify a register or memory location.

Algorithm—a method, or procedure, for solving a problem or accomplishing a task.

AND gate—hardware device that takes two logical signals as input, and produces a logical output of TRUE only if both input signals are TRUE.

Animation—in computer graphics, giving the appearance of smooth, continuous motion by rapidly producing a series of successive images.

Application—a program that can be run on a computer.

ASCII—American Standard Code for Information Interchange.

Assembler—a program that translates a source code file containing assembly language into an object code file.

Assembly language—a programming language that corresponds closely to the processor's machine language. In general, one assembly language statement translates into one processor instruction.

Attribute—in displays, a byte specifying the visual characteristics of the character to be displayed, e.g., blinking, inverse video, greenι

Base address—a starting address, to which offsets can be added.

BIOS—Basic I/O System.

Bit—Binary digIT, a basic unit of information in a computer, having one of two values, zero or one.

Bit rate—in data transfers, the number of bits that can be transfered per unit time, e.g., 1200 bits per second.

Boiler-plate—a fixed piece of material replicated and reused many times. In programming, a piece of code that is reused.

Boot—to start up the computer from scratch.

Branch—in programming, a control flow jump from one instruction sequence to another. In tree graphs, a connection from one node to another.

Breadth first—in search strategies, searching across the tree before going down the tree.

Buffer—a storage area for intermediate results, generally used to allow two parts of a program to proceed independently.

Bug—a program error introduced by the programmer.

Byte—eight bits.

Byte-backwards—bytes stored so that the top bit of a word is the same bit as the top bit of the second, rather than the first word, of the equivalent two bytes.

C—a high level programming language.

C File I/O—a set of routines for reading and writing data from a C program.

C Stream I/O—a set of routines for reading and writing variable sized blocks from a C program. The routines take care of buffering for the program.

Cache—a storage area used to hold in fast memory part of the data available in slower memory, in order to improve access time to the data.

Calling convention—the procedure used to call one function from another, particularly that used by a compiler.

CD—Color Display.

CGA—Color Graphics Adapter.

Character—a printed letter or special symbol; or, a value used in a computer to represent such a letter or symbol, usually stored as a byte.

Chip—an integrated circuit.

Cipher—a procedure for encrypting and decrypting information.

Cipher text—a message that has been encrypted.

Circular buffer—a type of buffer where data is entered and removed into memory sequentially; and when the end of the buffer is reached, entry starts over at the beginning.

Clip—in graphics, to limit an area to the part that lies within another area: e.g., to limit a rectangle to the part that is visible on the screen.

Code—instructions to be executed by a computer, or, a number representing an object or objects, for example a "character code."

Code segment—the processor memory segment that contains the instructions being executed by the processor.

Color Display—a color RGB monitor, used to display data from the Color Graphics Adapter.

Color Graphics Adapter—an add-on card for the IBM PC that displays text and graphics, in color, on the IBM Color Display.

Column—in a rectangular array, a set of elements vertically aligned, e.g., a column of characters on a display.

Command—input from a computer user to a program telling it what to do next.

Communications—transfer of data between two computers or computer elements.

Compact model—compiler memory model limiting the program code to 64K, but allowing more than 64K of data.

Compatible—able to work together; or able to run the same software.

Compiler—a program that translates a higher level language source code file into an object file.

Contiguous—adjacent.

Coordinate—in a graphic plane, the location of a point in terms of its distance horizontally and vertically from a special point called the "origin."

Co-processor—a second chip designed to work closely with the processor; particularly, a math co-processor that implements extended mathematical functions in the IBM PC.

Cursor—a location on a display showing where the next input or output will go; usually indicated visually by a block or bar which may flash on and off.

Cursor keys—The keys on the keyboard specifically designed to let the user manipulate the position of the cursor.

Data—information processed by a computer and stored as bits.

Data Encryption Standard—a National Bureau of Standards encryption/decryption algorithm.

Data segment—the processor memory segment that contains the data the executing program reads and writes.

Debug—to find and remove bugs from a program.

Decimal—base ten.

Decrypt—to translate an encrypted message back into a readable, text form.

Depth first—in search strategies, searching down the tree before going across the tree.

DES—Data Encryption Standard.

Device—a piece of hardware, particularly one external to the processor.

Device driver—a piece of software designed to manipulate a device, and to provide an interface between the operating system and the device.

Diagnostic—a piece of software designed to test a piece of hardware.

Direct memory access—a technique whereby the hardware transfers data into memory without disturbing the execution of the program.

Disk—a device for reading and writing data stored on a circular magnetic media that spins to allow access to all portions.

Disk operating system—an operating system designed to work specifically with a disk or other mass storage system, and to support a file system.

Display—a device for showing text and graphics to the user on a screen; similar to a TV

Display adapter—an add-on card that goes in the IBM PC, interfaces to a display, and generates the picture shown on the display.

Display border—the area of the display surrounding the main text and/or graphics area.

Display memory—RAM contained in the display adapter, which holds the information being displayed.

Display mode—the particular type of operation the display adapter is currently in: e.g., 200x640 graphics, 40x25 text, 80x25 text, and so on.

Display page—one of several sets of display information kept in display memory.

DMA—Direct Memory Access.

DOS—Disk Operating System.

Double word—two words, 32 bits.

ECD—Enhanced Color Display.

Editor—a program for creating text files, including program source code files.

EGA—Enhanced Graphics Adapter.

EIA—Electronic Industries Association.

Emulate—to behave like.

Encrypt—to translate a readable, plain text message into an unreadable, cipher text message.

End-of-file—the end of data in a file.

Enhanced Color Display—a high resolution color RGB monitor, used to display data from the Enhanced Graphics Adapter.

Enhanced Graphics Adapter—an add-on card for the IBM PC that displays text and graphics, in color, on the IBM Enhanced Color Display.

Environment—context; the elements surrounding an object, routine, or program.

EOF—End-Of-File.

Exclusive-or—"one or the other but not both," an operation that can be used to toggle a bit without knowing its original value.

Execute—to perform the instructions in a program.

Execution—the process of following the instruction in a program.

Execution speed—the rate at which a program executes.

Extra segment—the processor memory segment that contains extra data used by the program.

Far pointer—in C, a 32-bit pointer that can reference any location in physical memory.

Fatal error—a condition that prevents the program from continuing execution; or, a condition where continued execution would have serious negative consequences; usually, a condition that was unforseen by the programmer.

File—a set of data stored on a disk or other mass storage device.

File system—a set of routines and data that maintains a predefined structure on a disk or other mass storage device.

Floppy controller—hardware that interfaces to a floppy disk drive.

Floppy diskette—a removeable piece of magnetic media, which holds data written and read using a floppy disk drive.

Floppy disk drive—hardware that reads and writes data on a floppy diskette.

Fractal—an object with a fractional number of dimensions.

Front panel—an array of lights and switches used to enter and display data on a computer; generally used on older computers.

Function—what something does, or, a subroutine, particularly in a high level language such as C.

Functionality—the external impact of an object or function, as opposed to its internal implementation; i.e., what something does, not how it does it.

Global—available everywhere; in programming, available to all parts of the program.

Global variable—a piece of data that is available to all modules and subroutines of a program.

Graphics—the use of dots and lines, rather than only characters.

Grid—an array of evenly spaced vertical and horizontal lines.

Group—in segments, a collection of segments that can all be referenced using the same segment register value.

Hardware—the physical, unchanging, part of a computer; as opposed to the software or changeable part.

Hardware interrupt—a signal from a device external to the processor that some event has occurred that requires the processor's attention.

Heap—a block of memory from which blocks are allocated and deallocated; generally distinct from the stack, where blocks are also allocated, but in a strictly first-allocated-last-deallocated fashion.

Hex—an abbreviation for hexadecimal.

Hexadecimal—base sixteen.

Hierarchy—a vertical ordering of objects or concepts.

Histogram—a record of the frequency of occurrence of a set of discrete events.

Horizontal—in programming, at the same conceptual level in a design or system.

Huge model—compiler memory model allowing more than 64K of program code, more than 64K of data, and data elements that can each be more than 64K.

Human—generally, the operator of your programs; or an inhabitant of the "real world."

IBM—International Business Machines, Inc.

IBM PC—the first machine in the IBM PC family.

IBM PC/AT—IBM PC family machine that uses an 80286 processor.

IBM PC/XT—the second machine in the IBM PC family.

IBM PC clone—a non-IBM computer that operates like one of the IBM computers.

Implementation—the internal design and operation of an object or function, as opposed to the external functionality; i.e., how something does what it does, not what it does.

Index—a number used to select one element of an array.

Initialize—to set to an initial value or state.

Input/Output—reading and writing data to and from an external device or object.

Instruction—an individual command to the processor to take some action.

Instruction pointer—the processor register telling where in the code segment to find the next instruction to execute.

Intel—the integrated circuit manufacturer that makes many of the chips used in the IBM PC.

Interface—the connection between two parts of a system.

Interrupt—a mechanism for invoking a special type of subroutine, called an interrupt service routine.

Interrupt service routine—the code responsible for handling a particular interrupt.

Interrupt table—the set of interrupt vectors stored in low memory, one for each potential interrupt.

Interrupt vector—new values for the CS and IP registers, to be used when this interrupt is invoked.

IP—Instruction Pointer.

I/O—Input/Output.

I/O Address—the number of an I/O port.

I/O port—an interface to a device external to the processor.

Jump—in program execution, to change the order of control flow, to change the location from which instructions are being taken.

Key—one pushable object on the keyboard.

Keyboard—a collection of keys used by the user to control the computer and enter text.

Keystroke—one press of a key.

Label—a name attached to a statement, which can be used in a branch instruction to specify a control flow jump to that statement.

Language—a means by which programmers specify algorithms in a form that can be translated into instructions to be executed by the computer.

Large model—a compiler memory model allowing more than 64K of program code and more than 64K of data, but limiting individual data elements to 64K.

Library—a set of previously developed subroutines that can be called from a program.

Light pen—a device, not widely used, that allows a user to select a point on a display.

Line—in graphics, a set of dots connecting two points; in text, a group of characters terminating in an end-of-line sequence: carriage return, line feed, or carriage return/line feed.

Linker—a program that combines object modules to produce a runnable application program.

Local variable—a variable accessible only within the function in which it is declared.

Loop—a statement or set of statements that is executed repeatedly.

Low memory—that part of the physical memory of a machine having low addresses; in the IBM PC, the area where the interrupt vectors and ROM BIOS data is stored.

MA—Monochrome Adapter.

Machine—a computer or associated device.

Macro assembler—a program that translates a source code file containing assembly language into an object code file, and which allows macros in the source file.

Mask—when manipulating bits, a value that has ones in the bit positions of interest, and zeros in all other positions; can be used with the AND operation to isolate the bits of interest.

MASM—Macro ASeMbler (by Microsoft).

Mass storage—large capacity, long term data storage, e.g., disks.

Media—an object upon which data is stored, e.g., a diskette.

Medium model—a compiler memory model allowing more than 64K of program code, but only 64K of data.

Megabyte—1,048,576 bytes.

Memory—in computers, that part of the computer that retains data; particularly the main ROM and RAM.

Memory model—the default conventions for the maximum size of program and data in a compiled program. It determines whether subroutines and pointers are declared NEAR or FAR by default.

Microcomputer—a small computer, generally dedicated to a single user.

Microsecond—1,000,000th of a second.

Microsoft—a software manufacturer; maker of the C compiler, macro assembler, and linker used in this book, not to mention MS-DOS, the standard IBM PC operating system.

MicroSoft C—the C compiler sold by Microsoft and used in this book.

Millisecond—1,000th of a second.

Minicomputer—a medium sized computer, generally used by more than one person.

Modem—"MOdulator/DEModulator," a device for converting serial data to and from modulated signals suitable for transmission over phone lines.

Modular—composed of multiple pieces, or modules.

Module—one component of a system of interconnected pieces.

Monitor—a display similar to a television; or, the process of watching and/or recording some activity.

Monochrome Adapter—an add-on card for the IBM PC that displays text on the IBM Monochrome Display.

Monochrome Display—a monochrome monitor, used to display data from the Monochrome Adapter.
Motorola—the integrated circuit manufacturer that makes the 6845 chip used in the MA and CGA.
MS-DOS—MicroSoft Disk Operating System; the standard IBM PC operating system.

Near pointer—in C, a 16-bit pointer that can reference any location in the data segment.
Node—in tree graphs, either the end points of the graph or the intermediate points connected together by branches.
NSA—National Security Agency.

Object code—an intermediate code produced by a compiler or assembler, and combined together by the linker to form a complete application program.
Octal—base eight.
Offset—the distance, usually measured in bytes, from a base address to an object of interest.
Op-code—in assembly language, an abbreviation used to specify a machine language instruction.
Operand—in assembly language, a parameter to a machine language instruction or to a pseudo-op.
Operating system—a piece of software that coordinates the execution of application programs, and provides resources useful to those applications; usually also includes the software that implements the file system.
Optimize—to make better; which usually means faster.
Overhead—the cost of accomplishing a task; especially, that part of the process that does not directly contribute to the result.

Page—in displayed text, data that fits on one display screen; in printed text, a block of text that fits on one physical sheet of paper.
Paragraph—in memory segmentation, a sixteen-byte block.
Parallel—multiple activities occurring simultaneously. In data transfer, transferring more than one bit of data at a time.
Parallel port—a parallel interface from a computer to the external world; usually used to send data to a printer.
Parameter—data transferred to a subroutine, either to modify the function of the routine, or on which the routine works.
Pattern—in graphics, a design used repeatedly, usually to fill in an area.
PC—personal computer.
PC-DOS—the version of MS-DOS specifically for the IBM machines.
Performance—The measurement of the operation of some activity, according to some criteria such as speed.
Personal computer—a small computer dedicated to a single user.
Pixel—PICture ELement, one dot on a graphics display.
Plain text—a readable message either before or after being encrypted and decrypted.
Pointer—a variable that contains the address of location in memory.
Pop—to remove an element from a stack.
Port—an interface to a device within the computer (I/O port); or, an interface to a device outside the computer (e.g., serial port or parallel port); or, to make a piece of code run on a different computer, including making any changes needed in the code.

Portability—the ease (or difficulty) with which a piece of code can be made to run on a different computer.

Porting—the process of making a piece of code run on a different computer.

Printer—a device for writing text and/or graphics on a piece of paper.

Processor—The part of a computer that interprets and carries out the instructions provided in the code.

Processor interrupt—an interrupt that occurs when some special condition arises in the processor itself; e.g., divide-by-zero.

Program—a collection of code and data, ready to be loaded and run by the computer.

Programmer—a person who writes programs.

Protocol—a procedure or set of conventions whereby two elements of a system cooperate to accomplish some goal.

Pseudo-op—an assembly language statement that controls the operation of the assembler, rather than directly corresponding to a machine instruction.

Push—to put an element on a stack.

RAM—Random Access Memory; read-write memory.

RAM sort—an algorithm that sorts elements while keeping them entirely in RAM.

Raster display—a display which is composed of dots.

Read—to input data from some external source.

Read/write head—the part of a disk drive that contacts (or nearly so) the disk itself, and that inputs and outputs the data.

Real world—the place where non-programmers live; or, anything outside the computer.

Recode—to rewrite a set of instructions or a routine; usually changing its function or performance in some way.

Recursion—the process whereby a function calls itself, in order to accomplish its task.

Register—a special area of data storage, which is actually within the processor chip, and which can be accessed very quickly; or, a data storage area within an I/O device, which is accessed via an I/O port.

Register variable—in C, a variable that has been declared to be register type using the register keyword. Such variables are kept within processor registers.

Return address—in a subroutine call, the location in memory where the execution continues when the subroutine is finished. The address is generally pushed on the stack when the subroutine is called.

ROM—Read-Only Memory; used to hold code which is preset at the factory.

ROM BIOS—Read-Only Memory Basic I/O System; a code built into the IBM PC, which is responsible for booting the computer and also providing an interface to several parts of the hardware.

Routine—same as subroutine.

Row—in a rectangular array, a set of elements horizontally aligned: e.g., a row of characters on a display.

RS-232—an EIA standard for pin assignments and electrical signal levels and usage for connecting two computers together, or for connecting a computer to a modem.

Run-time—the time when a program is executing; as opposed to when it is being designed, compiled, assembled, or linked.

Run-time library—a set of routines that can be linked with a program and called when the program is executing.

Scan code—a value that identifies one of the keys on the IBM PC keyboard.

Scroll—to move a block of characters on a display up or down.

Sector—a block of data on a disk.

Segment—in the IBM PC, a 64K block of memory accessible from the processor.

Segment register—a processor register which holds the base address of a segment. In the IBM PC, there are four such registers: CS (code segment), DS (data segment), SS (stack segment), and ES (extra segment).

Sequential—occurring in sequence, or one after another.

Serial—multiple activities occuring sequentially; in data transfer, transferring only one bit at a time.

Serial port—a serial interface from a computer to the external world; usually used to exchange data with a modem or another computer.

Simulate—to act like.

Slot—one of several connectors inside the IBM PC, by which add-on boards can be connected to the system board.

Small model—a compiler memory model limiting both the program code and data to 64K.

Software—the part of a computer that is changeable (unlike hardware), and that controls the operation of the machine.

Software interrupt—an interrupt generated by the executing program code.

Sort—to order a set of elements according to some criteria.

Sound effects—interesting or unusual noises produced by design.

Source code—the human-readable input to a compiler or assembler.

Stack—a data structure that allows two operations, push and pop, to occur in such a way that the last element pushed is the first element popped (like a stack of plates).

Stack segment—the processor memory segment that contains the stack used by the executing program.

Stand-alone—capable of operating without external support; in programming, usually a program that executes without using an operating system.

Statement—in programming, a basic unit of source code.

String—a block of characters; in C, ending in a zero byte (null-terminated).

Subroutine—a set of instructions that can be called from another part of the program. "Calling" means saving the caller's location (the return address), executing the instructions, and then returning to the saved location.

Substitution—to replace one object with another; in cryptography, replacing each symbol in a message with a different, but unique symbol.

Supercharging—in this book, to improve a program by either speeding it up or making it do something it couldn't do previously.

Supercomputer—a very large computer, generally stretching the limits of state-of-the-art computing performance.

Syntax—in programming, the form of a program or other input to a computer.

System—a collection of interacting elements; or, in programming, sometimes the same as "operating system."

System board—the main printed circuit board in the IBM PC.

Telecommunications—the process and technology of transferring data between two locations, such as between two computers.

Terminal—a keyboard and display; used primarily to interact with multi-user computers.

Text—a set of characters.

Text file—a data file composed entirely of characters and intended to be readable by humans.

Timer—a device that keeps track of the passage of time.

Track—one band on a disk.

Transposition—rearranging a set of objects; in cryptography, rearranging the symbols in a message according to a specific algorithm.

Tree—in programming, a graph that expands as it goes from the base to the leaves. (See "squirrel" in the index to Kernighan & Ritchie.)

TTY—TeleTYpe; a mechanical terminal widely used in early computer systems.

TTY-style output—to display data in the same way that a TTY would display it, where the ASCII carriage return code causes the cursor to go to the start of the line, the line feed to go down one row, the bell to ring a bell, etc.

User—the person interacting with a running program.

Variable—a changeable piece of data, used by a routine to hold intermediate results.

Vector—see "interrupt vector."

Vertical—in programming, to be in the same functional area, but at a different conceptual level in a design or system.

Video—a visual display.

VLSI—Very Large Scale Integration; technology used to produce many of the chips used in the IBM PC.

Word—16-bits.

Worst case—the input or conditions that generate the least favorable conditions for a program.

Write—to output data to some external destination.

XModem—a protocol for reliably transferring data between two computers.

Index

A

B

C

D

E

F

G

H

I

T

U

V